RELIGION AND SOCIETY IN MODERN JAPAN

NANZAN STUDIES IN ASIAN RELIGIONS
Paul L. Swanson, General Editor

1 Jan NATTIER, *Once Upon a Future Time:*
   Studies in a Buddhist Prophecy of Decline, 1991.
2 David REID, *New Wine:*
   The Cultural Shaping of Japanese Christianity, 1991.
3 Minor and Ann ROGERS, *Rennyo:*
   The Second Founder of Shin Buddhism, 1991.
4 Herbert GUENTHER, *Ecstatic Spontaneity:*
   Saraha's Three Cycles of Dohā, 1993.

Religion and Society in Modern Japan

Selected Readings

edited by

Mark R. MULLINS

SHIMAZONO Susumu

Paul L. SWANSON

ASIAN HUMANITIES PRESS
[An imprint of Jain Publishing Company]
Web Site – www.jainpub.com

ASIAN HUMANITIES PRESS

Asian Humanities Press offers to the specialist and the general reader alike the best in new translations of major works and significant original contributions to our understanding of Asian religions, cultures, and thought.

Printed in the United States of America

Library of Congress Cataloging-in-Publication Data

Religion and society in modern Japan: selected readings / edited by Mark R. Mullins, Shimazono Susumu, and Paul L. Swanson.
   p.   cm.   — (Nanzan Studies in Asian Religions)
   Includes bibliographical references.
   ISBN 0-89581-935-X. — ISBN 0-89581-936-8 (pbk.)
   1. Japan—Religion—1868–1912. 2. Japan—Religion—20th century. 3. Religion and sociology—Japan. I. Mullins, Mark, 1954– . II. Shimazono, Susumu, 1948– . Swanson, Paul Loren, 1951– . IV. Series.
BL2207.5.R5 1993   93-23877
306.6'0952—dc20   CIP

Contents

PREFACE, **vii**

PART 1 JAPANESE RELIGIOSITY

Introduction, **3**

Shinto in the History of Japanese Religion
KURODA Toshio, **7**

Religious Rituals in Shugendō
MIYAKE Hitoshi, **31**

Religion in Contemporary Japanese Society
Jan SWYNGEDOUW, **49**

PART 2 RELIGION AND THE STATE

Introduction, **75**

Background Documents, **81**
  1 Meiji Constitution (1889), Article 28, **81**
  2 Imperial Rescript on Education (1890), **81**
  3 Memorandum on State Shinto, 3 December 1945, **82**
  4 Directive for the Disestablishment of State Shinto,
      15 December 1945, **97**
  5 Emperor's Imperial Rescript Denying his Divinity,
      1 January 1946, **102**
  6 Constitution of Japan, Articles 20 and 89, **104**

The Revitalization of Japanese Civil Religion
K. Peter TAKAYAMA, **105**

Yasukuni-Jinja and Folk Religion
Klaus ANTONI, **121**

PART 3 TRADITIONAL RELIGIOUS INSTITUTIONS

Introduction, **135**

Buddhism as a Religion of the Family
Ian READER, **139**

Religious Rites in a Japanese Factory
David C. LEWIS, **157**

Mizuko Kuyō and Abortion in Contemporary Japan
HOSHINO Eiki and TAKEDA Dōshō, **171**

Pokkuri-Temples and Aging
Fleur WÖSS, **191**

Sōtō Zen Nuns in Modern Japan
Paula K. R. ARAI, **203**

PART 4   NEW RELIGIOUS MOVEMENTS

Introduction, **221**

Sōka Gakkai and the Slippery Slope from Militancy to Accommodation
Anson SHUPE, **231**

Magic and Morality in Modern Japanese Exorcistic Technologies
Richard Fox YOUNG, **239**

Christianity as a New Religion
Mark R. MULLINS, **257**

The Expansion of Japan's New Religions into Foreign Cultures
SHIMAZONO Susumu, **273**

CUMULATIVE BIBLIOGRAPHY, **301**

Preface

RELIGION AND SOCIETY in modern Japan is such a vast field that one cannot hope to exhaustively cover every facet in one volume. Instead, this anthology seeks to provide readers with a selection of interpretations and perspectives on the significance of religion in modern Japan. Emphasis is placed on the sociocultural expressions of Japanese religions or religion in everyday life rather than on religious texts or traditions. Without denying the importance of doctrines and textual studies, in this volume we have chosen studies that show the diverse forms of Japanese religiosity today and the continuing role of religion in this modernized society. Therefore, most of the studies have a social science orientation, and are based on extensive field research and participant observation.

The readings were also selected and edited primarily with the undergraduate student in mind, after consultation with many people who teach courses on Japanese religion at the university level. Some of the readings, however, may require guidance from a teacher, either because the content requires background knowledge, or because the perspective is controversial. The classroom instructor should be able to provide further details and different perspectives. Further suggested readings have also been provided to offer such assistance.

In the selections we have aimed for a combination of contemporary Japanese and Western scholarship. Although the anthology is designed for use as a textbook in university classes, the editors hope that it will find an even wider audience. It is hoped that through these readings the reader will gain a deeper understanding of both the continuity and change in Japanese religions, and the religious dimensions of issues and challenges in Japanese society today.

Perhaps we could venture to say that this anthology is like a few meals at a colossal smorgasbord. The array of religions and religious phenomena in Japanese society is staggering in its richness and variety. The readings in each section are like picking a few selections from many possible topics and approaches—like choosing a salad here, an entrée there, a drink, and hopefully a couple of rich desserts. The reader should be aware, however, that there is much more waiting to be discovered. It is hoped that the reader will be inspired to use these studies as springboards for further inquiry.

OUTLINE OF THE SECTIONS

To give some structure to this great variety of topics, the anthology is divided into the following four sections: Japanese Religiosity, Religion and the State, Traditional Religious Institutions, and New Religious Movements. These divisions are somewhat arbitrary and there is much overlap between the content of articles in different sections. Sub-themes include life-cycle rituals, the role of religion in the family, abortion, decline and adaptation of religious institutions, religion and politics, religion and state issues, and the growth of Japanese New Religions outside Japan. Each section opens with a short introduction to the topic by one of the editors, and a supplementary reading list of important books and articles on the topic for further reading. The original source of each selection, or that of an earlier version, is given before the first note at the end of each reading.

EDITORIAL GUIDELINES

The readings have been edited and abridged with the idea that the primary reader is an undergraduate student or a reader with little or no previous knowledge of religion in Japan. Many of the original publications contain more details, fuller bibliographical references (often with the *kanji* for Japanese references), and/or more Japanese *kanji* within the text, and the reader interested in these details is advised to consult the original publication, usually in an academic journal such as the *Japanese Journal of Religious Studies*. Some readings have been considerably rewritten and updated. In general we have left out most of the *kanji*, adding in the margin only those that clarify the meaning of the text and would be helpful to those familiar with *kanji*. Readers with no acquaintance of *kanji* can safely ignore them.

Japanese names are given in Japanese order, that is, surname first and personal name second.

Major words that can be considered to have entered the English language—at least in the academic community—have been put in roman type: e.g., kami. A Japanese word that appears frequently in an article is given in italics the first time it appears (along with an explanation in parentheses), and subsequent appearances are given in roman type: e.g., yamabushi and matsuri. Other Japanese words are given in italics.

References have been collected in a Cumulative Bibliography in the back of the book, as many of the references are referred to in more than one reading. References included in the Cumulative Bibliography are referred to in the text by the author's name in small caps, the date of publication, and page numbers (e.g., HARDACRE 1989: 123–25). Some references (such as Japanese articles that would not be accessible to an undergraduate student, or specialized works limited to a single reading) are given full bibliographical treatment in the notes and not included in the Cumulative Bibliography. Note that the Cumulative Bibliography is not meant as a comprehensive selection on the subject of Japanese religion, a goal that would require a considerable amount of attention. As mentioned above, further suggested readings are given in the introduction to each section.

ACKNOWLEDGMENTS

The editors would like to thank the various sources (listed at the end of each reading) that gave permission to reprint previously published material, and the individual authors for permission to use their work and to adapt it for use in this volume. Our thanks to Thomas L. Kirchner and Edmund R. Skrzypczak for their help with the copy editing, and a special thanks to James Heisig for invaluable help with the layout, design, and innumerable details involved in preparing the camera-ready copy. Several individuals provided photographs for illustrating the text. Photo credits are listed on the copyright page.

We also wish to thank the many people who answered our questionnaire, shared their syllabi, and suggested useful readings for this volume. We regret that we were unable to accommodate all the suggestions, and hope that we have provided an acceptable compromise from among the many available choices. We are also grateful for advice from a number of individuals—including David Reid, Richard Fox Young, and Ian Reader—that proved very useful at various stages in the compilation of this volume. Of course the responsibility for faults that remain lies with the editors.

April 1993

Mark R. MULLINS
SHIMAZONO Susumu
Paul L. SWANSON

PART 1

Japanese Religiosity

Introduction to Part I

Japanese Religiosity

Paul L. SWANSON

I

N THE PREFACE we have already mentioned the great variety of religious phenomena in Japan, but it bears repeating, not the least because the Japanese people are often simplistically and mistakenly portrayed as homogeneous and lacking in creativity. In spite of all the talk about the "homogeneous" Japanese, there have always been a great variety of ways of being religious in Japan—from individual ascetics who practiced in the mountains to various group-oriented ceremonies and festivals, from private observances to state-sponsored public religious rituals—and the current scene is also a mixture of diverse forms of religiosity that reflect both continuity and discontinuity with the past.

Even the use of the term "folk religion" (which we decided not to use for this section header) is often no more than an attempt to categorize a bewildering array of customs and beliefs that have been, and are still, constantly evolving and developing—and just as often declining and disappearing. Talk of "traditional" religion or religiosity gives the mistaken impression that there were certain practices or beliefs that have always been that way. Although many contemporary religious practices can be traced back to earlier periods, this does not mean that so-called traditional practices have always and everywhere been the same and a part of the "Japanese" religious life. With that caveat in mind, in this section we present a few aspects of Japanese religiosity that indicate something of the long and complicated historical background of religion in Japanese society, and some of the current aspects of religiosity in contemporary Japanese society.

The essay by **Kuroda Toshio** on "Shinto in the History of Japanese Religion" gives a powerful revisionist reading of the role and meaning of "Shinto" while discussing how Buddhism and Shinto have changed and developed through history. Readers should be aware that this is a revolutionary (or perhaps we should say "restorational") view, and they will find much that is different from the "traditional" presentation of Shinto in most previous publications. Most Shinto scholars would vehemently object to this interpretation, and yet it is finding increasing acceptance among scholars at large. In any case, it is clear that the simplistic understanding of Shinto and Buddhism as two independent religions is misleading at best for much of Japanese history, and the same is just as true for contemporary Japanese society.

Miyake Hitoshi's presentation of "Shugendō" ritual makes the same point but in a much more circumspect manner. Shugendō is a syncretistic religion based on mountain asceticism—it evolved through a combination of ancient practices and beliefs centered on the mountains, esoteric Buddhism, shamanistic practices, Taoist or Yin-Yang magic, and more. Shugendō in itself no longer possesses the powerful religious organization or direct social authority that it once had, but the influence of Shugendō-type rituals and practice continues in many forms. Much of the ritual described by Miyake is still quite recognizable by all Japanese, who have participated in and will participate in or view such matters often during their lives. Most of the rituals described here have been adapted by and become a part of many of the so-called New Religions, and thus continue to be used in a "new" setting.

The broad sweep of **Jan Swyngedouw**'s article helpfully shows the "division of labor" in Japanese religious life, and should clarify why Japanese find it perfectly natural to visit "Shinto" shrines on New Year's, celebrate Christmas and get married in a Christian church, and be buried in the family Buddhist temple. It deals with religion for the "everyday" Japanese—the large number of Japanese who claim that they have nothing to do with religion. Japan has often been described as a living museum of religions or religiosity, with a vast array of religious traditions, teachings, and practices found in almost every corner of society. On the other hand, however, there are many (including many Japanese) who claim that Japan is the most secular of all modern societies, pointing to the decline of traditional religious institutions and the fact that a majority of Japanese claim to be "irreligious." Can both these observations be true? Jan Swyngedouw's article provides the information and analysis to clarify these seemingly incompatible interpretations.

As Jan Swyngedouw himself points out, however, his analysis is based on concepts such as *musubi* ("linkage") that are most current among Shinto scholars. Information and analysis from other perspectives, e.g., Buddhist, are given in other sections. Also, in spite of the harmonious picture that emerges from this interpretation, the reader should be aware that there are many areas of dissension and conflict associated with Japanese religions. The second section, on "Religion and the State," illustrates this point.

FURTHER SUGGESTED READINGS

BLACKER, Carmen. *The Catalpa Bow: A Study of Shamanistic Practices in Japan*. London: George Allen and Unwin, 1975.

DAVIS, Winston. *Japanese Religion and Society: Paradigms of Structure and Change*. Albany, NY: State University of New York, 1992. (See Chapter One: "Japanese Religious Affiliations," pp. 15–41.)

EARHART, H. Byron. *A Religious Study of the Mount Haguro Sect of Shugendō*. Tokyo: Sophia University, 1970.

———. *Japanese Religions: Unity and Diversity*. Belmont, CA: Wadsworth, 1982.

HORI Ichirō. *Folk Religion in Japan: Continuity and Change*. Chicago: University of Chicago Press, 1968.

KANEKO Satoru. "Dimensions of religiosity among believers in Japanese folk religion." *Journal for the Scientific Study of Religion* 29/1: 1–18, 1990.

KITAGAWA, Joseph M. *On Understanding Japanese Religion*. Princeton: Princeton University Press, 1987.

MIYAKE Hitoshi. "Folk religion." In *Japanese Religion*, Hori Ichirō, et al., eds. Tokyo: Kodansha, 1972.

MURAKAMI, Shigeyoshi. *Japanese Religion in the Modern Century*. Translated by H. Byron Earhart. Tokyo: University of Tokyo Press, 1980.

READER, Ian. *Religion in Contemporary Japan*. London: Macmillan, 1991.

———. "Letters to the gods—The form and meaning of *ema*." *Japanese Journal of Religious Studies* 18/1: 23–50, 1991. (See also the response to this article by Richard W. Anderson and Ian Reader's counter-response in "What constitutes religious activity?" (I) and (II) in *Japanese Journal of Religious Studies* 18/4: 369–76, 1991.)

SMITH, Robert J. *Ancestor Worship in Contemporary Japan.* Stanford: Stanford University Press, 1974.

SWANSON, Paul L. "*Shugendō* and the Yoshino-Kumano pilgrimage: An example of mountain pilgrimage." *Monumenta Nipponica* 36/1: 55–79, 1981.

Shinto in the History of Japanese Religion

KURODA Toshio

S HINTO HAS LONG been regarded as a crucial element in Japanese religion that gives it distinctiveness and individuality. The common person's view of Shinto usually includes the following assumptions: Shinto bears the unmistakable characteristics of a primitive religion, including nature worship and taboos against *kegare* (impurities), but it has no system of doctrine; it exists in diverse forms as folk belief but at the same time possesses certain features of organized religion—for example, rituals and institutions such as shrines; it also plays an important role in Japan's ancient mythology and provides a basis for ancestor and emperor worship. In short, Shinto is viewed as the indigenous religion of Japan, continuing in an unbroken line from prehistoric times down to the present.

Many people have discussed the role of Shinto in Japanese history and culture, but depending on the person there are slight differences in interpretation. These can be divided into two general categories. The first includes those who believe that, despite the dissemination of Buddhism and Confucianism, the religion called Shinto has existed without interruption throughout Japanese history. This has become the common view, and it is the conviction of Shinto scholars and priests particularly.

The second category includes those who think that, aside from whether it existed under the name Shinto, throughout history there have always been Shinto-like beliefs and customs (*shinkō*). This kind of interpretation is frequently found in studies of Japanese culture or intellectual history. This view can be traced back to the National Learning (*kokugaku*) scholar Motoori Norinaga in the eighteenth century, and it is reflected more recently in Yanagida Kunio's work on Japanese folklore. The same trend is discernible in the writings of Hori Ichirō, who claims an opinion similar to Robert Bellah's and Charles Eliot's.[1] Hori defines Shinto and

信仰

国学

"Shinto-ness" as "the underlying will of Japanese culture."
He argues that Shinto has been the crucial element bringing
the "great mix" of religions and rituals absorbed by the
Japanese people into coexistence. Moreover, it has forced
them to become Japanese in character.

Maruyama Masao, speaking as an intellectual historian on
the historical consciousness of the Japanese people, is also of
this school. He maintains that the thought processes found in
the myths of the *Kojiki* and the *Nihon shoki* continue to exist
as an "ancient stratum," even though other layers of thought
have been superimposed in subsequent ages.[2] Maruyama is
somewhat sympathetic to "Shinto thinkers of the Edo period"—including of course Motoori Norinaga—"down to the
nationalistic moralists of the 1930's," and he even construes
their assertions to be "a truth born of a certain kind of intu-
ition."

Of these two groups, the views of the second demand special attention, but they should not be looked upon separately
from those of the first. The two represent in a sense the external and the internal aspects of the same phenomenon. The
views of the second group can be summarized as follows:

1 Shinto, with the Japanese people, is enduring. It is "the
    underlying will of Japanese culture," to borrow Hori
    Ichirō's phrase, an underlying autonomy that transforms
    and assimilates diverse cultural elements imported from
    outside. In the words of Motoori Norinaga, any cultural
    element of any period (even Buddhism and Confu-
    cianism) is, "broadly speaking, the Shinto of that peri-
    od."[3]

2 Even though one can speak of Shinto as a religion along
    with Buddhism and Taoism, "Shinto-ness" is something
    deeper. It is the cultural will or energy of the Japanese
    people, embodied in conventions that precede or tran-
    scend religion. Here, the "secularity of Shinto" is
    stressed. Whether people who maintain this position
    like it or not, what they advocate is akin to the Meiji
    Constitution, which did not regard State Shinto as a reli-
    gion and on that basis placed restraints on the thought
    and beliefs of Japanese citizens. It is also similar to the
    rationale adopted by certain movements today that seek
    to revive State Shinto.

3 Based on this line of thought, "the miscellaneous nature of Japanese religion," whereby a person may be Buddhist and Shinto at the same time, is taken as an unchanging characteristic of Japanese culture. When such a formula is applied to all cultural phenomena in history, then a miscellaneous, expedient, irrational, and non-intellectual frame of mind, more than any effort at a logical, unified, and integrated world view, is extolled as that which is most Japanese.

The views of the second group when compared to those of the first differ in conception and central argument, but insofar as they both regard Shinto as a unique religion existing independently throughout history, the two share a common premise and reinforce one another. This view, however, is not only an incorrect perception of the facts but also a one-sided interpretation of Japanese history and culture. It is hoped that this article will demonstrate that before modern times Shinto did not exist as an independent religion. The main points of my argument will be as follows:

1 It is generally held that an indigenous self-consciousness is embodied in the word *shintō*. I would argue that the original meaning of the word differs from how it is understood today.

2 The ceremonies of Ise Shrine, as well as those of the imperial court and the early provincial government, are said to have been forms of "pure Shinto." I would like to show that they actually became one component of a unique system of Buddhism that emerged in Japan and were perceived as an extension of Buddhism.

3 It is said that Shinto played a secular role in society and existed in a completely different sphere from Buddhism. I would maintain that this very secularity was permeated with Buddhist concepts and was itself religious in nature. The greater part of this paper will examine this question and the preceding two in their ancient and medieval contexts.

4 Finally, I would like to trace the historical stages and the rationale whereby the term Shinto came to mean the indigenous religion or national faith of Japan and to clarify how and when Shinto came to be viewed as an independent religion.

神道

The word *shintō* is commonly taken to mean Japan's indigenous religion and to have had that meaning from fairly early times. It is difficult, however, to find a clear-cut example of the word *shintō* (lit. "the way of the *kami* [gods]") used in such a way in early writings. The intellectual historian Tsuda Sōkichi has studied the occurrences of the word *shintō* in early Japanese literature and has divided its meaning into the following six categories:

1 "religious beliefs found in indigenous customs passed down in Japan, including superstitious beliefs";
2 "the authority, power, activity, or deeds of a kami, the status of kami, being a kami, or the kami itself";
3 concepts and teachings concerning kami;
4 the teachings propagated by a particular shrine;
5 "the way of the kami" as a political or moral norm; and
6 sectarian Shinto as found in new religions.[4]

From these it is clear that the word *shintō* has been used in a great variety of ways. Tsuda maintains that in the *Nihon shoki, shintō* means "the religious beliefs found in indigenous customs in Japan," the first definition, and that it was used from that time to distinguish "Japan's indigenous religion from Buddhism." He also claims that this basic definition underlies the meaning of *shintō* in the other five categories.

It is far from conclusive, however, that the word *shintō* was used in early times to denote Japan's indigenous religion,[5] and for that reason Tsuda's analysis of examples in the *Nihon shoki* should be re-examined. The following three sentences are the only instances of the word *shintō* in the *Nihon shoki*.

仏法

1 The emperor believed in the teachings of the Buddha (*buppō* or *hotoke no minori*)[6] and revered Shinto (or *kami no michi*). (Prologue on Emperor Yōmei)
2 The emperor revered the teachings of the Buddha but scorned Shinto. He cut down the trees at Ikukunitama Shrine. (Prologue on Emperor Kōtoku)
3 The expression "as a kami would" (*kamunagara*) means to conform to Shinto. It also means in essence to possess one's self of Shinto. (Entry for Taika 3/4/26)

In examples one and two it is possible to interpret Shinto as distinguishing "Japan's indigenous religion from Buddhism," but that need not be the only interpretation. Tsuda himself indicates that in China the word *shintō* originally meant various folk religions, or Taoism, or sometimes Buddhism, or even religion in general.[7] Therefore, the word *shintō* is actually a generic term for popular beliefs, whether of China, Korea, or Japan, even though in examples one and two it refers specifically to Japan's ancient customs, rituals, and beliefs, regardless of whether they were Japanese in origin. Since the *Nihon shoki* was compiled with a knowledge of China in mind, it is hard to imagine that its author used the Chinese word *shintō* solely to mean Japan's indigenous religion. Though there may be some validity in what Tsuda says, the word *shintō* by itself probably means popular beliefs in general.

In examples one and two *shintō* is used in contrast to the word *buppō*, the teachings of the Buddha. Tsuda takes this to mean "Japan's indigenous religion," but there are other possible interpretations of this without construing it to be the name of a religion. For example, it could mean "the authority, power, activity, or deeds of a kami, the status of kami, being a kami, the kami itself," Tsuda's second definition of *shintō*. In fact, during this period the character *dō* or *tō*, 道 which is found in the word *shintō*, meant not so much a road or path but rather conduct or right action.[8] Hence, *shintō* could easily refer to the conduct or action of the kami.

In example three there are two instances of the word *shintō*. While it is not unthinkable to interpret them as "popular beliefs in general," Tsuda's second definition, "the authority, power, activity, or deeds of a kami,..." is perhaps more appropriate, since the word *kamunagara* in the quotation means "in the nature of being a kami" or "in the state of being a kami." The sentences in example three were originally a note explaining the word *kamunagara* as it appeared in the emperor's decree issued on the day of this entry, and according to Edo-period scholars it was added sometime after the ninth century when the work was transcribed.[9] Therefore, it is not reliable as evidence for what *shintō* meant at the time the *Nihon shoki* was compiled. Even if it were, it is more likely that the compiler did not use the same word in two different ways but rather applied the same definition, "the authority, power, activity, or deeds of a kami..." in all three examples.

Another possible interpretation of *shintō* in the *Nihon shoki* is Taoism. Based on recent studies, it is clear that *shintō* was another term for Taoism in China during the same period.[10] Moreover, as Taoist concepts and practices steadily passed into Japan between the first century A.D. and the period when the *Nihon shoki* was compiled, they no doubt exerted a considerable influence on the ceremonies and the beliefs of communal groups bound by blood ties or geographical proximity and on those that emerged around imperial authority.

真人

Among the many elements of Taoist origin transmitted to Japan are the following: veneration of swords and mirrors as religious symbols; titles such as *mahito* or *shinjin* (Taoist meaning—"perfect man," Japanese meaning—the highest of eight court ranks in ancient times which the emperor

仙
天皇

bestowed on his descendants), *hijiri*[11] (Taoist—immortal, Japanese—saint, emperor, or recluse), and *tennō* (Taoist— lord of the universe, Japanese—emperor); the cults of Polaris and the Big Dipper; terms associated with Ise Shrine such as

神宮
内宮
外宮
太一

jingū (Taoist—a hall enshrining a deity, Japanese—Ise Shrine), *naikū* (Chinese—inner palace, Japanese—inner shrine at Ise), *gekū* (Chinese—detached palace, Japanese—outer shrine at Ise), and *tai'ichi* (Taoist—the undifferentiated origin of all things, Japanese—no longer in general use except at Ise Shrine, where it has been used since ancient times on flags

大和

signifying Amaterasu Ōmikami); the concept of *daiwa* (meaning a state of ideal peace, but in Japan used to refer to Yamato, the center of the country); and the Taoist concept of immortality.

Early Japanese perhaps regarded their ceremonies and beliefs as Taoist, even though they may have differed from those in China. Hence, it is possible to view these teachings, rituals, and even the concepts of imperial authority and of nation as remnants of an attempt to establish a Taoist tradition in Japan. If that is so, Japan's ancient popular beliefs were not so much an indigenous religion but merely a local brand of Taoism, and the word *shintō* simply meant Taoism. The accepted theory today is that a systematic form of Taoism did not enter Japan in ancient times,[12] but it is not unreasonable to think that over a long period of time Taoism gradually pervaded Japan's religious milieu until medieval times, when Buddhism dominated it completely.

Three possible interpretations of the word *shintō* in the *Nihon shoki* have been presented above. It is not yet possible to say which of these is correct, but that should not preclude certain conclusions about Shinto. What is common to all three is that none view Japan's ancient popular beliefs as an independent religion and none use the word *shintō* as a specific term for such a religion. Also, there is no evidence that any other specific term existed. Moreover, when Buddhism was introduced into Japan there was a controversy over whether or not to accept it, but there is no indication that these popular beliefs were extolled as an indigenous tradition. Hence, Shinto need not imply a formal religion per se, and it need not indicate something that is uniquely Japanese.

THE SIGNIFICANCE OF SHINTO DEITIES IN THE ANCIENT PERIOD

In the previous section the word *shintō* was analyzed to show how it was used and what it meant in ancient times. Now it is necessary to consider the institutional significance and place of kami in Japan during that period, especially as evidenced in the *jingiryō* laws and in Shinto-Buddhist syncretism. 神祇令

The *jingiryō* is a set of laws of ancient Japan that instituted ceremonies to the kami. Needless to say, these laws include only those rites that had state sponsorship, but they nonetheless represent a fair sampling of the ceremonies current at that time. In brief, the *jingiryō* laws cover the following topics:

1 the season, title, and content of official annual ceremonies;
2 imperial succession ceremonies and *imi* (seclusion to avoid things tabooed); 斎
3 the supervision and administration of ceremonies;
4 *ōharai* (an official ceremony to exorcise evils and offenses from people); and 大祓
5 the administration of government shrines.

It is well known that the *ritsuryō* law code of ancient Japan was modeled on the codes of Sui and T'ang China. Many scholars have already pointed out that the *jingiryō*, one section of the *ritsuryō*, was based on the Chinese *tz'i-ling* code, which has been reconstructed in forty-six articles.[13] When compared to the T'ang code, the *jingiryō* is seen to occupy an 律令

祠令

identical position in the overall order of the law code and to correspond to the Chinese code in topic and sentence structure. The official ceremonies described in the *tz'i-ling* include:

祀
祭
亨
釈奠

1 *shi* or, in Chinese, *ssu* (veneration of kami of heaven);
2 *sai* or *chi* (veneration of kami of earth);
3 *kō* or *heng*, (deification of the spirits of the dead); and
4 *sekiten* or *shih-tien* (deification of ancient sages and masters).

From these the *jingiryō* of Japan incorporated only the first two and then added imperial succession ceremonies and *ōharai* ceremonies, not found in the Chinese code. These changes probably reflect differences in the use of ceremonies in Japan and China that the compilers of the *ritsuryō* code took into account. Notwithstanding these differences, both codes are alike in that they record popular ceremonies of society at that time, even though they include only those ceremonies that had official or political significance. The importance that Japan's *ritsuryō* code placed on kami derived ultimately from such ceremonies. Originally, kami were popular local deities connected to communal groups bound by blood ties or geographical proximity, and later to the imperial concept of state as well. The *kami* associated with ancestor worship are one example of such local deities. As the section following the *jingiryō* in the *ritsuryō*, the government drew

僧尼令

up the *sōniryō*, laws for Buddhist institutions, to regulate priests and nuns. By compiling the *sōniryō* separately from the *jingiryō*, the government placed ceremonies for kami in a different dimension from religions such as Buddhism, which exerted a special influence on society through its high doctrines.

In subsequent centuries the significance of kami changed somewhat from what it had been under the original *ritsuryō* system. During the eighth century the state enthusiastically embraced Buddhism, and the Empress Shōtoku, in collusion with the priest Dōkyō, established a policy that was pro-Buddhist in the extreme. Recent scholars have shown how this policy met with opposition in aristocratic and court circles, and they claim that in conjunction with political reforms at the beginning of the ninth century there emerged the concept of Shinto as an independent indigenous religion.[14] Certainly, it was during these ninth-century reforms that court Shinto ceremonies and Ise Shrine's organization were formalized. Nonetheless, it is highly unlikely that Shinto was perceived as an independent religion in opposition to Buddhism at this time.

As is already well known, between the late eighth century and the eleventh century Shinto and Buddhism gradually coalesced with each other (*shinbutsu shūgō*)—or, more precisely, veneration of the kami was absorbed into Buddhism through a variety of doctrinal innovations and new religious forms. Among the doctrinal explanations of the kami were the following: 神仏習合

1 the kami realize that they themselves are trapped in this world of samsara and transmigration and they also seek liberation through the Buddhist teachings;
2 the kami are benevolent deities who protect Buddhism;
3 the kami are transformations of the Buddhas manifested in Japan to save all sentient beings (*honji suijaku*); and 本地垂迹
4 the kami are the pure spirits of the Buddhas (*hongaku*). 本覚

Among new religious forms were the *jingūji* (a combination shrine and temple) and Sōgyō Hachiman (the kami Hachiman in the guise of a Buddhist monk). Such religious 神宮寺 forms typify ceremonies and objects of worship that could not be distinguished specifically as Shinto or as Buddhist. The first stage in this process of Shinto-Buddhist syncretization covered the late eighth and early ninth centuries. During that period the first two doctrinal explanations of kami, mentioned above, became current.

It is only natural that at this stage people became more cognizant of the kami, especially in relation to the Buddhas. Examples of this are found in the *Shoku nihongi*. The entry there for 782/7/29 states that Shinto cannot be deceived and that numerous recent calamities are retribution meted out by the great kami of Ise and all the other kami in return for the negligent use of mourning garb widespread among men. Such disrespect for decorum, and by extension for the kami, indicates implicitly the popularity of the Buddhas over the kami.

Another example from the *Shoku nihongi* is an imperial edict of 836/11, which states that there is nothing superior to Mahāyāna Buddhism in defending Shinto and that one should rely on the efficacy of Buddhist practices to transform calamity into good. This passage indicates that it is the Buddhas who guarantee the authority of the kami.

These examples reflect a heightened awareness of kami during this period, but they by no means imply that Shinto was looked upon as an independent and inviolable entity. On the contrary, there was more of a sense that Shinto occupied a subordinate position and role within the broader scheme of Buddhism.

THE MEANING OF THE WORD *SHINTŌ* IN MEDIEVAL TIMES

The *Konjaku monogatari-shū* (Tales old and new), composed around the eleventh century, contains the following two references. First, an old woman in China was possessed with heretical views: she served Shinto and did not believe in Buddhism. Second, there was an outlying province in India that was a land of kami, and to this day the words of Buddhism have not been transmitted there.[15] Here "Shinto" and "land of kami" have nothing to do with Japan but clearly indicate "local deities" and "a land devoted to its local deities." Although these references are from a collection of Buddhist tales, they show that even in this period the word *shintō* was used in its classical sense, as it was in China and in the *Nihon shoki.* In medieval times the word *shintō* generally meant the authority, power, or activity of a kami, being a kami, or, in short, the state or attributes of a kami. For example, the *Nakatomi no harai kunge*, a work on Ryōbu Shinto of Shingon Buddhism, discusses the relationship of kami and Buddha in the following way: "The Buddha assumes a state in which kami and Buddha are not two different things but are absolutely identical. The Buddha constantly confers his mark (*suijaku*) on Shinto."[16] Here *shintō* must mean kami or the state of being a kami. The word *shintō* is used in the same way in the *Shintōshū*, a collection of tales from the Sannō Shinto tradition of Tendai Buddhism:

> Question: For what reason do the Buddhas and the Bodhisattvas manifest themselves in the form of Shinto?

> Answer: The Buddhas and the Bodhisattvas manifest themselves in various forms out of compassion for and to save all living beings.[17]

Besides these sayings there are numerous other examples of *shintō* used to mean kami.

A saying in common parlance in medieval times was, "Shinto is a difficult thing to speculate about." This example, if any, is representative of what Shinto ordinarily indicated in that period. It does not mean that one cannot conjecture about the religion or doctrines of the kami but rather that it is difficult to fathom the conduct, the intentions, and the existence of the kami by human intellect. Such a definition of Shinto was current throughout the medieval period, and even the *Japanese Portuguese Dictionary* of 1603 contains the following entry: "Xinto (*camino michi*). Kami [*camis* in the original] or matters pertaining to kami."[18] The *camino michi* recorded here is the Japanese reading of the Chinese characters for *shintō*. It is clear that this word *michi* likewise does not mean doctrine. *Michi* in the medieval period, just as in ancient times, indicated conduct or ideal state, like the *michi* in *mononofu no michi* or *yumiya no michi* (the way of the warrior). Hence *kami no michi* means the state of being a kami or the conduct of a kami. Even when *michi* is compounded with another character and read *tō* or *dō* as in *shintō*, the compound can have the meaning of the other character alone. An example of this is found in the *Gishi wajinden*, which states in reference to Himiko that "she served the *kidō* (demons)." The same can be said of the *dō* and *tō* of *myōdō* (deities of the world of the dead) and *tentō* (deities such as Bonten and Taishakuten), words that appear in *kishōmon*, medieval documents containing oaths sworn before kami and Buddhas.

道

鬼道
冥道　天道

The next question that must be dealt with is what religious content this word *shintō* was said to have contained. As pointed out earlier, during medieval times Shinto was generally interpreted as one part of Buddhism. This was possible because the concepts contained in Mahāyāna Buddhism provided a rationale for absorbing folk beliefs. Just as a unique form of Buddhism evolved in Tibet, so in medieval Japan Buddhism developed a distinctive logic and system of its own.

Nominally, medieval Buddhism comprised eight sects, but it was not unusual for individuals to study the teachings and rituals of all the sects. The reason is the eight held a single doctrinal system in common, that of *mikkyō* or esoteric Buddhism (Skt. Vajrayāna). The Buddhist teachings that were recognized as orthodox during the medieval period had *mikkyō* as their base, combined with the exoteric teachings or *kengyō* (Buddhist and other teachings outside of *mikkyō*)

密教

顕教

of each of the eight schools—Tendai, Kegon, Yuishiki (Hossō),

顕密

Ritsu, etc. These eight sects, sometimes called *kenmitsu* or exoteric-esoteric Buddhism, acknowledged their interdependence with state authority, and together they dominated the religious sector. This entire order constituted the fundamental religious system of medieval Japan. Shinto was drawn into this Buddhist system as one segment of it, and its religious content was replaced with Buddhist doctrine, particularly *mikkyō* and Tendai philosophy. The term *kenmitsu* used here refers to this kind of system.[19] At the end of the twelfth century, various reform movements arose in opposition to this system, and there even appeared "heretical" sects that stressed exclusive religious practices—the chanting of

念仏 禅

the *nenbutsu*, *zen* meditation, and so forth. Nonetheless, the *kenmitsu* system maintained its status as the orthodox religion until the beginning of the sixteenth century.

In *kenmitsu* Buddhism, the most widespread interpretation of the religious content of Shinto was the *honji suijaku* theory, based on Tendai doctrine. According to this theory, the kami are simply another form of the Buddha, and their form, condition, authority, and activity are nothing but the form and the acts by which the Buddha teaches, guides, and saves human beings. Shinto, therefore, was independent neither in existence nor in system of thought. It was merely one means among many by which the Buddha guides and converts sentient beings. The *Shintōshū* cited earlier contains about fifty tales in which the Buddha takes the form of a kami and saves human beings. The word *shintō* in its title presupposes this meaning—i.e., conversion by the Buddha. With Shinto interpreted in this way and with people's beliefs based on this kind of interpretation, individual Shinto shrines sought to emphasize the distinctive capacities and lineage of their own kami as a manifestation (*suijaku*) of the Buddha, as well as the unique teachings and practices passed down in their shrine or school. These claims were expanded through complicated doctrines and tortuous theories into a

社家

class of teachings now called sectarian or *shake* Shinto (Tsuda's fourth definition of the word *shintō*, "the teachings propagated by a particular shrine"). Ryōbu Shinto of the Shingon tradition and Sannō Shinto of the Tendai tradition are typical examples of such teachings. Individual shrines in different areas adapted these teachings in such a way that during the medieval period countless theories of Shinto arose.

The theory of Shinto propounded by the Ise Shrine tradition, sometimes called Ise or Watarai Shinto, is of decisive importance in a consideration of medieval Shinto. Modern intellectual and Shinto historians have generally regarded Ise Shinto, which became active in the thirteenth century, as evidence of Shinto's tenacious, though hidden, existence as "Japan's indigenous religion" throughout medieval times. Moreover, they see it as the starting point for subsequent medieval theories of Shinto as they began to break away from Buddhism.[20]

It is well known that even during Buddhism's apex in the medieval period Ise Shrine maintained ancient rites—whether uniquely Japanese or Taoist in origin—and upheld proscriptions against Buddhist terminology, practices, and garb. But it is equally important to realize that Ise Shrine did not completely reject Buddhism, for Buddhist priests would visit the shrine and Ise priests themselves possessed considerable knowledge of Buddhism. In this light, the proscription against anything Buddhist was probably regarded as a peculiar and mysterious practice, incomprehensible to society in general and even to the Shinto priests at Ise. This proscription, for example, is treated as strange in Mujū's *Shasekishū* and Tsūkai's *Daijingū sankeiki*, works closely associated with Ise Shrine, and in treatises by outstanding priests of Ise, such as the *Daijingū ryōgū no onkoto* by Watarai Tsunemasa. For the medieval mind this was only a natural response. The problem that arises here is how to explain in Buddhist terms what was a truly peculiar practice for the times, or even more so, how to advocate it in all good conscience as a praiseworthy feature of the shrine. The works mentioned above actually begin with this kind of question and end up expounding the immeasurable virtues of the kami at Ise. Also in Ise Shinto there is the expression "not to breathe a word about Buddhism." This in fact does not imply a rejection of Buddhism but rather indicates a special attitude or etiquette assumed in the presence of the kami. As I have explained in detail in a previous book, this view draws on the philosophy of innate Buddhahood (*hongaku shisō*) found in esoteric 本覚思想 Buddhism, which was popular at that time, the thirteenth century.[21] In the final analysis, Ise Shinto was nothing more than one form of sectarian Shinto, which took for granted the existence of the Buddhas.[22]

In the *Hieisha eizan gyōkōki* of the early fourteenth century, it states:

和光同塵

> There are identical as well as differing aspects in the method of conversion used by the *shinmei* (kami) in other lands and that used by Shinto in our own land. Our land, which is a land of the kami, is superior in that human beings are benefited by "the light of the Buddha melded to become one with our world of dust" (*wakō dōjin*, i.e., the power of the Buddha harmonized with our mundane world and manifested as kami).[23]

This passage is indicative of how the word *shintō* was interpreted in medieval times. It was not used to distinguish popular beliefs from Buddhism, but rather to signify the form in which the Buddha converts and saves human beings.

SHINTO'S SECULAR ROLE

神殿

If Shinto is a manifestation of the Buddha and one form in which he converts and saves human beings, there arises the question of whether kami play precisely the same role as the Buddha. Here it is important to note the secular character of Shinto in medieval times. Many of the representations of kami familiar to people in the medieval period were secular in form. Admittedly, there were also numerous examples of syncretism with Buddhism—for instance, Sanskrit letters used to symbolize invisible kami or a Buddhist image enshrined in the inner sanctuary (*shinden*) of a shrine, or again Hachiman portrayed as a Buddhist monk, or Zaō Gongen as the Buddhist deity Myōō (Skt. Vidhārāja). Nevertheless, in many of the Shinto statues, portraits, and narrative drawings that survive today, kami were depicted in such secular guises as noblemen, ladies, old men, young boys, Chinese gentlemen, travelers, and hunters. A number of these became formalized iconographically during the thirteenth century.[24]

The same can also be said of how the word *suijaku* (manifestation) was comprehended. *Suijaku*, as understood by the common people in medieval times, was not the abstract philosophical idea found in the doctrines of Mahāyāna Buddhism but was mythological in nature or perhaps associated with concrete places or events. The term *suijaku* literally meant to descend from heaven to a given spot and to become the local or guardian kami of that spot.[25] Hence, at that spot there would arise a legend of the mysterious relationship between men and kami, and the very area enshrining the kami would be looked upon as sacred ground where profound doctrinal principles lay concealed. The history of this manifestation—that is, its development over time—was related in the form of an *engi* (a historical narrative), and the 縁起 positioning of its enshrinement—that is, its location in space—was depicted in the form of a mandala (a rational layout). This indicates that the legends, the architectural form of early shrines, and the rituals of worship were interpreted as mysterious principles expressing Buddhist philosophy. In short, secular representations in Shinto actually expressed an essence that was strongly Buddhist. The link between Buddhism and Shinto in medieval times is exemplified by the Kike ("chroniclers") school at Enryaku-ji. This school, 記家 which specialized in chronicles, concentrated on mysterious legends, especially Shinto legends, as a means of plumbing the depths of Buddhism.[26]

Also in the medieval period Shinto was associated with numerous secular functions and duties. Shinto observances at court, such as the *Daijōe* (a rite performed by the emperor upon his succession), and the *Jingonjiki* (a biannual offering to the kami by the emperor) had no other purpose than to enshroud secular authority in mystery. Nonetheless, they derived their meaning from the fact that secular mystery lay within a world encompassed by Buddhist law. Eventually, the worship of kami became inseparable from secular authority, but at the same time it was incorporated into the multileveled *kenmitsu* system with its unique logic and structure resulting from Buddhism's development in Japan. Secular though it was, Shinto did not coexist aloof from Buddhism, nor did it constitute a non-Buddhist stronghold within the Buddhist sphere. Rather, its secularity functioned, in the final analysis, within a Buddhist world.

Because shrines were Buddhism's secular face, their upkeep was the responsibility of the secular authority, even though they themselves were integrated into Buddhism's system of control. For that reason, the imperial court made regular offerings to twenty-two specially designated shrines, and the provincial government bore the responsibility for ceremonies

**Buddhist priests chant sūtras in front of a "Shinto" shrine.
On the temple grounds of Zentsū-ji in Kagawa Prefecture.**

and maintenance at major shrines (*sōsha, ichinomiya,* and *ninomiya*) in the provinces. In the Kamakura period the bakufu government stipulated in article one of the *Goseibai shikimoku,* the Jōei law code, that "efforts must be made to keep shrines in repair and not to neglect their ceremonies," thereby stressing the importance of maintaining shrines in the provinces and on estates (*shōen*) under bakufu supervision. In article two it dealt with Buddhist temples and their functions. These indicate not only the responsibilities that the bakufu inherited from the provincial government of the previous period but also the obligations that secular administrative authority had to fulfill to religion.

As stated earlier, Shinto was looked upon as a skillful means by which the Buddha, in his compassion, might lead people to enlightenment or deliver them to his Pure Land. Nonetheless, it is important to note that in actuality Shinto played an important role in the administrative power upholding the secular order. As pointed out in the previous section, the ability of "the light of the Buddha to meld and to become one with our world of dust" (a phrase originally from the *Tao-te ching!*) was constantly stressed in medieval times,

A Gokoku-jinja ("country-protecting shrine")
in the city of Zentsū-ji, Kagawa Prefecture.

but that expression reflects an understanding of Shinto's ultimate significance or its final objective. On an everyday level,
people felt a strong sense of fear toward the kami. For example, in many medieval oaths (*kishōmon*) it is recorded, "If I
violate this pledge, may the punishments of Bonten and
Taishakuten, of the kami of the Provinces, and especially of
the guardian kami of this *shōen*, be visited upon this body of
mine." It goes without saying that what was sworn in such
oaths was, without exception, actions of worldly significance
or things relating to the preservation of the secular order,
rather than anything to do with religious affairs. It is true that
in Buddhism also people would petition the Buddha for
"peace in this world and good fortune in the next," but as a
general rule matters of this world were addressed to the kami
and those of the coming world to the Buddha. In times of
worldly difficulty one might pray for the protection of the
kami and the Buddha, but first and foremost for that of the
kami. Or, when heading into battle, one would beseech the
kami for good fortune in war. Concerning the kami and their
power, it was generally said that they were strict in both
reward and punishment. Such views simply highlight the

influence and control that religion exerted over secular life.

Though there is not enough space to deal with it adequately here, the belief that "Japan is the land of the kami," with both its political and religious implications, was based on the secular role of Shinto described above. The secularity of Shinto and the political applicability of the concept of "the land of the kami" does not indicate that Shinto was without any religious character but rather shows that the Buddhist system that lay behind it pervaded all aspects of everyday life. The present-day illusion that Shinto is not a religion derives historically from a misunderstanding of this point.

THE EMERGENCE OF THE CONCEPT OF SHINTO AS AN INDIGENOUS RELIGION

The following two sentences are found in the *Shintōshū*:

1 Question: On what basis do we know that Shinto reveres the Buddha's teachings?

2 Question: How are we to understand the statement that the Buddha's realm and Shinto differ in their respective forms but are one and the same in essence?[27]

Both of these questions pose kami and Buddha against one another. In the first Shinto clearly indicates the kami themselves, whereas in the second Shinto may be interpreted as the deeds, state, or authority of the kami, but it also conveys the idea of a realm of the kami by contrasting it with the Buddha's realm. A similar passage is found in the *Daijingū sankeiki* by Tsūkai:

> Amaterasu Ōmikami is paramount in Shinto and the Tathāgata Dainichi is paramount in Buddhist teachings. Hence in both *suijaku* (manifestation) and *honji* (origin or source) there is the supreme and the incomparable.[28]

In this case Shinto may be understood as the ideal state of being a kami, but it is also important that, as a concept juxtaposed to "Buddhist teachings," it assumes a sphere of its own, meaning "the realm of *suijaku*," teaching and converting in the form of a kami. This is especially true of the Ise school's theory of Shinto. For example, in the *Hōki hongi* Shinto is contrasted with the "three jewels" (the three basic components of Buddhism—the Buddha, the Buddhist teachings, and the Buddhist order), or in the *Ruishū jingi hongen* it is juxtaposed to *bukke* (Buddhist schools).[29] These imply that Shinto and Buddhism belong to separate spheres in the phenomenal world even though they are identical in essence. Examples that transfer emphasis to the word Shinto in this way are quite conspicuous in Ise Shinto. This was a natural tendency, since the Ise school's theory of Shinto had to stress the efficacy of Shinto above all, even more than other schools of sectarian Shinto.

The word *shintō*, when set up as an object of contrast in this way, emerged with a sectarian meaning or with a special sphere of its own, even though fundamentally it meant the authority of the kami or the condition of being a kami. This is not to say that it assumed the meaning of a separate teaching or religion immediately liberated from the framework of Buddhism. Rather, what Ise Shinto tried to do was to cast the kami of Shinto in a resplendent light. This was attempted by reducing the terms contrasted with Shinto to purely Buddhist phenomena and forms—i.e., Buddhist teachings, "three jewels," Buddhist schools, etc.—and by defining Shinto relative to them. All the while, Buddhism, the overarching principle that embraced and unified both, was left intact as the ultimate basis. The Ise school also attempted to aggrandize Shinto by diverse embellishments and additions to Shinto that were non-Buddhist, and by cloaking it in a dignity similar to that of the Buddhist scriptures. Nonetheless, in this case also the principles that Shinto held in common with Buddhism were likewise stressed.

In this way the word *shintō* came to refer to a Japanese phenomenon, school, or sphere of Buddhism qua religious truth. This meaning of the word paved the way for later stages in which Shinto became a term for Japan's indigenous religion. The writings of the priests at Ise as well as the theories of fourteenth-century Shinto thinkers such as Kitabatake Chikafusa, Jihen, and Ichijō Kanera (corresponding to Tsuda's third definition of Shinto, "concepts and teachings concerning kami") played a particularly important role in this process. Nevertheless, it was not because these thinkers were critical of *kenmitsu* Buddhism, which was the orthodox religion of the medieval period. Rather, they were all adherents of the orthodox teachings, so that any statements they made, which might at first seem to oppose those teachings, were nothing more than an attempt, extreme though it may have been, to enshroud in mystery the authority of the governing system at a time when it was isolated and in decline. With the rise of the Shinto-only school (Yuiitsu or Yoshida Shinto) at the end of the fifteenth century, the word *shintō* became more and more identified as an indigenous form of religion. It was even interpreted as the highest religion, though identical in essence with Buddhism and Confucianism.

At this point the meaning of the word began to depart from the orthodox meaning of *kenmitsu* Buddhism. It just so happened that during this period the power of the orthodox religious order was in a state of decline because of the strength of various heretical movements of so-called "new Buddhism," 一向一揆 particularly of Shinshū uprisings (*ikkō ikki*). The Shinto-only school, which was one branch of sectarian Shinto, simply took advantage of this situation for its own unfettered development.

Beginning in the seventeenth century a Confucian theory of Shinto, with much the same structure as medieval theories, was formulated by Hayashi Razan and other Edo-period scholars. Based on this interpretation of Shinto, the definition of Shinto as the indigenous religion of Japan, as opposed to Taoism, Buddhism, or Confucianism, became firmly fixed. Moreover, the Confucian concept of *dō*, the way, also influenced the word *shintō,* imbuing it with the meaning of "the way, as a political or moral norm" (Tsuda's fifth definition of Shinto). Of course, Confucian Shinto amounted to nothing more than theories of the educated class subordinating Shinto's true nature to Confucianism. Actual belief in the kami, however, as found among the common people at that time, remained subsumed under Buddhism.

The notion of Shinto as Japan's indigenous religion finally emerged complete both in name and in fact with the rise of modern nationalism, which evolved from the National Learning school of Motoori Norinaga and the Restoration Shinto movement of the Edo period down to the establishment of State Shinto in the Meiji period. The Meiji separation 神仏分離 of Shinto and Buddhism (*shinbutsu bunri*) and its concomi- 廃仏毀釈 tant suppression of Buddhism (*haibutsu kishaku*) were coercive and destructive "correctives" pressed forward by the hand of government. With them Shinto achieved for the first time the status of an independent religion, distorted though it was. During this period the "historical consciousness" of an indigenous religion called Shinto, existing in Japan since ancient times, clearly took shape for the first time. This has remained the basis for defining the word *shintō* down to the present. Scholars have yielded to this use of the word, and the population at large has been educated in this vein.

There is one further point to be made—that separating Shinto from Buddhism cut Shinto off from the highest level of religious philosophy achieved by the Japanese up to that time and inevitably, moreover artificially, gave it the features of a primitive religion. Hence, while acquiring independence, Shinto declined to the state of a religion that disavowed being a religion.

CONCLUSION

This essay is an attempt to trace Shinto throughout Japan's entire religious history by extracting samples dealing only with Shinto from each period. The reader may be left with the impression, contrary to the assertion at the beginning of this essay, that Shinto has indeed existed without interruption throughout Japanese history. This is only natural considering the sampling method used. Moreover, it is undeniable that there is a certain continuity to it all. Therein lies the problem. Up to now all studies of Shinto history have emphasized this continuity by means of such a sampling process. In doing so they have applied to all periods of history a sort of surgical separation of Shinto from Buddhism and thus from Japanese religion as a whole. By such reasoning, anything other than Shinto becomes simply a superficial overlay, a passing thing. The meanings of the word *shintō,* as well as changes over time in customs and beliefs, would indicate that Shinto emerged as an independent religion only in modern times, and then only as a result of political policy. If that is so, can this continuity be regarded as a true picture of history? Or could it be that what is perceived as indigenous, or as existing continuously from earliest times, is nothing more than a ghost image produced by a word linking together unrelated phenomena? Up to just one hundred years ago, what constituted the religion and thought of the Japanese people in most periods of history was something historical—that is, something assimilated or fabricated by the people, whether it was native or foreign in origin. This thing was something truly indigenous. In concrete terms, this was the *kenmitsu*

Buddhist system, including its components, such as Shinto and the Yin-yang tradition, and its various branches, both reformist and heretical. It, rather than Shinto, was the comprehensive, unified, and self-defined system of religious thought produced by Japan in premodern times. Even today it is perpetuated latently in everyday conventions as the subconscious of the Japanese people.

Throughout East Asia, Mahāyāna Buddhism generally embraced native beliefs in a loose manner, without harsh repression and without absorbing them to the point of obliteration. The question here is how to understand this process in Japan. While acknowledging Japan as an example of this East Asian pattern, should one consider the separation of Shinto and Buddhism to be an inevitable development and, in line with Meiji nationalism, perceive Shinto as the basis of Japan's cultural history? Or, should one view *kenmitsu* Buddhism's unique system of thought, which evolved historically from diverse elements, including foreign ones, as the distinguishing feature of Japanese culture?

The magnitude of this subject is too great to adequately address in one short article. It is hoped, however, that the above discussion has served to dispel fictitious notions about Japan's religious history and religious consciousness, and about Japanese culture in general.

NOTES

* The author thanks Suzanne Gay and James C. Dobbins for their suggestions during the writing of this article, and for translating it into English. (This essay first appeared in *Journal of Japanese Studies* 7/1: 1–21, 1981. Reprinted by permission. Kuroda Toshio was professor at Osaka University. He passed away while this book was being prepared for publication.)

1 Hori Ichirō, *Hijiri to zoku no kattō*, Tokyo: Heibonsha, 1975.

2 See Maruyama Masao, ed., *Rekishi shisōshi*, Tokyo: Chikuma Shobō, 1972.

3 Taken from the *Tōmonroku* by Motoori Norinaga, thought to have been written between 1777 and 1779. This work is a compilation of answers to questions asked by his students. See *Motoori Norinaga zenshū*, vol. I, Tokyo: Chikuma Shobō, 1968, p. 527.

4 Tsuda Sōkichi, *Nihon no Shintō*, Tokyo: Iwanami Shoten, 1949, chapter one. *Kami* is the Japanese word for a deity or spirit. The word

shintō, which is of Chinese origin, is made of two characters: *shin* meaning *kami*, and *tō* meaning way or upright conduct.

5 *Nihon shoki* II, vol. 68 of *Nihon koten bungaku taikei*, Tokyo: Iwanami Shoten, 1965, note on "Shinto," p. 556.

6 In an early manuscript, the Japanese gloss *hotoke no minori* is added to the Chinese characters *buppō*. Of course this was written after the ninth century, but it may have been read that way from the time of the manuscript.

7 Tsuda, *Nihon no Shintō*, chapter one.

8 *Jidaibetsu kokugo daijiten*, Tokyo: Sanseidō, 1967; *Iwanami kogo jiten*, Tokyo: Iwanami Shoten, 1967. Both works give examples of *michi* used to refer to Buddhist doctrines, but this is not to say that the meaning "doctrine" is included in the word *michi*.

9 *Nihon shoki*, II, p. 574.

10 Fukunaga Kōji, "Dōkyō ni okeru kagami to tsurugi—sono shisō to genryū," *Tōhō gakuhō* 45 (1973); Fukunaga Kōji, "Tennō to shikyū to shinjin—Chūgoku kodai no Shintō," *Shisō* 637 (1977).

11 Editor's note: Reading this character as *hijiri* is highly unusual and suggestive, but is clearly indicated as such by the author in the original Japanese. It is usually pronounced *sen*, as in the compound *sennin*. 仙人

12 Shimode Sekiyo, *Nihon kodai no jingi to dōkyō*, Tokyo: Yoshikawa Kōbunkan, 1972.

13 *Ritsuryō*, vol. 3 of *Nihon shisō taikei*, Tokyo: Iwanami Shoten, 1976, p. 529.

14 Takatori Masao, *Shintō no seiritsu*, Tokyo: Heibonsha, 1979.

15 *Konjaku monogatarishū*, fasc. 7, story 3; fasc. 3, story 26.

16 *Kōbō Daishi zenshū*, vol. 5, Tokyo: Yoshikawa Kōbunkan, 1909, p. 160.

17 *Akagi bunkobon Shintōshū*, vol. 1 of *Kichō kotensekisōdan*, Tokyo: Kadokawa Shoten, 1968, p. 12.

18 *Vocabvlario da Lingoa de Iapam* (Nagasaki, 1603); *Nippo jisho*, Tokyo: Iwanami Shoten, 1960.

19 Kuroda Toshio, *Nihon chūsei no kokka to shūkyō*, Tokyo, Iwanami Shoten, 1975, chapter three.

20 Ōsumi Kazuo, "Chūsei Shintōron no shisōteki ichi," *Chūsei shintōron*, vol. 19 of *Nihon shisō taikei*, Tokyo: Iwanami Shoten, 1977.

21 Kuroda Toshio, *Nihon chūsei*, chapter four.

22 Kuroda Toshio, "Chūsei shūkyōshi ni okeru Shintō no ichi," in *Kodai chūsei no shakai to shisō: Ienaga Saburō kyōju taikan kinen*, Tokyo: Sanseidō, 1979, p. 151 ff.

23 Okami Masao hakase kanreki kinen kankōkai, ed., *Muromachi gokoro—Chūsei bungaku shiryōshū*, Tokyo: Kadokawa Shoten, 1978, p. 366.

[24] See *Enryaku-ji gokoku engi* in *Dai Nihon bukkyō zensho*, chapter one; and Kageyama Haruki, *Shintō bijutsu*, Tokyo: Yūzankaku, 1973, p. 170.

[25] See Kuroda, *Nihon chūsei*, p. 451.

[26] Hazama Jikō, *Nihon bukkyō no kaiten to sono kichō*, vol. 2, Tokyo: Sanseidō, p. 245 ff.

[27] *Akagi bunkobon Shintōshū*, pp. 226–27.

[28] *Jingū sankeiki taisei*, in *Daijingū sōsho*, p. 70.

[29] *Watarai shintō taisei*, I, in *Daijingū sōsho*, pp. 54, 695.

Religious Rituals in Shugendō

A Summary

MIYAKE Hitoshi

S HUGENDŌ REFERS TO a religious tradition, still alive today, that developed a specific religious structure when the beliefs and faith with regard to mountains in ancient Japan were influenced by foreign religious traditions such as Buddhism, Taoism, and shamanism. The core of this religious tradition consists of magico-religious activities performed in response to the religious needs or demands of people in local communities by *shugenja* or *yamabushi*, Shugendō practicers who have acquired supernatural spiritual powers through cultivation of various ascetic practices, mainly in the mountains.

修験道

修験者 山伏

Shugenja traveled widely throughout the mountains and plains of Japan during the medieval period, but in later times, in part because of the restrictive policies of the Tokugawa government, they settled down and became a regular part of local communities. By this time local communities in Japan already had shrines that housed the local guardian deities, and temples that took care of funerary rites. The role undertaken by shugenja who settled in these communities was to respond to the various mundane needs of the common people in the areas of disease and problems of daily life, offering religious services such as fortunetelling and divination (*bokusen*), obtaining oracles through mediums (*fujutsu*), offering prayers (*kitō*), and performing exorcism (*chōbuku*). Thus, in the Edo period the shugenja were responsible for offering "this-worldly benefits" within the context of the religious activities of the common people, and played a major role in these religious activities. It can also be said that Shugendō provided the central model for the religious activities of many of the "new" religions (e.g., sectarian Shinto) that proliferated from the latter part of the nineteenth century and continue to this day.

In this sense it can be said that it is impossible to understand popular religion in Japan without taking Shugendō into consideration. The importance of research on Shugendō is not limited to religious studies but is also imperative for the areas of historical and folk studies. However, Shugendō studies so far have, with few exceptions, concentrated on such limited aspects of Shugendō as sectarian history or mountain practices. There have been no comprehensive studies of the religious rituals of Shugendō, which include festivals, fortunetelling, divination, prayers and incantations, exorcism, spells, charms, and so forth. These are religious rituals that are performed by shugenja in response to the daily needs and requirements of the people. They are the key to understanding Shugendō as a popular religion. In order to study Shugendō as a single religious system, it is important to grasp the aggregate relationships between and among these religious rituals. However, much of the information concerning these rituals is hidden behind the veil of oral and secret transmissions. Thus these activities have been inaccessible to academic research through normal research methods.

In my work I have examined the written documents concerning these religious rituals that are available, and then analyzed and clarified them further through on-the-spot observation of the practices of various Shugendō organizations, and have thus attempted to grasp the symbolic meaning of Shugendō rituals as a whole. Here I will attempt to summarize my conclusions.[1] I have identified various categories of religious rituals that have an organic relationship with the entire system of Shugendō religious rituals.

入峰修行   **• PRACTICES IN THE MOUNTAINS (nyūbu shugyō)**

There are three types of nyūbu. First is entering the mountains to make offerings of flowers, read or bury sūtras, and so forth, in honor of various buddhas or other deities, based on the belief that the mountain is a sacred area like a mandala. Examples of this type of nyūbu are the offerings of flowers at Kinpusen, Hongū, and Shingū; the Higan ceremonies at Nachi in Kumano; the nyūbu by the Honzan-ha at Katsuragi for the purpose of burying sūtras; and the summer nyūbu (natsu no mine) at Mt. Haguro. This first type of nyūbu eventually developed into ceremonies performed in preparation for the second type of nyūbu, i.e., entering the mountains for a certain period of time. Examples of this second type include the *nyūbu* of yamabushi from around the country at Kinpusen, the summer ascetic practices at Nachi in Kumano, the fall *nyūbu* (*aki no mine*) by the Honzan-ha and Tōzan-ha, and by ascetics at Haguro-san. All of these retreats in the

Confession time during the summer *nyūbu* on Mt. Ōmine.

秘法

mountains occur for a set length of time, during which various ascetic practices are cultivated, culminating in the transmission of secret lore (hihō) or performance of initiations. This kind of nyūbu is an essential experience for any serious shugenja. At the present time, however, there are few transmissions of secrets or initiations during nyūbu, and there is increasing participation by lay people. This type of nyūbu was and remains the central and most popular practice of shugenja at major Shugendō centers throughout Japan.

The third type of nyūbu is the most severe, consisting of a difficult ascetic retreat in the mountains during the wintertime. Examples include the nyūbu of the misoka ("end of the year") yamabushi of Kinpusen, Hongū, and Shingū; the practices of toshigomori ("retreat over new year's day") at Nachi; and the winter nyūbu (fuyu no mine) of Haguro. At Haguro-san only the most advanced yamabushi participate in this nyūbu. The purpose of this kind of nyūbu was to acquire special spiritual powers.

正灌頂

• CONSECRATION CEREMONIES (shōkanjō)

Shugendō, as a movement very much influenced by esoteric (mikkyō) Buddhism, involves a great variety of consecration ceremonies (kanjō, Skt. abhiṣeka). The central and most important consecration, however, is the shōkanjō performed at the end of a nyūbu. Shōkanjō is a distinctive Shugendō consecration performed at Jinzen towards the end of the Ōmine nyūbu. It is performed on the assumption that the shugenja has passed through the "ten realms" from hell to buddhahood during the person's practice in the mountains, and symbolizes the final attainment of "buddhahood in this body" (sokushin sokubutsu).

験術

• DEMONSTRATION OF MAGICO-SPIRITUAL POWERS (genjutsu)

The spectacular demonstration of spiritual powers attained through the cultivation of ascetic practices in the mountains is perhaps the best-known aspect of Shugendō in present-day Japan. These demonstrations once included flying through the air, walking on swords, walking on fire, "hiding" one's body, and entering boiling water. The details concerning some of these powers, such as flying through the air and hiding one's body, are unknown, with only scant information concerning them in surviving Shugendō records. Other demonstrations such as walking on fire are still performed today, often with much fanfare, in places such as Mt. Takao outside Tokyo, Mt. Ishizuchi in Ehime, and Mt. Ontake in Nagano/Gifu.

• COMMEMORATION RITES (kuyōhō)

供養法

By kuyōhō I refer to rites of worship whereby the shugenja expresses his reverence toward certain deities through the performance of the chanting of sūtras or other offerings. Ui Hakuju classifies kuyō into three types: offerings of respect (kei kuyō) such as the decoration and cleaning of the worship hall; offerings of action (gyō kuyō) such as the chanting of sūtras and performance of worship; and offerings of "benefit" (ri kuyō), such as the offerings of food and water (Ui 1980: 206). The kuyō offerings in Shugendō follow the same pattern. The central Shugendō kuyō is that performed for Fudō Myōō (Fudō hō), in which the presence of Fudō is solicited, offerings are made, and the shugenja becomes symbolically identified with him.

敬
行

利

• PARTICIPATION IN MATSURI FOR THE KAMI, FOR THE SUN, MOON, AND STARS (hi-tsuki-hoshi no matsuri), AND FOR SMALL SHRINES (shōshi no matsuri)

日月星の祭
小祠の祭

Shugenja have always been involved in "Shinto" matsuri (festivals) for the kami. These activities include chanting sūtras in front of the kami, "calling" on the kami and making offerings, visiting shrines and participating in worship, performing rites of purification, and so forth.

One type of matsuri in which shugenja were particularly active were those connected with the sun, moon, and stars. Matsuri for the sun include rituals whereby shugenja and other believers gather together to worship the sun for the purpose of averting disasters or promoting prosperity. The rituals involve undergoing purification and then staying awake all night making offerings, reading sūtras, and performing other rites until the sun rises in the morning. Matsuri that involve worship of the moon include gatherings of shugenja and believers at certain phases of the monthly cycle to eat and drink together, watch for the rising of the moon, and pray for the realization of certain requests. Festivals for the stars include worship of the North Star and performance of various forms of divination based on the calendar and astrology.

Another kind of matsuri in which shugenja are often involved is matsuri for small shrines. In Japan there are innumerable small shrines throughout the country that house and honor, for example, the kami of the hearth, the family deities, and especially the unpredictable *kōjin* ("fierce deity") of the kitchen. Shugenja were often called upon to participate in matsuri or rituals connected with these small shrines.

荒神

卜占 • **FORTUNETELLING AND DIVINATION (*bokusen*)**

Shugenja were and are involved in many types of fortunetelling and divination: the analysis of good and bad days of the calendar, yin-yang divination, the determination of lucky and unlucky directions, divining a person's fate through astrological signs or guardian deities based on a person's birthdate, and so forth.

巫術 • **THE ART OF OBTAINING ORACLES THROUGH MEDIUMS (*fujutsu*)**

In addition to the aforementioned methods of divination, some shugenja obtain oracles by acting as mediums, calling on the spirits of the kami or buddhas to possess them and give oracles. However, I believe that the shugenja as medium is a marginal role within Shugendō. It is also difficult to draw a line between mediums who are affiliated with Shugendō and those who are not. Nevertheless, the art of obtaining oracles through mediums is not an uncommon occurrence within the framework of Shugendō.

憑り祈禱 • **PRAYERS OF POSSESSION (*yorigitō*)**

Yorigitō is a form of obtaining oracles peculiar to Shugendō. In this ritual a shugenja uses a medium as a vehicle for possession by a deity, which is then asked to reply to various queries or requests concerning the next harvest or one's personal fortune.

息災護摩 • **FIRE CEREMONIES FOR AVERTING MISFORTUNES (*sokusai goma*)**

The *goma* fire ritual is a form of Shugendō prayer. A certain liturgy is performed, including various chants, before and while a fire is burnt. Offerings are burnt in the fire for the object of worship, usually Fudō Myōō, and prayers are offered for the realization of certain requests. These cere-

A *saitō goma* performed at the beginning of a summer *nyūbu* on Mt. Ōmine.

monies are much the same in content as the *Fudō hō* discussed earlier.

The *saitō goma* is a fire ceremony unique to Shugendō. This ceremony often forms the central part of major Shugendō ritual performances, especially before, during, or after a *nyūbu*.

• RITUALS CENTERED ON VARIOUS DEITIES (*shosonbō*) 諸尊法

In addition to fire ceremonies, Shugendō rituals include many ceremonies utilizing hand gestures (*mudrā*) and spells (*shingon*; *dhāraṇī*) for the purpose of attaining what one prays for. These ceremonies address certain deities: buddhas such as Yakushi and Amida, bodhisattvas such as Monju and Kokūzō, various forms of Kannon, various Myōō such as

Fudō, originally Indian deities such as Benzai-ten (Sarasvatī), Japanese kami such as *kōjin* (untamed spirits), Inari, and Daikoku. An examination of the ceremonies listed in Shugendō manuals shows that these ceremonies are most often addressed to the Myōō or the Indian deities and their retinue, with Fudō Myōō the most common figure.

加持 ## • INCANTATIONS (*KAJI*)

The word *kaji* is often combined with *kitō* ("prayers") to form the compound *kaji-kitō*, and in the popular mind this is believed to be the most common activity or function of a shugenja. However, *kaji* and *kitō* are not the same. *Kitō* refers to the prayers offered to a deity as a form of request in ceremonies such as the *Fudō hō, sokusai goma,* and *shosonbō. Kaji,* on the other hand, refers to the identification (*ka*) of the shugenja with the deity in order to realize (*ji*) a certain purpose.[2] Therefore *kaji* is a religious ritual wherein the shugenja achieves identification with the deity and manipulates the power thus obtained in order to gain certain benefits.

調伏 ## • EXORCISM (*tsukimono otoshi, chōbuku*)

Shugenja also perform rites of healing by determining the cause of a disease (such as the spirit of an evil deity, the dead, or an animal), and then perform ceremonies to exorcise these spirits. Shugenja were known as figures who could control or manipulate such spirits of possession (*tsukimono*).

There are some cases of possession, however, which cannot be resolved through ceremonies of *tsukimono otoshi* and require the more demanding ritual of exorcism called *chōbuku* ("subduing" of spirits). An example of this ritual is the *kuji* ("nine letters") ceremony that utilizes nine mudrā and nine formulas to draw on the power of supernatural deities. This ceremony is based on a Taoist practice but is one of the most fundamental practices of Shugendō.

符呪 呪い ## • SPELLS AND CHARMS (*fuju, majinai*)

Finally, shugenja utilize various forms of charms and spells in response to simple requests by people for healing, safe childbirth, protection from theft, and so forth. These spells are simpler than the aforementioned prayers and incantations, often consisting of a short phrase (the gist of a sūtra, an

---

esoteric formula, or the name of a deity) written on a small amulet. These amulets are carried by people in their pockets or around their neck, or placed somewhere such as near the oven in a house, and so forth, in order to divert misfortune or solicit good fortune.

On the basis of the concrete examples outlined above, I understand the structure and function of Shugendō religious rituals as follows: each of these individual religious rituals assumes a symbol system that reflects a specific religious worldview. In other words, the activity undertaken in each of these rituals is symbolic action, and the various devices used in the rituals are symbols. These numerous symbolic actions and symbols combine to form a symbolic system that reflects a certain religious worldview.

The symbol system of the religious rituals, and the religious worldview, of Shugendō is revealed through the activities of the shugenja themselves. The rituals as a symbol system must have a motif, which is based on the religious worldview of Shugendō. By analyzing and clarifying this religious worldview in light of the concrete religious rituals, we can avoid the pitfall of an overly abstract or inconsistent analysis.

Each of the individual rituals, in order to symbolize a religious worldview, fulfills a proper ritualistic function within that religious worldview, and forms a symbol system centered on a motif that is close to the daily lives and concerns of the shugenja and the faithful. A set of numerous symbolic actions or symbols are the elements that form this symbol system. The elements that form each religious ritual have a nucleus—a central motif—from among these elements. These elements are bound together and mutually related, and thus form a single, ordered mechanism. My study of these individual Shugendō rituals involves analyzing this mechanism and clarifying the central motifs. In the other direction, the religious worldview of Shugendō is re-interpreted through the motifs from the perspective of the religious rituals.

THE STRUCTURE OF SHUGENDŌ RITUALS

Let us first concentrate on the structure and the central nucleus—the motif—from among the elements of these individual Shugendō rituals, and clarify them in light of the religious worldview of Shugendō.

First, practices in the mountains (*nyūbu shugyō*) and consecrations (*shōkanjō*) involve spiritual identification with the central deity, Fudō Myōō, through reception of a secret transmission while the shugenja is in the mountains. These rituals signify the rebirth of the ascetic as a buddha who has acquired the ability to control or utilize the power of Fudō. Therefore the central element in both of these rituals is the symbolic action exhibited in a state of identification with the central deity, Fudō Myōō. The performance of various practices and rituals in the mountains assumes that the mountains are a supernatural spiritual realm, the dwelling of various deities and objects of worship such as Fudō Myōō, separate from the realm of our daily lives. This belief is based on a religious worldview that considers the mountains to be a symbol of the universe.

The demonstration of magical/spiritual powers (*genjutsu*) involves rituals in which the shugenja who has achieved symbolic identification with Fudō Myōō then demonstrates this identification by entering the spiritual realm. Identification is the central element of these activities. An underlying assumption of these activities is the shamanistic idea that the shugenja who has become identified with the figure of Fudō Myōō can in fact enter the spiritual realm.

Next, commemorative rituals (*kuyōhō*) and services for kami, for the sun, moon, and stars (*hi-tsuki-hoshi no matsuri*), and for small shrines (*shōshi no matsuri*), are rituals often performed by shugenja. A typical example of *kuyō hō* is the service for Fudō, a ritual in which Fudō Myōō is invited by the shugenja as a guest to the altar (*shūhōdōjō*) for the purpose of achieving identification with the deity. The "object of worship" (*sūhai taishō*) is welcomed and favored with the chanting of scriptures (*dokyō*) or performance of matsuri for the kami. Thus the structure of this ritual consists of the elements of communication and identification between the shugenja and the object of worship.

Rites in honor of the sun, moon, and stars consist of bringing down these heavenly bodies and achieving their identification with Fudō Myōō, for the purpose of "extinguishing the seven kinds of adversities" (*shichinan sokumetsu*) and "arousing the seven kinds of blessings" (*shichifuku sokushō*).[3] The festivals of small shrines, which celebrate local kitchen gods, deities of the earth, and so forth, involve the

七難即滅
七福即生

shugenja achieving identification with Fudō Myōō, where-
upon the shugenja removes evil influences by exorcising evil
deities or evil spirits that are causing misfortune, and invites
good spirits to take their place. In a broad sense these two rituals both have prayers for the removal of evil influences as
their central structural element. And both rituals are based on
a religious worldview that accepts as normal the possibility
of the shugenja, through identification with Fudō Myōō,
removing misfortunes by exorcizing evil spirits or modifying
the unfortunate influences of heavenly bodies.

Various forms of divination and fortunetelling are used to
discover the causes of misfortune and the fates of human
beings. Fortunetelling methods such as *kikkyō* and *unsei* use   吉凶　運勢
the motif of analyzing the smaller realm of human beings
within the larger universe through the structure of the five
elements of Yin and Yang and the ten calendar signs and
twelve signs of the zodiac. In this case the religious worldview involved is that, for example, daily fortunes depend on
the power of various deities or vengeful spirits, or that the
fates of human beings depend on the astrological influences
of the stars. There are also rituals for determining the cause of
disease, and so forth, through *bokusen*, *kikkyō*, or *unsei*.
These rituals are based on the assumption that disease is
caused by angry spirits or spirits of the living or dead that
hamper the proper and normal course of the universe.

The practice of obtaining oracles through mediums (*fujutsu*) involves rituals through which a shugenja makes his or
her guardian spirit possess him or her in order to obtain an
oracle. In the case of *kuchiyose* oracles by Itako-type medi-   口寄せ
ums, the mediums achieve identification with their guardian
spirit and use the power thus acquired to call forth the
requested spirit (of the living or dead), which then takes possession of the medium. "Prayers of possession" (*yori-kitō*) are
a specifically Shugendō-type practice that consists of a
shugenja achieving identification with Fudō Myōō in order to
manipulate deities (usually tutelary deities) so the medium
is possessed by them and grants an oracle.

Fire ceremonies for averting misfortune (*sokusai goma*) are
rituals wherein a shugenja achieves identification with Fudō
Myōō in order to manipulate the deity of fire (*katen*) and the   火天
fates (*yōshuku*) for the purpose of removing evil influences.   曜宿
This activity is based on the religious worldview that it is

Symbolically burning away passionate delusions during a *saitō goma* fire ceremony.

possible to obtain good fortune by determining the cause of misfortune through divination, and that one can then "burn away" misfortune. *Shosonbō* involves a shugenja attaining identification with a certain object of worship and then performing certain actions that symbolize salvific activity. The central structural element of both these rituals is prayer. *Kaji* prayers or incantations, on the other hand, are rituals that utilize the power of the object of worship in order to remove or exorcize evil influences, or that seek the protection of the object of worship by transferring its power into a tool, weapon, clothing, and so forth.

Another type of religious ritual that shugenja often perform is exorcism (*tsukimono-otoshi* and *chōbuku*). *Tsukimono-otoshi* is a ritual of exorcism wherein a shugenja drives out a possessing spirit by teaching it the error of its ways or by threatening it. *Chōbuku*, on the other hand, involves identification of the shugenja with Fudō Myōō so that the shugenja can control Fudō Myōō's retinue of servants and have them bind, kick, beat, or otherwise subdue evil deities or evil spirits. Both of these rituals are based on the religious worldview that evil deities or evil spirits are the cause of misfortune, and that the shugenja through identification with Fudō Myōō can directly utilize his supernatural power, or can manipulate Fudō Myōō's retinue, in order to control and defeat these evil deities and spirits.

On a simpler level various charms (*fuju*) and spells (*majinai*) are also utilized. The motif here is the removal of evil influences by using charms onto which the shugenja has transferred the supernatural power of a deity, or by manipulating magical instruments. Thus the last four types of rituals, i.e., incantations, exorcism, charms, and spells, all have the removal (or exorcism) of evil influences as their central motif.

THE LOGIC OF RELIGIOUS RITUALS IN SHUGENDŌ

The individual religious rituals of Shugendō outlined above have the following interrelationship within the total structure of Shugendō rituals.

The primary Shugendō rituals are those associated with *nyūbu* and consecration, through which shugenja achieve identification with a deity and gain the ability to control the power thus attained. Next, these powers are manifested to the shugenja's followers through rituals such as *genjutsu*, the demonstration of magical powers. The identification and communication with deities continue in rituals such as *kuyō hō* and various activities connected with matsuri. On the basis of these preparations, shugenja respond to the requests of their followers by performing divination and the art of obtaining oracles through mediums to avert misfortune by clarifying the causes of these misfortune, whether evil deities, evil spirits, or unlucky stars. Evil influences are removed and blessings solicited through the performance of *goma* fire ceremonies, rituals centered on various deities, and services for the heavenly bodies and small shrines. At other times evil deities or evil spirits are exorcized. Other accessible means for averting misfortune or soliciting blessings include *kaji* incantations, charms, and spells.

I have attempted to grasp the whole of the Shugendō ritual system as one that is structured from central elements found in these individual rituals. I have concluded that Shugendō rituals as a whole are made up of seven major elements:

1 Rituals for the purpose of identification with the object of worship (*nyūbu*, consecration, the demonstration of magical powers, rites for Fudō Myōō).
2 Rituals for the purpose of communication with the object of worship (chanting of sūtras, matsuri for deities).
3 Rituals as means to achieve identification with the object of worship (divination, obtaining oracles through mediums, prayers of possession, *goma* fire ceremonies, rites for deities, *kaji* incantations, exorcism).
4 Rituals to achieve the power to manipulate these deities (prayers of possession, *goma* fire ceremonies, *kaji* incantations, exorcism, charms, spells).
5 Rituals to receive oracles (divination, oracles through mediums, prayers of possession).
6 Rituals of prayer (services for the sun, moon, and stars, and small shrines, *goma* fire ceremony for averting misfortunes, rites for various deities).
7 Rituals of exorcism or removing evil influences (*kaji* incantations, removing a possessing spirit, "defeating" spirits, charms, spells).

When considering the interrelationship between these elements, we can reach the following conclusions concerning the structure of Shugendō rituals as a whole.

Shugendō rituals begin with the shugenja attaining a spiritual identification with Fudō Myōō, the main deity, and the attainment of the ability to control this spiritual power. When a shugenja receives a request from a follower, he must first determine the cause of misfortune through divination. There are many possible causes for misfortune: the spirits of animals, the spirits of the living or the dead, evil deities, and so forth. The most common means for putting an end to this evil activity is to pray to a deity. In Shugendō the more common approach is to have the shugenja experience identity with Fudō Myōō, and have the evil activity cease through manipulating the supernatural power of Fudō Myōō or his retinue.

Thus it can be said that the structure of the Shugendō ritual system is as follows. First, the shugenja identifies himself with a deity in order to learn, through an oracle, which evil deity or evil spirit is causing misfortune. He then wields the supernatural power of his deity or its retinue, and finally exorcizes or removes the evil influences. Within this structure one can see that the three elements of identification, manipulation, and exorcism are the three central motifs of the Shugendō ritual system.

These three motifs are particularly suitable to the function of Shugendō rituals from the perspective of the religious worldview of Shugendō. The explicit function of the religious rituals of Shugendō, especially the people's appeal for "this-worldly benefits," is to remove evil influences and misfortunes from their daily lives. The implicit functions of these rituals for the believers, on the other hand, include the transmission of the teachings and supernatural revelations possessed by the shugenja, and integration with already-existing forms of folk religion.

The fact that an explicit function of Shugendō rituals is to remove the cause of misfortunes is a reflection of the "exorcism" motif. Next, implicit functions such as the revelation of the shugenja's supernatural power to the believers and the dissemination of teachings reflect the "identification" motif, i.e., that the shugenja is identified with Fudō Myōō and his activity. A particularly graphic illustration of this motif is *genjutsu*, the demonstration of magical powers, in which the shugenja symbolically enters the spiritual realm after his identification with Fudō Myōō. Also, these teachings of Shugendō, the religious worldview that has been authorized by its organization, is expressed in manifestations or often clearly expounded in the course of various rituals.

The idea that Shugendō rituals have served to integrate Shugendō with previously existing forms of folk religion is reflected in the role shugenja play at shrines or at matsuri such as those for small shrines. An interesting aspect of this idea, in connection with the "manipulation" motif of Shugendō rituals, is that the retinue of powers manipulated by the shugenja after his identification with the deity often turn out to be the tutelary deities of the local society wherein the ritual is being performed. By controlling these powers the shugenja could succeed in having his religious activity accepted by the local community, and his rituals could eventually achieve a more prestigious status than the religious activities that existed previously within the local society.

In this way the motifs of identification, manipulation, and exorcism are intimately related to the function of the religious rituals of Shugendō. It must be noted, however, that these motifs are ways to symbolize the religious worldview of Shugendō through the form of religious rituals. With this in mind let us take another look at the motifs of identification, manipulation, and exorcism from the perspective of the religious worldview of Shugendō and revealed in Shugendō rituals.

THE RELIGIOUS WORLDVIEW OF SHUGENDŌ AND SHUGENDŌ RITUALS

First, the religious worldview that underlies Shugendō rituals assumes the existence of at least two realms of existence, that of the daily lives of human beings, and a separate, supernatural spiritual realm behind it, that controls the daily lives of human beings. The mountains are seen either as a sacred space that is part of both of these worlds, or seen to be an actual part of the spiritual world. The altar space during the fire ceremony, or the area of a matsuri, is also considered to be this kind of sacred space.

The supernatural spiritual world of Shugendō contains a large syncretistic pantheon of various kami, deities, buddhas, spirits, and so forth, all of which are believed to control the daily lives of human beings. Fudō Myōō plays a central role in this pantheon. The residents of this spiritual realm, with Fudō Myōō in the center, can be classified into three types of entities.

First are various buddhas and other Buddhist *mikkyō*-type figures such as Fudō Myōō and Dainichi Nyorai (Mahāvairocana), specifically Shugendō objects of worship such as Zaō Gongen, and kami that are enshrined by many shrines all around Japan or that have a universalistic character. These kami often serve to symbolize the universe as a whole.

Second, kami with a more individual or local character, such as tutelary deities, guardian deities, the retinue of more powerful figures, and so forth. The members of this second group often serve as the retinue of those in the first group. Zaō Gongen and some of the kami enshrined in many shrines around Japan were originally local figures like those in the second category, but later took on a more universalistic character.

Third, the evil deities and evil spirits that are the actual causes of various misfortunes. When these evil deities and spirits are brought under control by the shugenja and "enshrined " in a small shrine, these deities take on the character of those in the second category.

Shugendō teaches that a human being is a product of the universe and is himself a "small" universe. All things, including human beings, are thought to have the same nature or character as the divine, the primary and original form of all things. Therefore it is possible for a human being to become a divine being. A shugenja, by cultivating ascetic practices in the mountains (symbolic of the supernatural spiritual world or of the universe itself) and by receiving secret transmissions, can become spiritually identified with Fudō Myōō, who already possesses a universalistic character.

If you will recall the structure of Shugendō ritual as outlined above, shugenja first enter the mountains and receive consecration in order to achieve identification with Fudō Myōō and gain the ability to control Fudō Myōō's spiritual power. The shugenja who have obtained this spiritual power can communicate with the more local and individual spiritual entities who are believed to have a more intimate relationship with the daily lives of the people, and can thus discover the causes of the people's misfortunes, and identify which evil deities or spirits are to blame. On this basis the shugenja use their universalistic spiritual power to manipulate the individual deities (category 2) and control the evil deities and evil spirits (category 3), and thus exorcise or remove evil influences.

In conclusion we can say that the three motifs of identification, manipulation, and exorcism in Shugendō rituals are based on the following religious worldview. First, the structure of the universe is such that behind the world of daily human life there is a separate spiritual realm that transcends yet controls our lives. Second, this spiritual world is inhabited by a syncretistic pantheon of various buddhas, kami, deities, and so forth, which can be categorized into three types: those having a universalistic character, those having an individualistic or local character, and evil deities or spirits. Third, shugenja, by cultivating ascetic practices in the mountains, can attain spiritual identification with figures of universalistic character and directly utilize their power to manipulate the deities of individual character and control the evil deities and spirits to exorcise or remove evil influences. This religious worldview is revealed and symbolized in and through Shugendō rituals.

NOTES

* This article was translated by Paul L. Swanson from the concluding summary of *Shugendō girei no kenkyū*, Tokyo: Shunjūsha, 1985, pp. 686–95, a massive and detailed study of Shugendō ritual. It was supplemented during translation (with the author's support and approval) with details from the main body of this book. The translation appeared originally in the special issue on "Shugendō and Mountain Religion in Japan," edited by Royall Tyler and Paul L. Swanson, *Japanese Journal of Religious Studies* 16/2–3: 101–16 (June–September 1989). Miyake Hitoshi is Professor at Keiō University in Tokyo and a leading specialist in Shugendō studies.

¹ For details concerning the argument in this article and concrete examples of Shugendō rituals see MIYAKE 1985a.

² Nevertheless, one must admit that in practice there is a mixture of these concepts. For example, various forms of *kaji* are incorporated into ceremonies of "prayer" such as the *Fudō hō*.

³ This phrase is found in a passage from the *Jên-wang ching* (Jpn. *Ninnō-kyō*), a Buddhist scripture. The "seven kinds of adversities" are calamities connected with the sun and moon, astrological calamities, fires, floods, strong winds, overly-luminous sunlight, and violent insurgences or revolts; the "seven kinds of blessings" are not listed. It is best to understand these in a general sense of gaining relief from all adversities and attracting all blessings.

Religion in Contemporary Japanese Society

Jan SWYNGEDOUW

I N A GUIDEBOOK by a well-known cartoonist with the English-language subtitle "Well-mannered Japanese Tourists: Overseas Travel Tips through Pictures," one page is devoted to the problem that arises when asked abroad about your religion. Depicted to the left of the cartoon is a tall foreign couple, the wife with a crucifix hanging from her neck; above their heads is a thought balloon with a Buddha statue inside. To the right stands a little Japanese who, apparently hesitating, answers: "Buddha" and "Zen." The explanation beneath the cartoon is clear. "The trend away from religion seems to be a worldwide phenomenon. Yet, since there are countries where the answer 'No' elicits mistrust, it is still a good idea to answer 'Buddha' or 'Zen' when asked."

It is hard to gauge the extent to which guidebooks like this have helped Japanese to realize that, after all, they themselves have something to do with religion in general and with Buddhism and Zen in particular. But it cannot be denied that the problem of religion is part and parcel of the ongoing boom of "navel-gazing," exemplified in the plethora of books on what it means to be Japanese. As is normal in such cases, the mass media have jumped on the bandwagon. They conduct surveys and engage in that other beloved pastime of the Japanese, comparisons with other countries in order to know where Japan ranks on the scale of religiosity—who is above and who is below. Some have even gone so far as to create new "religious needs." Witness the various new magazines catering to and nurturing the undifferentiated desire for magic and mystical experiences, not least alive among middle-aged housewives.

Nevertheless, it remains a difficult task to find one's way through the maze of religiosity and non-religiosity that typifies the Japanese. Scholars of religion—both Japanese and non-Japanese—have come up with all kinds of interpretations, some of them diametrically opposed. Others, such as Westerners on a search for Oriental enlightenment, easily become lost and disillusioned upon discovering that even the highly cultured Zen is in reality often entangled in a web of folk beliefs and practices of a questionable standard. Again, others enjoy participating in the "celebration of life" that permeates both Japanese culture and the many religious traditions handed down from ages long gone. In a word, there seems to be such diversity in Japanese religion and such a possibility for different approaches that no definite answer can be given to all the questions this situation elicits. Let us first have a look at some statistics as one key for deepening our insight into Japanese religion.

THE NHK SURVEY OF JAPANESE RELIGIOSITY

It has always been a moot question whether Japan is really the most secularized and irreligious country in the world. It certainly remains a fact that, according to all surveys, up to two-thirds of the total population claim to have no personal religious affiliation; and this percentage rises still further if we focus on the younger generation. In a survey on "The Religious Consciousness of the Japanese," conducted by the NHK Broadcasting Corporation in 1981,[1] the results about personal religious faith show 65.2% answered in the negative. But when we compare the statistics with data from previous years, we notice an interesting phenomenon (see Figure 1): the number of believers hit a low of 25% in 1973, but has been gradually increasing since that time.[2]

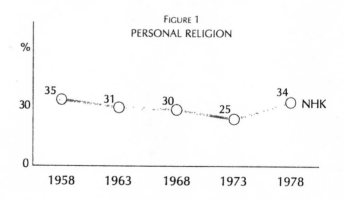

FIGURE 1
PERSONAL RELIGION

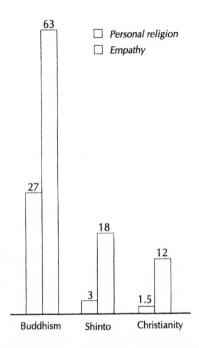

FIGURE 2
PERSONAL RELIGION AND
EMPATHY FOR OTHER RELIGIONS

63

□ *Personal religion*
□ *Empathy*

27

18

12

3

1.5

Buddhism   Shinto   Christianity

Besides an item on the "need for religion"—with 71.9% of the total number of respondents declaring that religion is certainly needed, or at least that it is good that religion exists, the NHK Survey included an interesting question asking the respondents towards what religion (including their own personal religion) they feel a certain empathy (*shitashimi*) (see figure 2). Worth noticing in this respect is that, for Shinto and Buddhism, this empathy increases with age. The figures for Shinto ranged from 11.4% in the 16–19 age bracket to 24.1% among those over 70 years old. This is still relatively low when we take religious observances connected with Shinto into account. For Buddhism, Sōka Gakkai excluded, the figures were respectively from 47.9% to 74.1%. On the other hand, Sōka Gakkai was steady at 4 to 6% over the whole line, a score that lies only a little higher than its actual membership; Christianity shows a completely reverse pattern. In the 16–19 age bracket, favorable ratings reached 29.7%, to go gradually down to 4.5% and 5.4% for, respectively, the 69 and the over-70 age brackets. Moreover, Christianity evoked *shitashimi* among 14% of the so-called unbelievers, almost equal to Shinto; but this drops to about 5% with the believers.

As shown in figure 3, however, belief (or unbelief) in a specific religion does not necessarily mean a rejection of all faith in supernatural beings. When we add the number of those who believe that *kami* (God or gods) or *hotoke* (Buddha or buddhas) certainly exist, and the number of those who think that these beings "perhaps" exist, we come to an aver-

神 仏

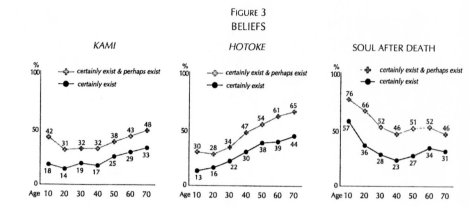

FIGURE 3
BELIEFS

age of, respectively, 35.9 and 42.8%. Belief in the existence of the soul after death averaged 54%. Striking here is the fact that the younger generation appears to be much more believing than their grandparents!

If religious beliefs are to be found among people who claim not to have any personal religion, it is especially in the area of ritual-related practices that Japan's religiosity comes to the fore. For the Japanese—as for most other people outside the strictly monotheistic traditions—religion has always been primarily a matter of participation in religious rituals rather than a matter of holding firmly to specific beliefs. The NHK Survey reveals that a little more than 60% claim to have prayed in times of distress. In other words, the expression *kurushii toki no kamidanomi* ("turn to the gods in time of distress") is indeed a living reality in Japan. Present-day youths in particular are not ashamed to acknowledge their "use" of the divine for concrete, immediate problems.

お守り
お札 御神籤

Related to this is the use of charms, oracle-lots, divination, and the like. As figure 4 shows, charms (*o-mamori* and *o-fuda*) and fortunetelling by means of oracle-lots (*o-mikuji*) are quite popular. Only about one-fifth to one-fourth of the respondents in all age groups expressed a negative attitude towards charms, although those who rely on them "often" are to be found particularly among the older generation, and those who do so "sometimes" in the young age brackets. As for oracle-lots, the younger generation is much more zealous than older people. Only about 23% of teenagers and those in their 20s were negative towards oracles, in contrast to 60% and more of the people over 60 years old who were negative.

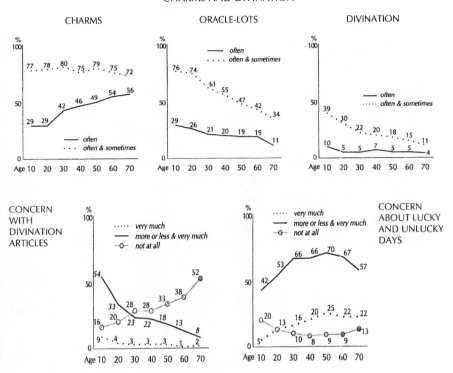

FIGURE 4
CHARMS AND DIVINATION

The attitude towards divination (*uranai*) seems to be gen- 占い
erally more negative. On the whole, 78% of the respondents
do not engage in the practice. But while 46.5% say they do
not care too much about articles on divination in newspapers
and journals, only 29% confess that they do not care at all,
with again the lowest score (16.1%) for the youngest generation and the highest score (51.8%) for the oldest. This shows
quite clearly that the young are more open to the "mysterious."

Matters are a little different when it comes to lucky and
unlucky days, important especially for fixing wedding dates.
A total of 63% pay attention to this question—18% very
much and 45% more or less. The score for the younger generation is the lowest (about 45% who care about it in one way
or another), gradually rising to about 70% for those in their
fifties. But as figure 4 also shows, the percentage of those who
do not care at all is extremely low for all age groups.

Besides these practices of a personal nature, practices inside the household are worth noticing. In 60% percent of the homes surveyed there was a *kamidana*, or Shinto god shelf, 神棚 and in 61% a *butsudan*, 仏壇 or Buddhist altar. About 45% had both and only 24% neither. Not surprisingly, the percentage was lowest for people between 25 and 40 years old, rising sharply for the older generation.

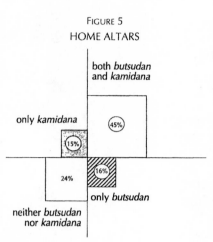

FIGURE 5
HOME ALTARS

both *butsudan* and *kamidana*

only *kamidana*

45%

15%

24%

16%

only *butsudan*

neither *butsudan* nor *kamidana*

To the question whether they ever worshiped at their home altars, 53% answered in the affirmative (16% daily and 22% sometimes) for the *kamidana* and 57% (28% daily and 19% sometimes) for the *butsudan*. In this respect, of course, members of the younger generation lag far behind their elders. The rate is especially low for *kamidana* worship (only 3% of teenagers do so daily and 11% sometimes), while *butsudan* worship scores a little higher (5% of the teenagers worship daily, but 20% sometimes and another 27% at least once in the past).

The picture is rather different when it comes to religion-related practices outside the home and of a communal nature,

FIGURE 6
ANNUAL OBSERVANCES

%
100

50

—— regularly

0
Age 10 20 30 40 50 60 70

GRAVE VISITS

%
100

50

····· regularly
------ regularly & sometimes

0
Age 10 20 30 40 50 60 70

HATSUMŌDE

%
100

50

····· regularly
------ regularly & sometimes

0
Age 10 20 30 40 50 60 70

CHRISTMAS CAKES

such as visits to ancestral graves and, particularly, annual 初詣
observances like *hatsumōde* (the first New Year visit to
Shinto shrines or Buddhist temples).

As seen in figure 6, paying a visit to the ancestral tombs at 御盆 彼岸
o-bon ("the feast of the dead" in July or August) and *higan*
(the spring and autumn equinoxes) is a custom that 89%
(69% regularly and 20% sometimes) observe. Almost all
older people pay such visits, but half of the younger generation participates also.

Also, *hatsumōde* scores 81% (54% regularly and 27%
sometimes), with little difference between the younger and
older generations except for the fact that those who do not
observe the custom ranged from only 14 to 18% for those
under 60 years old, rising suddenly to 30% and 36% for
those above that age (see figure 6).

Another popular observance, which in itself may seem to
have little to do with religion but which in Japan is often considered to be on a par with grave visits and *hatsumōde*, is the
celebration of Christmas by, for example, buying a Christmas
cake. In any case, this was an item taken up in the NHK
Survey. The survey shows that this custom is regularly
observed by 65%, while another 18% have at least experienced it. As seen in figure 6, the younger generation takes the
lead over the older.

Let us add for the moment only that a comparison of surveys of religion-related practices over the years shows a slow
rise in this respect since 1973. This is apparently correlated
to the slow increase in the total number of religious "believers" mentioned above.

RELIGION AND JAPANESE COMPANIES

Statistics like those of the NHK Survey can be interpreted in
various ways. It is possible to read into them that most
Japanese indeed do not care much for religion and that the
relatively high participation in religion-related rituals has no
meaning other than mere conformity to popular custom.
Others would argue that low consciousness of religious
affiliation and ignorance about doctrine do not necessarily
mean a lack of religious feelings as such. On the contrary, the
tenacity that most Japanese manifest in sticking to those
popular customs is evidence that such feelings are indeed
present.

The young and the old celebrate the birth of the Buddha.

In all discussions on Japanese religion, the problem boils down to precisely this question: what is the meaning of performing these religion-related customs? Foreign observers of Japan's religious scene who ask the Japanese about their religion will most probably receive negative answers, as exemplified in the NHK statistics. Or they might be told "Buddha" or "Zen," as advised by the cartoonist, and be left completely in the dark when asking for further explanation. Yet, if they happen to be in Japan during the New Year period or at festival times, they will certainly be impressed by the crowds streaming to shrines and temples and by the brief yet fervent praying to the gods and buddhas they witness then. Is this behavior just a sham, or does it point to an experience that in one or the other way deserve to be regarded as "religious"?

Before trying to answer this question, let us have a look at another domain that, although not covered by the NHK Survey, manifests religion Japanese-style in a very clear way, and that is therefore of great importance for deepening our understanding of Japanese society and culture. It is the relationship between religion and Japanese *kigyō* or business enterprises.

In Japanese folk beliefs, Inari or the Fox Deity is not only the guardian god of grain cultivation but also of modern business. No wonder that most business shops in Japan have a small Inari shrine established somewhere on the premises. And many, if not most, of Japan's big department stores have a small Inari shrine on their roof, a symbol of a faith of ages past that has somehow survived and is now flourishing amidst the bustle of Japan's mammoth cities.

Inari is the guardian deity of several very large companies such as the Mitsubishi Group. There the deity is enshrined in the Tosa Inari Shrine, commonly called Mitsubishi Inari, in Osaka, where the company was established by a certain Iwasaki Yatarō of the feudal Tosa clan at the beginning of the Meiji Era.[3] One Mitsubishi shrine is on the roof of the West Osaka Branch of the Mitsubishi Bank, where the annual festival is held on the Day of the Horse in February, sponsored by the two hundred members of the Society for the Support of the Mitsubishi Inari, mainly customers of the bank. Another shrine is located next to the main entrance of the Osaka Refinery of Mitsubishi Metal Corporation. This shrine has three annual festivals: a New Year Prayer Festival, a Safety Prayer Festival, and an Inari Festival. The last one is held on 1 November, the Founding Day of the company. It is a grandiose event, attended by the company president, who functions as the master of ceremonies, by employees, and by people from the vicinity.

But a recent survey of company shrines[4] has revealed that Japan's big companies seem to have also followed a number of other patterns in their choice of a guardian deity. Besides the 20% that chose Inari because of his alleged powers in procuring business success, there is a group of enterprises that revere the local deity of the place where the company was founded. Famous examples of this pattern are Hitachi and Nippon Oil Co. The former has taken for itself the guardian deity of the Kumano Shrine, who was the tutelary deity of Hitachi City, where the first Hitachi factory was built. Since then, every Hitachi factory has established a shrine to the same kami, who has become the guardian deity of the whole company. Even in allied companies like Hitachi Chemical Co. there are shrines in his honor.

Festivals are held six times per year, among which Founding Day (16 July) and Extinction Day (1 December) are the most important. The latter was occasioned by the destruction of the Hitachi factory by fire in 1920, and provides an opportunity for praying that such an accident may never happen again.

Nippon Oil Co., on the other hand, has had a special relationship to the local Iyahiko Shrine ever since it was established in Niigata Prefecture during the Meiji Era. In 1926, the company established its own shrine as a branch of the local one. This was destroyed in the earthquake of 1964, but the company restored it to its previous splendor under the rationale that the faith of the local people and their prayers for safety are a prerequisite for safety at the company's refineries. Regularly, and especially in the New Year period, the company's managers and employees worship at both shrines.

Another pattern is that in which the kami worshiped by the company is the deity (or deities) personally venerated by the company's founder or some other influential person. For example, the soy sauce company Kikkōman was founded in 1789 in Noda City, Chiba Prefecture. It still possesses in the precincts of its head office a Kotohira Shrine, where the kami of the Kotohira Shrine of Kagawa Prefecture (Shikoku) is venerated. This is because its second president was a fervent worshiper of that specific shrine. Also, many branches of the company have a Kotohira Shrine and have ceremonies performed on 9 and 10 November with the office heads acting as masters of ceremonies. Especially in the year of the monkey—the last was in 1992—special celebrations are held, with side entertainments such as dances, sumo wrestling, and the like performed for the company employees and their families as offerings to the kami.

In the same way, in 1963 the Idemitsu Kōsan Co. established a Munakata Shrine near its new main offices on reclaimed land in Chiba Prefecture. The shrine is a copy on a reduced scale of the shrine of the same name in Munakata County, Fukuoka Prefecture. Again, Munakata branch shrines have been established in the other refineries of the company. The reason is that the founder of the company, Idemitsu Sazō, was born in Munakata County, and was a fervent worshiper of the shrine of his native place. Festival days at the company shrines follow the calendar of the shrine in Fukuoka—annual festivals in April and October, and monthly ceremonies on the first and fifteenth day of each month.

In a third pattern, the kami worshiped at the company shrines have a special relationship to the type of work done. Along this line, it is not surprising to find several mining companies in Japan, such as Japan Mining Co. and Hitachi Kōsan (not related to the Hitachi group mentioned above), or pharmaceutical companies, such as Kyūshin Co., that respectively worship mountain gods (*yama no kami*) and kami famous for their curative powers.

But perhaps the most interesting example is the Toyota Motor Co. in Toyota City near Nagoya, which has had its own shrine—the Hōkō Shrine, also called Toyota Shrine—since 1939, one year after the completion of what is still today its main office and plant. The guardian deities worshiped there are, besides the kami of the Atsuta Shrine in Nagoya, Kaneyama-hiko and Kaneyama-hime, both considered "gods of iron." The annual festival is held on 3 November, the "Foundation Day." But there is also a New Year's Festival on 4 January. This latter festival used to be held on New Year's Day itself, but the date has recently been changed to make it possible for company people living in Tokyo to attend. In typical Japanese fashion, the chairman of the company and most managers of the various allied companies attend the ceremony, in which a Shinto priest solemnly recites prayers for the safety and prosperity of Toyota.

Examples of this kind could be multiplied indefinitely. Even when the companies do not possess their own shrine, they have often "infiltrated" the existing local shrines. It is no longer an exception to find that traditional festivals have become affairs sponsored more by business enterprises than by the local population. Moreover, the custom of holding Shinto rituals at ground-breaking ceremonies, completion of new buildings, and similar occasions, usually followed by the "enshrinement" of a kami who is supposed to protect the place, is becoming increasingly popular. Whether it is the launching of a communications satellite from the Tanegashima Space Center or the ground-breaking for an international event like the Science Exposition at Tsukuba in 1985, the kami of Japan are invoked. Very often, a small *kamidana* or god-shelf is set up where one can pray to the deities for benign protection over all earthly endeavors.

However, it is not only the Shinto gods who are mobilized. Japan's other religions are also given a share. Established

Buddhism is, of course, the first after Shinto. Its contribution seems to be most appreciated in April, the season when hordes of "freshmen" join the companies. There have been an increasing number of reports about companies that offer their new recruits a Zen meditation session, often at a Zen *dōjō* or training hall set up in the company compounds.[5] The companies openly state that the purpose of the sessions is "to deepen human relationships and to teach proper etiquette and strict adherence to the company rules through common attendance at those sessions."

道場

Even Christianity sometimes comes into the picture. Since Christianity in Japan possesses the excellent credentials of high morality and of *kokusai-kankaku* ("international sensitivities"), more than a few companies have invited Christian ministers to give pep talks on those subjects for company employees. Even in a "secularized" Japan, the future of religions is guaranteed if they do not object to being "used" in this fashion for company purposes.

THE STRUCTURE OF JAPANESE RELIGIOSITY

As already indicated, the interpretation of these various kinds of data is not an easy task. Although at first sight the Japanese seem to have very little interest in things religious, rituals connected with religion, whether private or public, are everyday events, and there are very few Japanese who are not in one way or another involved in them. But can this involvement be called "religious"?

One characteristic of Japanese religiosity is that it is very often, if not mostly, limited to the very time the religious events are held. Once they are over, normal life seems to go on without any further connection to religious matters. Moreover—and in the eyes of non-Japanese, this is apparently the most difficult thing to understand—even when the Japanese engage in religious acts, there seems to be no coherency in their behavior. Except for Christians and people belonging to certain new religious movements, most Japanese do not see any contradiction in asking for "benefits" from various religious organizations. On some occasions they will worship at Shinto shrines. On other occasions a Buddhist temple becomes their refuge. And it is not at all exceptional that the same person would visit a Christian church at yet another time. In all those different religious

RELIGION AND SOCIETY IN MODERN JAPAN

establishments, the worshipers will adapt themselves to the atmosphere and the rules of the place and behave as convinced believers of the religion they are visiting.

Whether in the case of individual persons or in that of groups such as present-day Japanese business enterprises, religions are evaluated primarily in a pragmatic or utilitarian way. The salvation they promise is mainly interpreted in this-worldly terms, as benefits of a material and/or psychological nature with specific self-chosen time limits. It is this pragmatic attitude that explains the seemingly fervent religious behavior at some times of the year and at some junctures in the course of a life. But, as mentioned above, religion does not seem to be needed before these occasions arise or after they have passed.

What this means in the first place is that the question of religious "truth" is far from an important preoccupation; it certainly should not interfere with the flow of everyday life. Far more than such questions of metaphysical import, the flow of everyday life itself constitutes the primary focus of attention and consideration. And all gods, buddhas, and organizations that represent them are welcome insofar as they fit into and serve this pattern.

Many theories have been propounded to explain this state of affairs, the most famous holding for the existence of a so-called *Nipponkyō*, or "religion of Japaneseness."[6] According to this view, the supreme sacred value to which all others are subordinated is to be a loyal member of Japanese society, from the smallest family unit to the country as a whole, and to work for the preservation and enhancement of its harmony. In other words, being a Japanese seems to carry with it a significance that makes appropriate the attribute of "sacred." This is, of course, reminiscent of the old adage that Japan is "the land of the kami"; it connects with the core of the traditional belief that the divine dignity of the nation lies at the basis of national unity and social solidarity. To be sure, the religious terminology connected with this belief is generally avoided nowadays—though attempts to revive it are not altogether rare. Moreover, many Japanese would firmly deny that there is anything "religious" in the affirmation of their national self-identity.

Nevertheless, many phenomena in contemporary Japanese society, such as the repeated emphasis on Japan's uniqueness, indicate that what we have to do with here is the value of "sacredness," that is, a value that encompasses and surpasses the individual, giving a meaning and direction to one's existence that transcends the possibilities inherent in one's own limited being. In this connection, many observers 和 of Japanese culture mention *wa* or "harmony" as one of the most appropriate terms for expressing Japaneseness.

Another related term that aptly expresses it and that can also give us new insights into the religiosity of the Japanese people is *musubi*.[7] *Musubi*, or "the power of becoming and growth that links all things together," refers first to the idea of fertility, the life-power that sustained life in Japan's traditional rice-growing communities. This life-power was thought to pervade the whole cosmos, which comprised not only the 八百万の神 *yaoyorozu no kami* (myriads of gods) and "the family of the living and the dead," but also animals and plants, not to mention objects like waterfalls and unusual rocks. All people of the community participated in this fertile life-power and contributed to it, each member fulfilling his or her role as one ring or link in both the vertical chain of ancestors and descendants and in the horizontal chain of fellow rice producers. Therefore *musubi* also has the connotation of strengthening the solidarity or *wa* (harmony) of the community through common labor.

It was this *musubi*-faith that to a great extent defined the spiritual outlook of the people living in the traditional agricultural communities, and that gave rise to the gradual establishment of a specific religious system called Shinto or "way of the gods." Important in this respect is that, even if an organized Shinto religion gradually came into existence, the real carriers of the *musubi*-faith were still the people themselves. Where a professional priesthood emerged, it mainly functioned as a kind of "service agency" for the local community. For example, it was the people themselves—and not the priests—who decided to rest from their rice-growing activities at regular times and who were the main actors in celebrating the life-power with rituals of thanksgiving and petition. In other words, organized Shinto performed a service function, offering the specific symbols that made the celebration possible. And this pattern was so strong that, when Buddhism was introduced in the country, it had to accommodate itself to it and become one of the elements sharing in the contribution to the maintenance and enhancement of the community's life-power or *musubi*.

Indeed, the problem Japan always faced in the course of its history has been how to preserve and enhance *musubi*, the life-power of harmonious communities on all levels of society, while continuously absorbing new, and sometimes conflicting, alien values. It has done this in various ways. One method, in the realm of ideas, has been to positively evaluate this plurality as being superior to unity. Another, more practical, method has been to cope with the influx of alien values by invoking what can be called "selective adoption and adaptation." Especially worthy of notice is the way this has been traditionally done, through a method that we can call "compartmentalization." This method can best be illustrated and expressed by referring to still another Japanese concept, namely that of *bun*, meaning "part," "share," 分 "segment."[8] In other words, all incoming values have been reduced to the status of a *bun*, i.e., assigned a proper place, a proper compartment or field of action. The concept of *bun* indeed implies that each value, put into its compartment, is to be considered not as integral in itself but only as a part or fraction of the whole, lent its proper worth and identity by subordination to the whole. The concept further implies that all the different *bun* or values are interdependent and contribute to the overarching value that keeps the whole together by acknowledging one another's (limited) roles and claims and by not overstepping the assigned boundaries of any given individual. This overarching value is nothing else than *musubi*, the life-power mentioned above.

Perhaps the most striking example of this pattern is to be seen in the fate of Buddhism in Japan. It is also seen in the more general plurality of ethico-religious values in Japan and in the more or less harmonious way they are related, or are made to relate, to each other. Admittedly, it is true that in the course of Japan's religious history the different traditions—Shinto, Buddhism, Confucianism, and later Christianity and other religions—were not always strictly kept apart but often blended into a more or less amorphous amalgam, a syncretism in the fullest sense of the word. It also happened that their supposedly harmonious coexistence was broken and that the celebrated tolerance of the various religions towards one another gave way to bloody inter- and intra-factional

A ritual burning of used *daruma* dolls before the New Year. Note the division of labor: the Buddhist priests performing the ritual, the Shinto symbols on the pile of *daruma* dolls, and the syncretistic yamabushi-like figure holding the torch in between.

strife, a fact sometimes overlooked by all-too-zealous Western admirers of things Oriental. Yet, throughout all these vicissitudes and notwithstanding numerous cases of amalgamation, Japanese society gradually developed into a patterned structure in which the various religious traditions and the institutions have preserved a relatively high degree of self-identity, each of them occupying a specific *bun* or compartment of action in the whole of Japanese religiosity.

Concretely, what has the preservation of this relative self-identity meant? What are the boundaries defining the *bun* in which the different religious traditions of Japan have performed their role? Westerners, inclined to think of religion primarily in terms of ideational elements and doctrinal orthodoxy, will point out immediately that on this level no clear boundaries are to be discerned. Indeed, most Japanese religions display a remarkable tolerance and flexibility in matters of doctrine. But this gives us a clue for discerning the boundaries of the *bun*, and, at the same time, for deepening our insight into the structure of Japanese religiosity and of Japanese culture in general.

As already mentioned in passing and as exemplified in the statistics above, for the Japanese religion is not primarily adherence to a particular set of rationalized beliefs but the acting out of religious feelings and aspirations in a wide spectrum of rituals that accompany a person's life from birth to death and still further into his afterlife, in unison with the recurring and always developing rhythm of the seasons. It is here that the different religious traditions have met the people, not so much through the imposition of differentiated doctrines that are supposed to distinguish their own *bun* from that of the others, but rather through specializing in rituals and other activities, answering to the specific needs of their clientele and contributing through this to the *musubi* of the community.

The assignment of a proper *bun* to each of the different religious traditions can certainly be called syncretistic. But this syncretism is patterned. For rituals of birth and of the local community, people generally call on Shinto priests, while for everything related to death a Buddhist priest will be asked. Christian priests should be ready to offer their specific help at Christmas time and, increasingly in recent years, also for nuptial blessings. Westerners might be startled by this apparently simultaneous adherence to different religions.

Strictly speaking, however, the Japanese are not "simultaneously" adhering to or believing in different religions. In her *Chrysanthemum and the Sword*, Ruth BENEDICT pointed out that, in contrast to the integrated behavior of Westerners and other people, the Japanese have a flair for swinging from one behavior pattern to another according to the situation without too much psychic cost (1954: 195–227). The division into *bun*, therefore, exists not only on the level of societal institutions but also, in a certain sense, in the personality structure of the people. There is a compartment or *bun* for Buddhism, one for Shinto, and one for many other religious and non-religious traditions, even if this might not be consciously acknowledged. Inside one *bun*, the commitment is complete, to the extent that even the distinction between subject and object might become blurred. But once matters are settled in this specific area, e.g., a Buddhist funeral, one puts an end to this activity (in Japanese, *kejime o tsukeru*) and can easily switch to another one for another purpose, e.g., a Shinto birth celebration or an apparently non-religious activity, without being aware of any contradiction in beliefs. As long as the different *bun* do not infringe too much upon each other, a balanced psychic life is possible and the harmonious life-power of the individual contributes to that of the community and that of the Japanese nation as a whole.

The ritual usefulness of this division-of-labor explains a great deal not only about the results of the NHK Survey but also about the relation between religion and Japanese companies. Indeed, if we attribute a central significance to *musubi* and take into consideration how the various religious traditions have been mobilized for maintaining and further enhancing it, it is evident that, at least in this respect, not so much has changed in the transition from an agricultural to an industrial society. Focusing upon Japan's business enterprises, we can say that the *musubi* ethos that sustained rice-growing labor in traditional society has been transferred to labor in an industrial context seemingly without very much difficulty. Furthermore, it seems that this ethos is partially responsible for the economic success of this country.[9]

Admittedly, if we think in terms of an opposition between fertility and productivity, as many Westerners tend to do, i.e., between cooperation in the continuity of life-power through the natural process as in rice-cultivation on the one hand and the production of inanimate objects in industrial plants on the other hand, the transition has indeed meant quite a radical break. On this view, it would be questionable to apply the concept of *musubi* to what is done in, for example, Japan's business enterprises. Yet, there seems to exist within the psyche of the Japanese a tendency, if not to completely disregard this opposition, at least to soften it so that the transition from fertility to productivity can be made relatively easily.

Japan's traditional communities, bound together by *musubi* in its various meanings, have largely broken down. And while this has naturally caused psychic unrest in many cases, one result has been a sort of reorganization of the social structure around other, new forms of community. Some people have benefited from the breakdown by establishing strong individual personalities. But a majority have gradually migrated to places where their latent *musubi* faith can be nurtured and further sustained.

The role performed in this respect by Japanese companies cannot be denied. Of course, this does not mean that every single Japanese who no longer belongs to a traditional community has now become a member of a "company-community," or that the latter is a complete replica of the former except for the type of labor. Yet, the similarities are too many to be taken lightly. Especially in the case of people who belong to a company that promises them lifelong employment, a kind of company-faith can be found that in many points resembles the faith of the people in traditional society. But what is still more remarkable is that the specifically religious forms by which this faith is expressed resemble the old pattern very closely.

The examples given above show that also in those new communities the sacredness of life-power, i.e., production, can only be maintained by regular celebrations that glorify the work ethic and strengthen the communal bonds between workers and management. In present-day Japanese companies, recourse to gods and buddhas to symbolize the integration of the community and the labor done in it—the unconscious *musubi* faith—is increasing. The main actors are again the people themselves: primarily the managers and the workers, but their families are also often invited. Together with people's recourse to the sacred on a more personal or family level, crystallized in the rich diversity of religion-related practices, the popularity of company rituals seems to prove that Japan has not forgotten the heritage of religious tradition that sustains its culture and keeps it "Japanese."

PRESENT CHANGES IN JAPANESE RELIGIOSITY

In the field of religious studies, no question attracts more attention nowadays than that of "religion and social change." In Western countries this problem is usually discussed in terms of "secularization," by which one generally understands a decrease in the influence of religion, if not on the individual consciousness of people, at least on the structures of society. Japanese scholars of religion, prone to stress the differences between Japan and the rest of the world, are rather hesitant to employ this term. But they generally agree that in this country, too, the influence of social change on religion has to be seriously considered. Yet, when it comes to what this influence concretely means, opinions diverge widely.

Without going into details, we should mention that in this connection interpreters of Japan's religious situation invariably refer to people's attitudes towards science. About 73% of the NHK respondents answered that "science is not almighty," and 55% added that "the more science develops, the more people will have a longing for the mysterious." In these answers members of the younger generation, especially those in their late twenties, have the highest scores, over against the oldest generation, among whom many preferred not to answer that type of question. That this disbelief in science is accompanied by a sort of flight into the irrational or the occult is a fact that can be inferred from the data introduced above. It is further illustrated by the attention given in Japan's mass media to the popularity of what have recently been called the "new New Religions" (*shin-shin-shūkyō*).

新新宗教

This influence of the mass media in *creating* the "occult boom" is certainly not to be ruled out. But it is also true that the mass media have cleverly caught what was already alive among the populace, namely a yearning for things and experiences that belong to the sphere of the irrational. In recent years, several new magazines that deal with topics of the "spiritual world" have begun to attract a wide readership. For example, the magazine *Mū* started publication in November 1979 with a circulation of 100,000 copies. As of August 1984, it had attained a sale of over 400,000 copies. More than 60% of the readers of this and similar "mystery magazines" are young people—of whom high school students are the great majority. But many housewives also seem to be avid readers. One of the main motives for reading this kind of magazine, especially of housewives, has apparently to do with the "fear of a curse (*tatari*) from evil spirits." This is not without connection to another prominent phenomenon of recent years, namely the popularity of *mizuko kuyō,* or "praying for the souls of aborted children.

祟り

水子供養

The so-called "new New Religions" have precisely caught this turn in religious consciousness towards the irrational and the mysterious. For example, the two Mahikari organizations (split into Sekai Mahikari Bunmei Kyōdan and Sūkyō Mahikari) claim a combined membership of about 600,000 believers. (See the tables on the New Religions in the introduction to Part 4.) They teach their followers to radiate "true Divine Light" so that they become spiritually awakened to the true nature of salvation and able to cure physical disorders, not only those of human beings but also of animals, plants, and even machines. Another of the new religions, the Agonshū, founded in December 1976, claims to have quickly gained 300,000 members (though this figure has been revised to about 200,000 in 1990). It specializes in esoteric rituals that allegedly turn evil spirits instantaneously into good-natured ones. It has become famous for staging a grand-scale fire ceremony, called the "Star Festival," every February in Kyoto, as well as for the "Aura Festival," held at the Budōkan in Tokyo in May 1984 with the Dalai Lama in attendance, not to mention the widely publicized encounter of the founder with Pope John-Paul II in March 1985.

Other groups gaining popular attention include Kōfuku no kagaku (the science of happiness) and Byakkō Shinkō-kai, known for the "May Peace Prevail on Earth" plates put up all over the country. Many of the groups combine forms of magic and irrationality of a sometimes crude nature with—it should be acknowledged—lofty ideals of peace and worldwide brotherhood. Even if these "new New Religions" do not develop further in the future, they are certainly manifestations of a craving for something spiritual that transcends the drabness and monotony of everyday life, a trend in contemporary society that has to be reckoned with but to which the traditional religions seemingly do not know how to respond. (See the essay by Richard Young in this volume, pp. 239–56.)

The relation between a distrust of science and a resurgence of religious feelings, particularly in the sense of a quest for the irrational, is something that is not limited to Japan. There is in this country, however, still another aspect to religion that we must not overlook. Mention was made above of a so-called "religion of Japaneseness," i.e., of the sacred character of belonging to the community of the Japanese nation as an overarching value that also somehow pervades the subunits of this community, such as the companies.

Interestingly enough, the NHK survey took up this point in the context of explaining why 1973 seems to constitute a turning point in the religious revival. It refers to the new self-confidence that many Japanese have gained since that time about their own cultural traditions, including traditional religiosity. Indeed, 1973 was the year of the "oil shock." Although the rapid economic growth of the sixties came to an end, it was around that time that it became gradually clear how Japan, in contrast with the Western nations, was much better equipped to overcome its difficulties. From that time, Western nations started looking up to "Japan as Number One," and this contributed to giving the Japanese a renewed sense of self-confidence.

In a word, it was in the beginning of the seventies that the Japanese could finally afford to take a kind of spiritual rest. Various events had caused a loss of confidence in the values—such as extreme individualism and selfish freedom—that had been imposed upon them after defeat in World War II. Rediscovering their own "Japaneseness," they have again started to probe their spiritual roots.

Still, even if empirical research on changes in Japanese religion indicates a revival of tradition, this could be a symptom of precisely the opposite trend, namely, the slow erosion of this tradition under the impact of a combination of factors, among which growing internationalization might be the most influential. In this sense, the present reversal to tradition might in fact be nothing more than a kind of natural, to some extent even essential, mechanism of self-defense against the increasing inroads of alien values resulting from internationalization, and at the same time herald the advent of more fundamental changes, against which such a reaction of self-defense will ultimately prove to be on the losing side.

➤ ➤ ➤

In a textbook of religious studies, the late Yanagawa Keiichi, one of Japan's foremost scholars on religion, had this to say about Japanese religiosity:

> In Japan, the unit of religion is human relationships and religion is indistinguishably mixed with customs. Since the European Reformation, the idea that religion is a personal affair has been predominant. But I do not think that it is right, using this as a criterion, to criticize the religion of the Japanese as being in some way not genuine, since religion based on human relationships does in fact exist. On the other hand, we have also to be careful not to base our judgments onesidedly on the view that the average Japanese has of religion. The reason is that, if we do, we will misunderstand those who think that religion is an irreplaceable treasure for the individual.
> (YANAGAWA & ABE 1985: 20)

The question of the role of the individual and the community in matters of religion will most probably always be with us. But this should not prevent us from trying to understand and to appreciate forms of religiosity different from our own. If Yanagawa's remarks on the Reformation are correct—and I would think he has a valuable point—Christians need only look back at their own tradition as it was before that time, to acquire a better insight into the religiosity of the Japanese. Reflection on the so-called "folk" or "popular" element in all religious traditions of the world might be the most appropriate starting point for such an endeavor. This kind of religiosity is, after all, an element of the soul of every human being. In this sense, the religiosity of the Japanese is anchored in humanity itself and, indeed, in a "celebration of life-power."

NOTES

* An earlier version of this article appeared in *The Japan Foundation Newsletter* 13/4 (January 1986), pp. 1–14. Reprinted and revised by permission of the author. Jan Swyngedouw is a member of the Nanzan Institute for Religion and Culture, and Professor of Japanese Culture and Religion in the Department of Japanese Studies at Nanzan University, Nagoya.

1 NHK Hōsō Yoron-chōsa-sho, ed., *Nihonjin no shūkyō-ishiki* [The religious consciousness of the Japanese]. Tokyo: Nippon Hōsō Shuppankyōkai, 1984. Unfortunately there has been no recent update of this survey by NHK. Though some of the figures may appear dated, I believe my general conclusions are still valid.

2 In 1981, 33% of the respondents listed themselves as "believers"; Buddhism scored highest with 27% (including 4.1% for the Sōka Gakkai), followed by Shinto 3.4%, Christianity 1.5%, and other religions 1.1%. When we look at the age groups, the number of "unbelievers" reaches 85.5% among those in their early twenties and gradually decreases to 38% among those over 70 years of age. In this latter age group, half of the respondents claim to be Buddhists, while only 11.3% of the former group (among whom 4.4% are Sōka Gakkai members) does so. For Christianity, the percentage is between 1 and 2% over the whole line except for the 20–24 (0.6%) and the 60–69 (0.4%) age brackets and a remarkable 3.7% for the 35–39 age group (which, incidentally, shows the lowest percentage [2.7%] of all age groups for Sōka Gakkai). Moreover, each religious tradition has a higher percentage of women than men, although the total number of unbelievers among men (70%) is only 5% higher than that of unbelieving women.

[3] This and other data given in this section are based upon a series of articles on "Kigyō no jinja" (company shrines), which appeared in 1984 in *Jinja shinpō*, the weekly newspaper of the Association of Shinto Shrines, and which was published under the same title in book form in 1986. See also NAKAMAKI 1992.

[4] See Note 3.

[5] See the Buddhist newspaper *Chūgai nippō*, No. 23184 (19 March 1984), p. 11.

[6] This term was made popular by Isaiah Ben-Dasan, the nom de plume of a mysterious writer of several bestsellers in the beginning of the 1970s, and further developed by Yamamoto Shichihei.

[7] The importance of this concept has been emphasized by the scholar of Japanese folklore, Honda Sōichirō, in his *Nippon Shintō nyūmon* [Introduction to Japanese Shinto]. Tokyo: Nihon Bungeisha, 1985.

[8] I have taken this concept from T. K. LEBRA (1976: 67–69), where it is applied to the position of Japanese individuals in the organic whole of a social group or society as such.

[9] It goes without saying that the problem of the roots of the work ethic that has played an important role in Japan's economic success is an extremely complex one and should not be explained exclusively in terms of *musubi*. The contributions of Confucian thought and of Buddhism in reinforcing this basic ethos must also be duly acknowledged.

PART 2

Religion and the State

Introduction to Part 2

Religion and the State

Mark R. MULLINS

THE READINGS IN Part 1 provided some historical background and explanation of the diversity and eclectic character of contemporary Japanese religiosity. Although diverse religious beliefs, practices, and forms of association have existed for centuries, one should not mistakenly assume that the religious economy of Japan has been a "free market" or that the "division of labor" in Japanese religions (Swyngedow) has always contributed to social harmony. The practice of religion in everyday life has often been controlled by those holding the reigns of political power, and religious beliefs have often been the cause of social conflict. During the Tokugawa period (1600–1867), for example, Buddhism received state patronage in exchange for services to the shogunate. By administering the *danka seido*, a system in which all the residents of a given area were required to register their household with a local temple and record births, marriages, and deaths, Buddhist priests were used by the Tokugawa regime to monitor and control the entire population. Priests also issued certificates (*tera-uke*) to individuals each year attesting that the person in question was not a member of the proscribed religion (Christianity).

檀家制度

寺請

Religious institutions and practices in the modern period have similarly been constrained by government policies. This section introduces several key historical documents that have defined the relationship between religion and state over the past century, and two articles that illuminate the debate concerning the renationalization of Yasukuni Shrine and the resurgence of civil religion in recent years.

Although the postwar period has been characterized by religious freedom, the religion-state issues being debated today cannot be fully appreciated without some understanding of the evolution of government policies toward religion since the Meiji Restoration. This is a complicated story with significant shifts in government policy and strategy (see HARDACRE [1989] and GARON [1986] for detailed historical analysis). The restoration of imperial rule in 1868 initiated a series of changes that radically transformed the role and status of religion in Japanese society. The most fundamental religious change resulting from the restoration was the development of an emperor-centered national religion. Buddhism lost the state patronage it had enjoyed during the Tokugawa period and Shinto was revived to provide the foundation for the new political order. In an effort to "purify" the ancient Shinto tradition from the centuries-old Shinto-Buddhist amalgam, the government issued an edict separating Shinto and Buddhism. As the **Memorandum on State Shinto** and additional readings clearly point out, the national religion created by the restoration bureaucrats differed considerably from the previous forms of Shinto belief and practice.

Largely because of foreign pressure, the government removed the notices proscribing Christianity in 1873 and included an article on religious freedom in the **Meiji Constitution** (1890). That same year, however, the **Imperial Rescript on Education** (*Kyōiku chokugo*) was issued and provided the normative framework that would define the limits of religious freedom for half a century. The Rescript on Education was distributed to all schools and quickly became a sacred text for religious socialization. Ceremonial readings of the Rescript were essentially religious events, which included rice-cake offerings to the scroll on which the Rescript was written. *Jinja sanpai* (shrine visits) became regular school-sponsored events and most schools maintained a *kamidana* (god shelf) and enshrined the imperial photo, various kami, and sometimes a talisman from Ise Shrine.

Until the end of World War II, the government used this "invented" (Hardacre) tradition and unifying ideology centered on a sacred emperor to integrate the heterogeneous population and mobilize the people for nation-building, modernization, and, eventually, military expansion. Comparative studies have indicated that civil religions emerge in periods of social crisis and political transition, and attempt to legitimize the new order with reference to a sacred or transcendent reality. The "family-state" ideology articulated by the

教育勅語

神社参拝
神棚

Meiji Constitution and the Rescript on Education was justified with reference to the divine origin of the emperor and the people of Japan. These documents not only reinforced the traditional Confucian virtues of loyalty and filial piety, but also were used to forge a strong national identity for the first time in Japan's history. By the 1930s this civil religion became increasingly totalitarian and members of every religious group were required to conform to the state-defined orthodoxy. In 1939, in fact, the Diet enacted the Religious Organizations Law, giving the state authority to disband any religious organization whose teachings were in conflict with "The Imperial Way." The government eventually defined Shinto as a "non-religious" institution of the state, and participation in its rituals came to be viewed as the "patriotic" duty of all Japanese, regardless of personal religious convictions. By the end of the war, most Buddhist and Christian religious bodies had also been coopted by the government and forced to promote and support militarism and nationalistic expansion.

All of this changed abruptly with Japan's defeat on 15 August 1945 and the arrival of the Occupation forces. Before the end of the year, the Supreme Commander for the Allied Powers (SCAP) issued the **Directive for the Disestablishment of State Shinto** (15 December 1945) and set in motion policies that effectively reduced Shinto to the status of a voluntary organization without special legal authority or financial support from the state. In order to achieve the "psychological disestablishment" of State Shinto, the Civil Information and Education Section of SCAP recommended that "His Majesty should be persuaded to disassociate himself entirely from any notion that he (the Emperor), the people, and the islands of Japan were superior to other rulers, people, or countries because of ancestry, descent, or alleged divine (special) origin." (WOODARD 1972: 259). The so-called "Declaration of Humanity" contained in the **Imperial Rescript** (1 January 1946) reflects this recommendation and the intention of the earlier Directive. An initial English draft was prepared by Dr. R. H. Blyth, a teacher of English Literature at Gakushūin (the Peers School), and revised by Japanese government officials in the process of translation. In the final version the emperor declares that he is not *akitsu-kami* (manifest deity).   現つ神

In accord with the Directive, the wartime laws regulating religion were subsequently abolished and all religious organizations, including Shinto shrines, were required to register as "religious juridical persons" and placed on equal footing as "voluntary" organizations. **Articles 20 and 89** of the postwar Constitution of Japan (1947) clearly articulated the principle of religious freedom and separation of religion and state, and thus fulfilled the constitutional reform objectives of the Occupation authorities.

祭政一致 Since Japan regained its independence in 1952, pro-Shinto leaders and groups have struggled to restore the prewar unity of religion and government (*saisei itchi*), arguing that the Occupation government overstepped its authority in forcing the Japanese to accept an unfairly restrictive interpretation of "separation" that was not applied in Western countries. This position was clearly stated by ASHIZU Yoshihiko, editor of the *Jinja Shinpō* (Shrine News), in 1960. Ashizu pointed out, for example, that the "separation of church and state" in the United States was interpreted in a manner that allowed for Christian ceremonies and prayers at the inauguration of presidents and other government officials and provided for the religious needs of the armed forces with a government-funded chaplain system. In Japan, on the other hand, the Shinto Directive had eliminated and prohibited similar religious ceremonies and activities related to government functions.

K. Peter Takayama's contribution to this section provides a review of the postwar situation, drawing attention to the efforts of religious and political leaders to renationalize Yasukuni Shrine and revise social studies and history textbooks for more effective patriotic education. Since 1969 the conservative Liberal Democratic Party (LDP) has made a number of attempts to renationalize Yasukuni, presenting bills to the Diet seeking state support for this shrine, which is dedicated to the war dead. This issue received international attention in 1986 when Prime Minister Nakasone Yasuhiro made an "official visit" to the shrine. This visit was followed by harsh criticism from several Asian nations that had suffered from Japanese military aggression as well by several lawsuits by Japanese citizens' groups. In spite of the negative press, the LDP has clearly not given up. As recently as August 1992, fifteen of the twenty members of Prime Minister Kiichi Miyazawa's Cabinet visited Yasukuni Shrine, several indicating publicly that it was an "official" rather than "private" visit. Thus far this movement has been successfully opposed by the Union of New Religions and various Buddhist and Christian groups.

The article by **Klaus Antoni** complements Takayama's socio-political perspective by providing historical background for understanding the religious dimensions of Yasukuni Shrine. Antoni explains that the religious rituals associated with Yasukuni and other *gokoku* ("protect the nation") shrines must be understood in relation to traditional folk beliefs regarding the need to pacify the spirits of ancestors who died an untimely, premature, or "bad death." 護国

The debate over the renationalization of Yasukuni Shrine is only one of many religion-state issues that have been deliberated by concerned citizens and the courts for the past several decades. These include the use of public funds for a *jichinsai* (Shinto grounds purification ceremony) in Tsu city, Mie Prefecture; the enshrinement of Nakaya Takafumi in the Gokoku Shrine of Yamaguchi Prefecture against the expressed wishes of his widow; and the use of public funds for the *Daijōsai*, a religious enthronement ceremony in which the emperor is believed to take on divine character. A helpful synopsis of the court cases and appeals surrounding these other areas of recent dispute may be found in REID (1991: 33–58) and HARDACRE (1989: 145–59). 地鎮祭 大嘗祭

NOTE

* The text of the Imperial Rescript on Education, the Directive for the Disestablishment of State Shinto, and the Imperial Rescript (1 January 1946) are from *Political Reorientation of Japan, September 1945–September 1948*, Report of Government Section, Supreme Commander for the Allied Powers, 2 vols., Washington D.C. Government Printing Office, 1949.

FURTHER SUGGESTED READINGS

ASHIZU Yoshihiko. "The Shinto directive and the constitution," *Contemporary Religions in Japan* 1/2: 16–34, 1960.

BELLAH, Robert. *Tokugawa Religion: The Values of Pre-Industrial Japan*. Boston: Beacon Press, 1970.

DAVIS, Winston. "Fundamentalism in Japan: Religious and political." In Martin E. Marty and R. Scott Appleby, eds. *Fundamentalisms Observed*. Chicago: University of Chicago Press, 1991.

———. *Japanese Religion and Society: Paradigms of Structure and Change.* (Chapter 8: "Japan Theory and Civil Religion, pp. 253–70). Albany, NY: State University of New York Press, 1992.

DOBBELAERE, Karel. "Civil religion and the integration of society: A theoretical reflection and an application," *Japanese Journal of Religious Studies* 13/3: 127–46, 1986.

GARON, Sheldon M. "State and religion in Imperial Japan, 1912–1945," *Journal of Japanese Studies* 12/2: 273–302, 1986.

GLUCK, Carol. *Japan's Modern Myths: Ideology in the Late Meiji Period.* Princeton: Princeton University Press, 1985.

HARDACRE, Helen. *Shinto and the State, 1868–1988.* Princeton: Princeton University Press, 1989.

HOLTOM, Daniel C. *Modern Japan and Shinto Nationalism.* Revised ed. New York: Paragon Books, 1963 (reprint of 1947 edition).

KETELAAR, James. *Of Heretics and Martyrs in Meiji Japan: Buddhism and Its Persecution.* Princeton: Princeton University Press, 1990.

NISHIKAWA Shigenori. "The Daijōsai, the constitution, and Christian faith," *The Japan Christian Quarterly* 56/3: 132–46, 1990.

NOSCO, Peter, ed. *The Emperor System and Religion in Japan.* Special issue of *Japanese Journal of Religious Studies* 17/2–3, 1990.

REID, David. *New Wine: The Cultural Shaping of Japanese Christianity.* Berkeley: Asian Humanities Press, 1991 (see especially chapter 2: "Religion and the state in Japan: 1965–1990").

TAKAYAMA, K. Peter. "Enshrinement and persistency of Japanese religion," *Journal of Church and State* 32/3: 527–47, 1990.

TAKIZAWA Nobuhiko. "Religion and state in Japan," *Journal of Church and State* 30: 89–108, 1988.

WOODARD, William P. *The Allied Occupation of Japan 1945–1952 and Japanese Religions.* Leiden: E. J. Brill, 1972.

Background Documents

1. Meiji Constitution (1889), Article 28

Article 28: Japanese subjects shall, within limits not prejudicial to the peace and order, and not antagonistic to their duties as subjects, enjoy freedom of religious belief.

2. Imperial Rescript on Education (1890)

Know ye, Our Subjects:

Our Imperial Ancestors have founded Our Empire on a basis broad and everlasting and have deeply and firmly implanted virtue; Our subjects ever united in loyalty and filial piety have from generation to generation illustrated the beauty thereof. This is the glory of the fundamental character of Our Empire, and herein also lies the source of Our education. Ye, Our subjects, be filial to your parents, affectionate to your brothers and sisters; as husbands and wives be harmonious, as friends true; bear yourselves in modesty and moderation; extend your benevolence to all; pursue learning and cultivate arts, and thereby develop intellectual faculties and perfect moral powers; furthermore, advance public good and promote common interests; always respect the Constitution and observe the laws; should emergency arise, offer yourselves courageously to the State; and thus guard and maintain the prosperity of Our Imperial Throne coeval with heaven and earth. So shall ye not only be Our good and faithful subjects, but render illustrious the best traditions of your forefathers.

The Way here set forth is indeed the teaching bequeathed by Our Imperial Ancestors, to be observed alike by Their Descendants and the subjects, infallible for all ages and true in all places. It is Our wish to lay it to heart in all reverence, in common with you, Our subjects, that We may thus attain to the same virtue.

The 30th day of the 10th month of the 23rd year of Meiji
[The 30th of October 1890]

3. Memorandum on State Shinto to the Chief of Staff (3 December 1945)

General Headquarters
Supreme Commander for the Allied Powers
Civil Information and Education Section
MEMORANDUM TO: Chief of Staff

I. THE PROBLEM PRESENTED

State Shinto has been used by militarists and ultra-nationalists in Japan to engender and foster a military spirit among the people and to justify a war of expansion. While the defeat, surrender, and subsequent occupation of Japan have undoubtedly done much to destroy the potency of Shintoism as a political force, until Shinto is separated from the state and instruction in Shinto is eliminated from the education system, there will always be the danger that Shinto will be used as an agency for disseminating militaristic and ultra-nationalistic ideology. In order to obviate this danger, the Supreme Commander for the Allied Powers has been directed to accomplish the separation of Shinto from the state and the elimination of Shinto from the education system.

II. FACTS BEARING ON THE PROBLEM

1. NATURE OF SHINTO

a. *A primitive religion put to modern uses.* Legends analogous to those which have become a vital force in the political and religious life of Japan are common to the early life of many peoples. No other modern nation, however, has attempted to secure social and political cohesion through the strength of a ceremonial nexus that was normal in occidental culture 2,000 to 4,000 years ago. Nor has any other modern religion attempted to utilize such ritualistic agencies for vivifying and achieving the primary ends of national life.

b. *Shinto variously interpreted.* The fact that Shinto has no clear-cut or precisely stated theology, dogma, or philosophy has led to diversity of interpretation and definition. It has been called the racial spirit of the Japanese people, the essence of the principles of imperial rule, a system of correct social and political etiquette, the ideal national morality, a system of patriotism and loyalty centering in emperor worship ("mikadoism"), a nature worship, an intermixture of the worship of nature and of ancestors.

c. *Close relation of Shinto to the Imperial Family.* In spite of the fact that Shinto has been variously interpreted and defined, there is wide agreement that the "fundamental and characteristic emphasis has always been ancestral and nationalistic." The whole history of Shinto has been intimated with members of the Imperial Family, real and mythological. In recent years Japanese political philosophy has become so closely involved with the Shinto cult that today it can hardly be understood apart from its interconnection with Shinto.

d. *Military elements.* Even though so conservative a scholar as Anesaki has referred to the militaristic aspects of Shinto and its emphasis on the moral virtue of submission,[1] the militaristic elements in early Shinto did not loom large by comparison with other primitive religions. Sir George Sansom has testified to the absence of menacing elements in early Shintoism.[2] Many of the more oppressive aspects of Japanese society, sometimes loosely attributed to Shinto and indeed somewhat intermingled with modern State Shinto, have their origin in other sources. The five human relationships specifically enumerated in the 1890 Imperial Rescript on Education were of Confucian origin. The Shushi Confucian heritage of rigorous morality, the subordination of everyone to a superior, and the assignment to every man and woman of a fixed place in the hierarchy of social and family life has dominated Japanese society. Introduced into Japan by Zen Buddhists, it was adopted as the orthodoxy of the ruling samurai class during the Tokugawa period and has served as an important factor in the development of what the Japanese since 1900 have glorified under the name of *bushidō*, "the way of the warrior." The Buddhist sect of Nichiren also has introduced militaristic elements into Japanese life, furnishing Japan with some of its most rabid nationalists.

2. EVOLUTION OF STATE SHINTO

a. *Recent origin.* As late as 1895 so keen a scholar as Aston believed that the ancient Shinto cult which the government had been so industriously cultivating for two decades was doomed to play only a small part in the life of the nation. "It has little vitality," he said. "As a national religion, Shinto is almost extinct. But it will continue to survive in folklore and custom, and in that livelier sensibility to the divine in its simpler and more material aspects which characterizes the people of Japan."[3] B. H. Chamberlain also attests to the newness of Shrine Shinto as a national religion. He refers to it as a manufactured religion "still (1912) in the process of being consciously or semi-consciously put together by the official class, in order to serve the interests of that class, and, the interests of the nation at large."[4]

b. *Factors utilized by the Government to make Shinto a vital force.* By what methods was this relatively unimportant religion—seemingly more in keeping with the needs of a primitive society than with the demands of a modern state—built up into the central force binding the Japanese people into a cohesive political and social unit?

1) *The schools.* By far the most important of the factors working to condition the people to an acceptance of a Shinto-centered state was the education system. From the time he first entered the schoolyard gate until he finished his formal schooling, all the techniques of modern education were utilized to weave into the student's mind the whole warp and woof of Shinto nationalist theory. Through the medium of textbooks, highly indoctrinated teachers, and deeply impressive ceremonies, Shinto was made the principal instrument for inculcating submissiveness, loyalty to the state, and unquestioning acceptance of the official views as to the proper nature of society and of political and social morality. The Shrine became the foremost agency for the promotion of "national morality" (*kokumin dōtoku*). Good citizenship was identified with the acceptance of Shinto mythology.

2) *Success in war.* Success in war has been attributed by everyone from the Emperor down to his most lowly subject as resulting from the intercession of the Imperial deities. The rescript issued at the conclusion of the Russo-Japanese War refers to Japan's victory as being "due in large measure to the benign spirits of our ancestors." The Japanese were taught that their invincibility

in war was due to their status as a "God-sent race." This idea has played a central part in Japanese military education.

3) *Nationalism*. Devolving from and solidifying the hold of Shinto on the public mind was the growing spirit of Japanese nationalism. Nationalists sought and found in Shinto a purely Japanese religion which could be utilized to stabilize and to protect native institutions against the destructive force of foreign ideologies. Soon passing to the offensive, extremists discovered that Shinto could provide justification for the "place in the sun" they were seeking. Shinto theorists were thus able to add sufficient ideological weight to the military side of the scales to tip it against the more peacefully inclined elements in Japanese society and to make the militarist the dominant force in the state.

4) *Repression*. Not necessarily the most effective, but certainly the most pernicious of the influences working to make State Shinto doctrine all pervasive was the negative policy of trying to black out every expression of opinion and every thought which might cast doubt upon its validity. For more than twenty years much effort has been spent in enforcing the official Shinto as a weapon against "dangerous thought." It has been used to prevent criticism of some of the least worthy Japanese officials and civilians who achieved a certain untouchability by invoking the blessing of the "Imperial Way." To deny the official mythology was to invite the attention of the thought police and, in some cases, the assassin. By the most carefully calculated effort, Japanese officialdom created out of the primitive religion, believed by Aston in 1895 to be on the road to extinction, a way of thinking and acting which all Japanese were compelled outwardly to profess and believe.

3. STATE SHINTO DOCTRINE

a. State Shinto doctrine, in spite of the persistent efforts of the government to overcome its diversities and integrate its various parts, does not present a unified and consistent whole.

b. State Shinto doctrine differs from that of other animistic religions chiefly in that its beliefs, narratives, traditions, and practices have been intimately linked up with the national history.

1) It does not, like a universal religion such as Christianity or Buddhism, center on the individual and thus transcend national boundaries. Of necessity, it is racialistic and nationalistic.

2) This relationship begins with the origin and foundation of the Japanese nation under the ruling family and continues, it is alleged, from time immemorial right down through the ages.

3) Shinto traditions are thus expressions of faith in the life and mission of the nation centered in the throne and shown in the loyalty of the people.

c. State Shinto supports a polytheism of great multitude and complexity.

1) According to its doctrines, the universe is inhabited by innumerable spirits (some 8,000,000 deities) in the air, the forests, and mountains, as well as in human homes and hearts.

2) There is one supreme deity, Amaterasu Ō-mikami, the "Heavenly-Shining August Goddess."

a) Born from the left eye of a sky-father, Izanagi, and sister of the moon and the storm, Amaterasu Ō-mikami is at one and the same time the world-soul, the racial head of the nation, the founder of the state, and the ancestress of the Imperial family.

b) This divine ancestress is the chief of the contemporary politically-inspired pantheon of Shinto deities, and her great shrine at Ise is the center of the devotion and worship of the entire nation.

c) The existence of the increasingly dominant sun goddess aspect of Shinto has been explained as the development of a primitive sun worship cult of probable southern origin.

3) Nearly all the Japanese claim to be descended from one of the deities.

a) The worship of these deities is, at one and the same time, a genuine nature worship and also the worship of ancestors and heroes, centering in the sovereign deity.

4) It is not improbable that some of these deities actually existed as real persons, around whom myths have developed.

a) Thus, according to one Japanese historian who tried to rationalize the traditional mythology, Amaterasu Ō-mikami was in reality a Mongolian princess.

d. Local rites and ceremonies present a wholly varied picture, depending upon diverse manners and customs, stages of development, needs, and characteristics of different geographical areas.
   1) Within the vast diversity of the Shinto complex exist such rites and ceremonies as those which
      a) Summon ancient storm-gods to mountaintops.
      b) Induce god possession.
      c) Drive away defilement from individuals and groups.
      d) Exorcise evil spirits.
      e) Expel insects from crops or protect them from wind and storm.
      f) Accompany the presentation of first-fruits.
      g) Dedicate children.

e. The government has made persistent efforts to resolve the problem of diversity of Shinto observance and practice by centering the prescribed rituals about the mythology of the Emperor's descent from the sun goddess Amaterasu Ō-mikami and by making belief in that mythology a test of good citizenship.
   1) As a direct lineal descendant of the sun goddess, the Emperor is to many Japanese an actual living god. As such, he is by divine right entitled to rule all lands and all peoples.

4. Distinction between State Shinto and Sect Shinto

a. Background of Distinction
   1) The Japanese Government carefully distinguishes between State Shinto (*Kokka Shintō*), National Shinto (*Kokutai Shintō*), or Shrine Shinto (*Jinja Shintō*), on the one hand, and Sect Shinto (*Shūha Shintō*) or Church Shinto (*Kyōha Shintō*) on the other. While Sect Shinto is recognized as a religion, the government has been unwavering in its declaration that State Shinto is not a religion—an obvious contradiction in fact. The reasons for the government's position are easily perceived.
   2) Early in the Meiji period, when Japan was being flooded by disintegrating foreign ideas, certain government officials saw in Shinto a purely native institution whose

intimate connection with the Imperial Family made it a heaven-sent medium for binding the Japanese people into a group sufficiently united to withstand any destructive influence.

3) But in order to appear well in the eyes of occidentals as well as satisfy some of the treaty requirements of western nations, Japan had proclaimed freedom of religion, even writing the doctrine into the Constitution. This proclamation of religious freedom precluded special favors to any one religion. Yet to promote official policy the government desired to teach Shinto doctrines in the schools while excluding all instruction in other religions. It also desired to compel people to attend observances at shrines, a further violation of freedom of religion. The solution adopted was to declare that State Shinto was not a religion—only a civic institution.

4) The situation is clearly stated by a Buddhist writer: "If we ask why the Meiji governments declared that shrines, which were clearly the objects of religious faith, were not the objects of religious faith,...then we must say in answer, that, if Shrine Shinto were a religion, both Buddhists and Christians, under the guarantee of freedom of religious faith as set forth in the Constitution, need not do reverence at the shrines, and a very serious problem would arise."[5]

5) Despite the official and some unofficial views, there is no doubt that State Shinto, though it is mixed with some purely secular elements, is a religion.

b. *State Shinto and Sect Shinto Distinguished.* The main features that distinguish State Shinto from Sect Shinto should be carefully noted, since the two are often confused, particularly in matters of doctrine. It must be frankly recognized, however, that some of the confusion exists in actual fact and could only be resolved by a more rigorous delineation of function than now exists.

1) Both branches of Shinto have received influences from the parent stream of an ancient and indigenous religion, State Shinto more directly and on the whole in more unmixed character than Sect Shinto. Interpreters of State Shinto are generally quick to assert that the ceremonies and beliefs connected with the shrines represent the true and uncontaminated line of pure Shinto; Sect Shinto has

been more or less modified through foreign influences and the contributions of the founders and other teachers, though some of the sects maintain that they alone preserve the true and original Shinto.

2) Taken as a whole and recognizing the dangers of over-generalization, the dominant characteristics of Sect Shinto are: popular folklore and magic; colorful imaginings of simple peasant-minded founders mixed with many wholesome ethical precepts and spiritual insights; elaborate regard for purification ceremonies, ranging from magic rituals that drive away demonic defilement to inner prayer that cleanses the heart; mountain worship and faith healing all intermingled with and supported by the beliefs and ceremonies of the traditional Shinto sanctuaries. The sects carry on definite religious propaganda, publish a vast amount of literature, and employ religious teachers and preachers. State Shinto has as its chief function the celebration of rites considered appropriate to the deepening of national sentiment, though it, too, involves religious elements such as ancestor worship, the selling of charms and talismans, and the conduct of marriage and funeral ceremonies. Its priests, however, are forbidden by law to "preach" to the people or to carry on missionary activities.

3) Sect Shinto exists in the form of 13 sects and numerous subsects and is accorded the status of a religion. State Shinto, because of its value to the state, enjoys a special status as a civic institution or cult.

4) State Shinto in the matter of legal control and coordination of activities is placed under the jurisdiction of the Bureau of Shrines in the Home Ministry. Special enactments and administrative orders issued in this ministry regulate the affairs of the shrines in matters of organization, priesthood, and ceremonies. The affairs of Sect Shinto, until the occupation, were under the jurisdiction of the Bureau of Religions in the Education Ministry. Thus, Sect Shinto is afforded the same legal treatment as Buddhism and Christianity and is completely on its own resources in matters of places of worship, finances, internal management, doctrines, etc.

5) The acceptance of the doctrines of State Shinto is required by national authority as the essence of loyalty.

The acceptance of the doctrines of Sect Shinto is left to voluntary choice.

6) Shinto shrines receive supervision and a measure of financial support from village, municipal, prefectural, or national governments, depending on the grade of the particular shrine concerned. Shinto sects, like all recognized religious bodies, maintain their own independent organizations and possess legal properties that are almost exclusively distinct from those of the shrines.

7) All State Shinto institutions, whether national or local, large or small, are given the title of *jinja*, meaning "God-house," or "dwelling-place of the *kami* (deity)." The institutions of Sect Shinto are legally classified as *kyōkai*, or "churches"; they cannot use shrines as meeting places and, except in special cases, are not permitted to use the *torii*, the distinctive gateway that stands outside of shrines.

4. CONCLUSIONS

a. *Overall Problem*

1) State Shinto is composed of both secular and religious elements, the latter predominating to such a great extent that there is no doubt that State Shinto is a religion. Indeed, the Professor of Comparative Religion at Tokyo Imperial University estimates that State Shinto is about 80 percent religious and 20 percent secular.

2) Shinto cannot be abolished as a religion: that possibility is precluded both by the doctrine of religious freedom and by the nature of religion itself. Actually, there is no need to attempt to abolish Shinto as a religion or to attempt to separate Shinto from the Emperor, which is to say practically the same thing. The danger in State Shinto lies (a) in its sponsorship, support, and propagation by the State, (b) in the uses to which Japanese governments and Shinto nationalists have put its more or less vague mythology of divine origin of land, emperor, and people, and (c) in the rigid compulsion enforced upon all Japanese to observe its rituals and outwardly to accept its premises as actual fact.

3) The danger lies not in the interconnection between the Emperor and Shinto; it lies in the peculiar nature of the political system which nominally places all civil and

military power in the hands of a priest-king but actually allows that power to be exercised by any powerful group that gets control of the machinery of government.

4) The solution is (a) to bring about as complete a separation of church and state as is consistent with our recent policy of permitting the Emperor to retain his throne and (b) to secure such a revision of the Japanese Constitution and laws as will place actual control of the state directly in the hands of representatives elected by the people. The second part of the solution is, of course, beyond the scope of this study.

b. *Abolition of State Support and Control*

1) All government support, direction, or control over the shrines, their priests, ceremonies, or rituals should be abolished so as to place State Shinto on exactly the same footing as other religions, permitting it to continue as a religion of individuals.

2) There is evidence that many Japanese who visit shrines should welcome the removal of state control and the recognition of the religious nature of shrines.

3) Those shrines having a real religious following would be able to exist on voluntary contributions. Those least important in the religious life of the people would perhaps deteriorate or even cease to exist. However, Professor Anesaki believes that many of the weaker shrines would be saved by voluntary unions....In fact, there is reason to believe that the majority of Shinto priests favor separation of Shrine Shinto from the state and feel that the shrines would profit rather than suffer by the separation....

4) Certain liberal Japanese, who favor complete separation in principle but who fear that the financial burden resulting from the severance of state support would be too great for some important shrines to bear, feel that a few shrines which are special sanctuaries of the Imperial House should be permitted special treatment. The Grand Shrine of Ise, especially, holds a position of such significance that any action which would force it to close for lack of financial support would undoubtedly come as a great shock to the Japanese people and cause deep resentment. They have suggested that, in the case of a few such shrines, the Imperial Household should be

permitted to make financial grants to supplement the voluntary contributions of the general public. The Secretary General of the *Kōtenkōkyūsho*, however, believes that even the shrines most intimately connected with the Imperial Family should be treated no differently from other shrines—a judgment in which, he says, most Shinto priests concur. The one exception to the above rule, he says, is that the government should be permitted to furnish the remaining 8,000,000 Yen needed to complete the reconstruction of the Inner Shrine of the Grand Shrine of Ise which is by custom rebuilt every 20 years.

5) There are in Japan certain monuments, structures, gardens, or parks whose artistic and cultural value to Japan and the world transcends their significance as shrines or as the location of shrines. The most notable of these is the Tokugawa sanctuary at Nikko (Tōshōgū) which was originally established by Buddhists (Buddhist priests are still at Nikko) and was made a Shinto shrine only after the beginning of the Meiji period. However, most of these shrines and particularly the Tokugawa sanctuary at Nikko are in good financial position and would not suffer from the withdrawal of state funds. It seems obvious, of course, that the withdrawal of financial support from shrines located on public reservations or parks should not preclude the Japanese Government from continuing to support the areas on which such shrines are located.

c. *Elimination of Shinto from the Education System*

1) *Instruction.* As the schools, particularly those of the elementary grade, have been the primary instruments for the inculcation of Shintoistic and ultra-nationalistic ideology, the dissemination of Shinto ideology, in any form and by any means in any educational institution supported wholly or in part by public funds should be prohibited. This is perhaps the most important single step in the separation of church and state. The teaching of Shinto in connection with elective courses in comparative religion at the university or college (*daigaku* and *senmon gakkō*) level should be permitted.

2) *The Imperial Rescript on Education*

a) The 1890 Imperial Rescript on Education is one of the most significant and influential documents ever issued in

Japan. It has become the most important single instrument for inculcating filial piety (a Confucianist touch) and loyalty to the Emperor. It is treated with an extreme degree of reverence bordering on sacrosanctity, and its reading in all schools on the Emperor Meiji's birthday is a deeply impressive ceremony. Its influence upon impressionable youth is enormous. Through official interpretation in works like *Kokutai no hongi*, it has been used in recent years to proclaim the superiority of Japan over other nations and to assert a divine mission for the Japanese state.

b) It should either be superseded, amended, or reinterpreted by a new imperial rescript expressly repudiating the ultra-nationalistic interpretation or be banished from the schools. If the latter course were followed, the banishment should be accompanied by the widest possible publicity explaining that such a move was dictated by the ultra-nationalistic uses to which the rescript had been put by Shinto theorists and militarists. This careful explanation would be required, according to several liberal Japanese, because of the great shock its banishment would otherwise bring to the mass of the Japanese people, who, it is asserted, are for the most part unaware of any ultra-nationalistic interpretation of the rescript and would consider its banishment a direct attack upon the position of the Emperor. An attempt to secure an authoritative statement from Japanese sources expressly repudiating the ultra-nationalistic interpretation seems the better policy for the present. All persons who were in any way responsible for writing the ultra-nationalistic interpretation into texts, teachers' manuals, or other books, papers, or pamphlets should be excluded from public office.

3) *The Imperial Portrait*

a) An extremely delicate question perhaps involving some Shinto elements is the matter of the Imperial portrait. Dr. Holtom believes that the ceremony of obeisance before the Imperial portrait should be abolished and that the special room or building in which the portrait is sheltered should be closed or turned to other uses. He would have the portrait hung in an easily accessible place where it would be brought into contact with the normal life of the school and thus gradually be divested of its sacrosanctity. Another view is expressed by Dr. Shafer who thinks that school principals should have the right to refuse to accept the portrait.

b) There is no doubt that many school principals would like to relieve themselves of the present heavy responsibility of caring for the Imperial portrait. The whole system of obeisance appears repugnant to a person of democratic sympathies who has not long been accustomed to it. Any directive at this time changing the system would be considered an attack upon the position of the Emperor. The problem is more closely connected with the revision of the Constitution and the whole governmental system than it is with the separation of Shinto and the state, and changes might more properly follow developments in that field.

4) *Kamidana.* All *kamidana* (Shinto god-shelves) should be removed from all public schools and from all public buildings.

5) *Compulsory attendance at shrines.* Compulsory attendance at shrines, previously required of all students and teachers, should be expressly prohibited, and no discrimination against any person for his views on Shinto will be allowed.

6) *Shinto schools*

a) The Kokugakuin Daigaku of Tokyo and the Jingū Kōgakkan of Ise are the principal Shinto schools. The former is primarily engaged in research in ancient literature, Japanese folklore, and Shinto. Both have been sources of ultra-nationalistic Shinto theory. The Kokugakuin is a private school but has received 30,000 Yen each year from the government. Some three years ago the property of the Kōgakkan was transferred to the Japanese Government by the Grand Shrine and it was made a college by the Ministry of Education. To the Kōgakkan of Ise is attached a Shinto preparatory school of middle school grade. There are 25 other minor Shinto schools.

b) The Kōgakkan and all other institutions which are wholly or in part supported by public funds and whose primary function is the investigation in and dissemination of Shinto or in the training of a priesthood should be abolished as Shinto schools.

c) Private educational institutions for the investigation of Shinto and the training of a Shinto priesthood should be permitted to exist and operate on exactly the same basis as educational institutions engaged in the propagation of other religions. Obviously the dissemination of militaristic and ultra-nationalistic doctrine will be forbidden in all schools, public or private.

d. *Abolition of the Shrine board*

The Shrine Board (*Jingi-in*) of the Home Ministry, the cetral agency of the Japanese Government for the support, administration, control, and promotion of State Shinto, should be abolished as one of the first steps in the elimination of the connection between the government and Shinto. There is little defense of the position of the Shrine Board nor support for its retention except among members of the Board itself. Indeed, many Japanese interested in the problem have recommended that it be abolished.

c. *Accomplishments and Remaining Problems*

1) If Japan is to assume a position of self-direction and a place among the family of nations, it is necessary to break completely not only the Shinto-inspired ultra-nationalistic beliefs of the Japanese people but also the whole complex machinery by which the Japanese Government has succeeded in propagating those beliefs.

2) Much has already been accomplished. Defeat, surrender, and the subsequent occupation have unquestionably gone far to remove the scales from the eyes of many of the Japanese who previously never seriously questioned the official views.

3) The new freedom of thought and expression has already relieved the more enlightened Japanese of the necessity for professing belief in theories which they always knew to be fantastic. It has done much and, if continued inviolate, will do still more to free the minds of the less enlightened of the more irrational interpretations of the old mythology which may in time revert to the status of

harmless folk tales. To speed this change, however, certain action is needed.

III. ACTION RECOMMENDED

1. In view of the authority which any declaration of the Emperor holds over the minds and actions of the Japanese people and in view of the perverted interpretations given to the Imperial Rescript on Education handed down in 1890, it is recommended that pressure be brought on the Imperial Government to secure a rescript from the Emperor, declaring, in effect, that :

   a. It is not an evidence of patriotism, nor is it a service to the Emperor or to the Japanese nation for any Japanese subject or citizen to believe, to profess to believe, or to advocate that others should believe that Japan has a mission to extend, or is in any way justified in attempting to extend, its rule over other nations or peoples by reason of:

      1) Superiority of the Emperor of Japan over the heads of other states because of ancestry, descent, or special origin;

      2) Superiority of the people of Japan over the people of other lands because of ancestry, descent, or special origin;

      3) Superiority of the islands of Japan over other lands because of divine or special creation.

   b. All Persons who have declared, on the basis of Shinto theory, doctrine, writings, or teachings, that Japan is or ever was justified in seeking to rule over or has a mission to rule over other nations or peoples, or who have interpreted any imperial rescript of previous emperors, especially the 1890 Imperial Rescript on Education, as an expression of Imperial sanction for such a mission, have done a grave disservice to the Emperor and to the nation.

   c. The Emperor definitely and expressly repudiates all such interpretations of imperial rescripts.

   d. It is the duty of good Japanese subjects to attempt to extend harmonious and peaceful relations between the Japanese and other peoples as fellow members of one great family of nations, working together, each in his own way, in a spirit of absolute racial equality, for the common and equal interests of humanity.

2. Since an imperial rescript would not of itself clear up the situation and since it is desirable to make our own official position clear beyond the possibility of misinterpretation, it is further recommended that a directive ordering the separation of Shinto from the state and the elimination of Shinto from the education system be handed to the Imperial Government.

Ken R. Dyke
Brigadier General, AUS
Chief, CI & E Section

NOTES

* Some portions of this document and its accompanying citations have been abridged for this volume. The full text and citations were published in *Contemporary Religions in Japan* 7: 321–46, 1966.

1 See ANESAKI 1930: 36–39.

2 SANSOM 1943: 46 ff.

3 ASTON 1905: 376–77.

4 CHAMBERLAIN 1927: 560. Appendix I of this work was first published in 1912 as a pamphlet entitled "The Invention of a New Religion."

5 *Tōkyō Nichi Nichi Shinbun*, 3 Feb. 1930, quoted in HOLTOM 1938: 295. See also *Japan Christian Quarterly* V/5: 276 (July 1931), and HOLTOM 1938: 297.

4. Directive for the Disestablishment of State Shinto from the Supreme Commander of Allied Powers

GENERAL HEADQUARTERS
SUPREME COMMANDER FOR THE ALLIED POWERS
AG 000.3 (15 Dec 45) CIE   15 December 1945
Memorandum for: Imperial Japanese Government
Through: Central Liaison Office, Tokyo.
Subject: Abolition of Governmental Sponsorship, Support, Perpetuation, Control, and Dissemination of State Shinto (*Kokka Shintō, Jinja Shintō*).

1. In order to free the Japanese people from direct or indirect compulsion to believe or profess to believe in a religion or cult officially designated by the state, and

In order to lift from the Japanese people the burden of compulsory financial support of an ideology which has contributed to their war guilt, defeat, suffering, privation, and present deplorable condition, and

In order to prevent a recurrence of the perversion of Shinto theory and beliefs into militaristic and ultra-nationalistic propaganda designed to delude the Japanese people and lead them into wars of aggression, and

In order to assist the Japanese people in a rededication of their national life to building a new Japan based upon ideals of perpetual peace and democracy,

It is hereby directed that:

a. The sponsorship, support, perpetuation, control and dissemination of Shinto by the Japanese national, prefectural, and local governments, or by public officials, subordinates, and employees acting in their official capacity are prohibited and will cease immediately.

b. All financial support from public funds and all official affiliation with Shinto and Shinto shrines are prohibited and will cease immediately.

   1) While no financial support from public funds will be extended to shrines located on public reservations or parks, this prohibition will not be construed to preclude the Japanese Government from continuing to support the areas on which such shrines are located.

   2) Private financial support of all Shinto shrines which have been previously supported in whole or in part by public funds will be permitted, provided such private support is entirely voluntary and is in no way derived from forced or involuntary contributions.

c. All propagation and dissemination of militaristic and ultra-nationalistic ideology in Shinto doctrines, practices, rites, ceremonies, or observances, as well as in the doctrines, practices, rites, ceremonies, and observances of any other religion, faith, sect, creed, or philosophy, are prohibited and will cease immediately.

d. The Religious Functions Order relating to the Grand Shrine of Ise and the Religious Functions Order relating to State and other Shrines will be annulled.

e. The Shrine Board (*Jingi-in*) of the Ministry of Home Affairs will be abolished, and its present functions, duties, and administrative obligations will not be assumed by any other governmental or tax-supported agency.

f. All public educational institutions whose primary function is either the investigation and dissemination of Shinto or the training of a Shinto priesthood will be abolished and their physical properties diverted to other uses. Their present functions, duties and administrative obligations will not be assumed by any other governmental or tax-supported agency.

g. Private educational institutions for the investigation and dissemination of Shinto and for the training of priesthood for Shinto will be permitted and will operate with the same privileges and be subject to the same controls and restrictions as any other private educational institution having no affiliation with the government; in no case, however, will they receive support from public funds, and in no case will they propagate and disseminate militaristic and ultra-nationalistic ideology.

h. The dissemination of Shinto doctrines in any form and by any means in any educational institution supported wholly or in part by public funds is prohibited and will cease immediately.

1) All teachers' manuals and textbooks now in use in any educational institution supported wholly or in part by public funds will be censored, and all Shinto doctrine will be deleted. No teachers' manual or textbook which is published in the future for use in such institutions will contain any Shinto doctrine.

2) No visits to Shinto shrines and no rites, practices, or ceremonies associated with Shinto will be conducted or sponsored by any educational institution supported wholly or in part by public funds.

i. Circulation by the government of "The Fundamental Principles of the National Structure" (*Kokutai no hongi*), "The Way of the Subject" (*Shinmin no michi*), and all similar official volumes, commentaries, interpretations, or instructions on Shinto is prohibited.

j. The use in official writings of the terms "Greater East Asia War" (*Dai Tōa Sensō*), "The Whole World under One Roof" (*Hakko ichi-u*), and all other terms whose connotation in Japanese is inextricably connected with State Shinto, militarism, and ultra-nationalism is prohibited and will cease immediately.

k. God-shelves (*kamidana*) and all other physical symbols of State Shinto in any office, school, institution, organization, or structure supported wholly or in part by public funds are prohibited and will be removed immediately.

l. No official, subordinate, employee, student, citizen, or resident of Japan will be discriminated against because of his failure to profess and believe in or participate in any practice, rite, ceremony, or observance of State Shinto or of any other religion.

m. No official of the national, prefectural, or local government, acting in his public capacity, will visit any shrine to report his assumption of office, to report on conditions of government, or to participate as a representative of government in any ceremony or observance.

2. a. The purpose of this directive is to separate religion from the state, to prevent misuse of religion for political ends, and to put all religions, faiths, and creeds upon exactly the same basis, entitled to precisely the same opportunities and protection. It forbids affiliation with the government and the propagation and dissemination of militaristic and ultra-nationalistic ideology not only to Shinto but to the followers of all religions, faiths, sects, creeds, or philosophies.

b. The provisions of this directive will apply with equal force to all rites, practices, ceremonies, observances, beliefs, teachings, mythology, legends, philosophy, shrines, and physical symbols associated with Shinto.

c. The term State Shinto within the meaning of this directive will refer to that branch of Shinto (*Kokka Shintō* or *Jinja Shintō*) which by official acts of the Japanese Government has been differentiated from the religion of Sect Shinto (*Shūha Shintō* or *Kyōha Shintō*) and has been classified a non-religious cult commonly known as State Shinto, National Shinto, or Shrine Shinto.

d. The term Sect Shinto (*Shūha Shintō* or *Kyōha Shintō*) will refer to that branch of Shinto (composed of 13 recognized sects) which by popular belief, legal commentary, and the official acts of the Japanese Government has been recognized to be a religion.

e. Pursuant to the terms of Article I of the Basic Directive on "Removal of Restrictions on Political, Civil, and Religious Liberties" issued on 4 October 1945 by the Supreme Commander for the Allied Powers in which the Japanese people were assured complete religious freedom,

1) Sect Shinto will enjoy the same protection as any other religion.

2) Shrine Shinto, after having been divorced from the state and divested of its militaristic and ultra-nationalistic elements, will be recognized as a religion if its adherents so desire and will be granted the same protection as any other religion in so far as it may in fact be the philosophy or religion of Japanese individuals.

f. Militaristic and ultra-nationalistic ideology, as used in this directive, embraces those teachings, beliefs, and theories which advocate or justify a mission on the part of Japan to extend its rule over other nations and peoples by reason of:

1) The doctrine that the Emperor of Japan is superior to the heads of other states because of ancestry, descent, or special origin.

2) The doctrine that the people of Japan are superior to the people of other lands because of ancestry, descent, or special origin.

3) The doctrine that the islands of Japan are superior to other lands because of divine or special origin.

4) Any other doctrine which tends to delude the Japanese people into embarking upon wars of aggression or to glorify the use of force as an instrument for the settlement of disputes with other peoples.

3. The Imperial Japanese Government will submit a comprehensive report to this Headquarters not later than 15 March 1946 describing in detail all action taken to comply with all provisions of this directive.

4. All officials, subordinates, and employees of the Japanese national, prefectural, and local governments, all teachers and education officials, and all citizens and residents of Japan will be held personally accountable for compliance

with the spirit as well as the letter of all provisions of this directive.

FOR THE SUPREME COMMANDER:

H. W. Allen
Colonel, A. G. D.,
Asst Adjutant General

5. Emperor's Imperial Rescript Denying his Divinity (1 January 1946)

In greeting the new year we recall to mind that the Emperor Meiji proclaimed as the basis of our national policy the five clauses of the charter at the beginning of the Meiji era. The charter oath signified:

1) Deliberative assemblies shall be established and all measures of government decided in accordance with public opinion.
2) All classes high and low shall unite in vigorously carrying on the affairs of State.
3) All common people, no less than the civil and military officials, shall be allowed to fulfill their just desires so that there may not be any discontent among them.
4) All the absurd usages of old shall be broken through and equity and justice to be found in the workings of nature shall serve as the basis of action.
5) Wisdom and knowledge shall be sought throughout the world for the purpose of promoting the welfare of the Empire.

The proclamation is evident in its significance and high in its ideals. We wish to make this oath anew and restore the country to stand on its own feet again. We have to reaffirm the principles embodied in the charter and proceed unflinchingly toward elimination of misguided practices of the past; and, keeping in close touch with the desires of the people, we will construct a new Japan through thoroughly being pacific, the officials and the people alike obtaining rich culture and advancing the standard of living of the people.

The devastation of the war inflicted upon our cities, the miseries of the destitute, the stagnation of trade, shortage of food, and the great and growing number of the unemployed are indeed heart-rending; but if the nation is firmly united in its resolve to face the present ordeal and to see civilization consistently in peace, a bright future will undoubtedly be ours, not only for our country but for the whole of humanity. Love of the family and love of country are especially strong in this country. With more of this devotion should we now work toward love of mankind.

We feel deeply concerned to note that consequent upon the protracted war ending in our defeat our people are liable to grow restless and to fall into the slough of despondence. Radical tendencies in excess are gradually spreading and the sense of morality tends to lose its hold on the people with the result that there are signs of confusion of thoughts.

We stand by the people and we wish always to share with them in their moment of joys and sorrows. The ties between us and our people have always stood upon mutual trust and affection. They do not depend upon mere legends and myths. They are not predicated on the false conception that the Emperor is divine and that the Japanese people are superior to other races and fated to rule the world.

Our Government should make every effort to alleviate their trials and tribulations. At the same time, we trust that the people will rise to the occasion and will strive courageously for the solution of their outstanding difficulties and for the development of industry and culture. Acting upon a consciousness of solidarity and of mutual aid and broad tolerance in their civic life, they will prove themselves worthy of their best tradition. By their supreme endeavors in that direction they will be able to render their substantial contribution to the welfare and advancement of mankind.

The resolution for the year should be made at the beginning of the year. We expect our people to join us in all exertions looking to accomplishment of this great undertaking with an indomitable spirit.

6. Constitution of Japan
(promulgated on 3 November 1946, and put into effect from 3 May 1947)

Article 20: Freedom of religion is guaranteed to all. No religious organization shall receive any privileges from the state, nor exercise any political authority. No person shall be compelled to take part in any religious act, celebration, rite, or practice. The state and its organs shall refrain from religious education or any other religious activity.

Article 89: No public money or other property shall be expended or appropriated for the use, benefit, or maintenance of any religious institution or association, or for any charitable, educational, or benevolent enterprises not under the control of public authority.

The Revitalization of Japanese Civil Religion

K. Peter TAKAYAMA

APAN IS NOW questioning the concept of nationality imposed upon it by the World War II victors almost fifty years ago, and examining whether the Japanese state can continue in a form different from all ordinary concepts of the nation-state. Major changes in the Japanese domestic and external environment have triggered a restless quest to redefine national priorities and create a new vision for the future. Among the central issues are the hotly debated issue of whether to remilitarize Japan and the perplexing matter of how to address what many people see as the country's increasing moral vacuum. Many argue that there is no consensus in Japan except on "economic achievement" values. Government and religious leaders blame the postwar "democratic" education for the self-oriented and "hedonistic" behavior of the younger generation, claiming that it has systematically cut people off from Japan's cultural heritage and has fostered a liberal social order that has lost sight of the concept of loyalty to the state.

Associated with these somewhat contradictory social phenomena is the movement to revitalize the Japanese civil religion, symbolized by the recent intensification of efforts to renationalize Yasukuni Shrine (the Shinto memorial to the nation's war dead). By revitalization I mean the effort to restore something sacred out of the past, spurred by a sense of decadence in the present. Many government leaders are convinced that Japan needs to restore the sacred Shinto symbols and historical legacies that once gave the Japanese a strong national identity and cosmic unity (ŌE 1984). To be sure, the movement to revitalize the Japanese civil religion rests on a resurgence of nationalistic and religious sentiments among many ordinary Japanese citizens, who accept Shinto as a "public" religion, as they did in prewar times.

A countermovement has also developed, one that opposes the infringement of the constitutional separation of state and religion. The new nationalistic and militaristic sentiments are of particular concern to many Buddhists, Christians, and intellectuals. This essay explores some aspects of this religio-political problem in Japan, devoting particular attention to the issues surrounding Yasukuni Shrine.

THE DYNAMICS OF CIVIL RELIGION

BELLAH's (1967) initial essay on civil religion in America opened a debate that has continued to this day. Much of the debate, as Bellah himself points out, has not been particularly productive, focusing more on form than content and on definition rather than substance. BELLAH and HAMMOND (1980) suggest that the comparative study of civil religions in different nation-states may be the best approach for examining and understanding the dynamic aspects of these religions. To further such study, Bellah and Hammond focus their inquiry upon what Hammond calls the structural analysis of civil religion—that is, the analysis of such institutional structures as public education systems and legal structures, and of the religious institutions through which patterns of belief and meaning regarding the polity are cultivated, maintained, and transmitted.

COLEMAN (1970) argues that civil religion—seen as a religious link between citizen and state—follows an evolutionary pattern of three stages: undifferentiation, state sponsorship in the period of modernization, and differentiation. In his cross-cultural comparisons of Japan, Imperial Rome, Turkey, France, the Soviet Union, and the United States, Coleman uncovers merits and demerits in each phase. Japan, which from the time of the Meiji Restoration until the end of World War II promoted State Shinto based on patriotism and veneration of the emperor, provides Coleman with a sample case of the state sponsorship of civil religion.

Earlier, BELLAH had postulated five phases of religious evolution: primitive, archaic, historic, early modern, and modern (1964). Advancing his comparative approach to civil religion through an extension of his theory and Coleman's typology, BELLAH writes: "Fairly distinct types of solution to the religio-political problem (or fairly distinct types of civil religion) seem to correlate with the phases of religious evolution...." (1980: viii). Bellah suggests that Japanese Shinto is particularly interesting because it is an example of a "full-fledged archaic solution to the religio-political problem that has survived into the twentieth century."

STATE SHINTO AND YASUKUNI SHRINE

State Shinto was essentially a religion of Japanese nationalism that was devised after the Meiji Restoration in 1868. Confronted with the double threat of Western civilization and internal disintegration, the new Meiji government needed a set of truly national symbols to help strengthen the concept of the new nation-state and develop a national patriotism strong enough to replace the local and parochial loyalties of the past. The government leaders resorted to the emperor system and Shinto, asserting that a spirit of national unity could be created only by reaching back to earlier historical periods, especially the seventh and eighth centuries, when the emperor and Shinto played prominent roles in governing the country.

The imperial family had existed for well over a millennium, but the imperial system that emerged during Meiji times was new, designed as an ideological weapon for controlling the Japanese population. "Mass media were employed to spread among commoners the archaic imperial mythology which in the past had been the serious make-believe of aristocratic and military alone" (DAVIS 1977: 69). It was to reinforce the veneration of the emperor that the Meiji government elevated Shinto to the status of a state religion, even creating a Department of Shinto, superior to all other departments. While the Meiji government promoted the establishment of a modern nation-state, what they really longed for was a semi-divine nation, a paternalistic and authoritarian state that could utilize the fruits of Western civilization. Thus, despite their passionate opposition to the shogunate, the architects of the Meiji regime inherited one significant characteristic of the Tokugawa feudal regime: its "immanental theocracy" (KITA-GAWA 1966: 185).

Whereas State Shinto centered on veneration of the emperor, early and communal Shinto centered around the animistic worship of natural phenomena—the sun, mountains, trees, rocks, and the entire process of fertility. Totemistic ancestors were included among the kami (deities), and no line was drawn between humanity and nature. The emperors were

現つ神 often spoken of as *akitsu-kami*, "visible gods." Historic Shinto never developed an orthodox doctrine, and remained tolerant of other religions such as Buddhism. Indeed, this historic Shinto readily absorbed Buddhist influences.

Yasukuni Shrine was established by the Meiji government as part of its effort to promote the emperor cult. Built in Tokyo in 1869 for the repose of those who had died fighting for the imperial cause at the time of the Meiji Restoration, the

招魂社 shrine was first named the Shōkonsha (literally, "spirit-invoking shrine"), then renamed ten years later as the

靖国神社 Yasukuni-jinja (shrine for the pacification of the nation). Enshrinement was limited to the soldiers who laid down their lives for the emperor and the state.

The shrine was a center for the glorification of militarism in the years before and during World War II. Kamikaze pilots during the war would say farewell to each other with the famous words, "We'll meet again under the cherry blossoms in Yasukuni." Describing the attitude of the Japanese toward Yasukuni, HOLTOM wrote: "It is probably safe to say that, with the exception of the shrine to the sun-goddess at Ise, no other spot in the entire country is so magnified in the national life or so closely bound up with the deepest sentiments of the people" (1947: 45). The occasion of deification (or enshrinement) was, and is, profoundly religious. In a solemn service of prayer and priestly ritual, the spirits of the dead soldiers first become kami and then guardian deities of the state, protecting soldiers on the field of battle and watching over the destiny of the nation.

Although the Meiji Constitution, as a concession to the Western powers, nominally guaranteed religious freedom, in reality State Shinto was considered an exception. The concept of "religious freedom" was meaningful only if State Shinto was viewed as nonreligious. Indeed, government leaders claimed that State Shinto had nothing to do with religion, that it was merely a part of being Japanese, a cult of national morality and patriotism that applied to all Japanese regardless of their religion. The Imperial Rescript on Education of 1880 affirmed the nonreligious character of Shinto, stating that Shinto and Confucian principles would be applied in the moral—not the religious—education of Japanese children.

However, a growing fanaticism and intolerance in State Shinto accompanied the mounting militarism of the 1930s, bringing a new brand of rightist nationalistic sentiment to the fore. This movement claimed that Japan was a sacred nation and demanded the prohibition of all other religions. In 1932 a major incident occurred when the students of a Catholic school in Tokyo refused en masse to participate in a special commemorative ceremony at Yasukuni Shrine for those who had died in the Manchurian Incident and the war in China. Thereafter the military perceived Christianity as an antagonistic force. In 1940 all Christian churches were forced to join a government-sponsored national organization that acknowledged—at least officially—the validity of State Shinto.

With Japan's unconditional surrender in 1945, the Allied powers demanded the abolition of the Japanese civil religion molded during the nationalistic and ultranationalistic periods. With this Japan lost more than the divine prerogatives of the throne and the immense institution of State Shinto. These were only the external symbols of something much deeper: the Japanese sense of identity and destiny based on the nation's ancient cosmological worldview. The loss was difficult, for this cosmology was linked to the fundamental Japanese conception of reality.

During the 1960s the GNP of Japan grew at an average annual rate of about ten percent higher than that of any other nation. As the Japanese devoted their energies to industrial production and commercial expansion, the average Japanese personal income doubled in the seven years after 1960. Japanese capitalism enjoyed unprecedented growth and penetrated markets throughout the world. Eventually the high quality and low price of Japanese products threatened European and American industry.

On the political front, however, a number of the New Left groups that emerged in the 1960s seriously questioned the economic expansion, attributing it to Japan's increased exploitation of East Asia, the source of raw material and cheap labor. In 1968 student insurgencies under the banner of political and educational reform spread throughout the university system. By June 1969 over forty percent of all Japanese university students were unable or unwilling to attend classes because of campus disorders.

Japan was then struck in the early 1970s by three successive shocks in the area of foreign affairs. The first was the so-called "Nixon shock" of 1971, when the American President announced his forthcoming plans to visit Peking; in spite of the supposedly close relations between Japan and the United States, the American government did not inform Prime Minister Satō Eisaku about this quite sensitive decision until only minutes before it was made public. The same year saw the "trade shock," resulting from the Nixon administration's efforts to curtail Japanese textile exports. In 1973 came the "oil shock," which followed the OPEC nations' 470 percent increase in the price of oil to $11.00 a barrel. The resulting severe inflation in Japan underscored the precariousness of the nation's foreign-procured energy supply. Japan entered a period of slow economic growth, accompanied by the emergence of a new international order shaped by the end of the Vietnam War, troubled relations between Japan's neighbors China and the Soviet Union, and the Japanese and the American restoration of relations with China.

It is difficult to show direct causal connections between the 1968–1971 student struggles, the subsequent economic troubles, and certain of the political and ideological developments that later took place, but such connections certainly did exist. There were signs throughout the nation of a new conservatism, along with the resurgence of a Japanese nationalism marked by strong elements of militarism (aspects that had never completely disappeared even during the American Occupation period).

Signs of the renewed conservatism had grown following the end of the Occupation, leading, for example, to novelist Mishima Yukio's ritual *seppuku* suicide in November 1970 following his calls for the remilitarization of Japan under a restored emperor system. A half-year later, in May 1971, the former prime minister Kishi Nobusuke made a speech in Tokyo, reported as follows in *The Mainichi Daily News*:

> Kishi Nobusuke, elder brother of former Prime Minister Satō, told a crowd of two thousand at Kyōritsu Hall that the present Constitution should be discarded in favor of one genuinely Japanese in nature. After the speakers there urged the revision of the Constitution, using such words as *yamato damashii* (the Japanese spirit) and "Greater East Asia Co-Prosperity Sphere," the meeting resolved, among other things, to place the Emperor at the center of the state, promote defense efforts, and map out a truly independent Constitution.

On 17 July 1973, twenty-four junior Liberal Democratic Party (LDP) Diet members gathered at the Ōkura Hotel to formally inaugurate a new nationalistic organization called the "Seirankai." The organization's primary missions were to revise the postwar peace constitution and promote Japanese patriotism. As evidence of his sincerity each member present sliced his little finger with a razor blade and wrote his signature in blood on the membership roster. Naturally, this bit of drama attracted much attention in the popular press.

During this period the movement to renationalize Yasukuni Shrine intensified. In June 1969 the conservative LDP, the ruling party for two decades, presented the Yasukuni Shrine Bill to the Diet. This bill, whose purpose was to establish Yasukuni Shrine as a nonreligious special foundation and to place it under the jurisdiction of the prime minister, was regarded by many as a violation of the constitutional principle of the separation of state and religion (ŌE 1984). The Association of War Bereaved Families, the Association of Shinto Shrines, and right-wing groups such as the Seirankai were the major forces behind the movement (MURAKAMI 1980: 158). Bills to restore state support to the shrine were introduced to the National Diet six times by June 1974, but were defeated on each occasion due to strong opposition from a variety of religious groups, including major Buddhist sects and Christian denominations.

On 15 August 1975, the anniversary of Japan's World War II surrender, Prime Minister Miki Takeo visited Yasukuni Shrine, the first postwar visit for a prime minister. He insisted that he visited as an individual citizen, not in an official capacity; nevertheless, visitations have become customary for Japan's prime ministers.

Movements to revise the peace constitution and restore the Japanese civil religion were further intensified by a series of events during the late 1970s. On 10 November 1976, the Japanese government sponsored the National Celebration for the Fiftieth Year of the Imperial Reign. Prime Minister Miki led an estimated 7,500 people gathered at the Tokyo Budōkan in the triple banzai salute to the emperor. This celebration was held under the tightest security as a divided nation watched. The Shōwa Emperor was in fact enthroned in 1928, so that the fiftieth year of his reign actually fell in 1978. Yet, for political reasons, the government held the event two years early. The date has a special meaning—in 1940, during World War II, it was this day that Japan declared the official date of its founding and celebrated its 2,600th anniversary as a nation.

Legal support for the idea that Yasukuni Shrine is "nonreligious" was provided by a 1977 Supreme Court decision 地鎮祭 that a ground-breaking ceremony (*jichinsai*) by the Tsu City government did not violate the constitutional separation of religion and state.[1]

On 19 April 1979, Yasukuni Shrine officials made a surprising announcement. Fourteen military leaders who had been found guilty of war crimes by the Allied Tribunal had been enshrined on 17 October 1978. They were called the "Shōwa Martyrs" (after the Shōwa Emperor) and were placed with 2,450,000 other war dead at the shrine (ŌE 1984: 18). The fourteen included General Tōjō Hideki, Supreme Commander of the Army. The shrine staff said that the enshrinement was done without consultation with family members, since some were certain to oppose the decision. Seven of the fourteen had been executed and seven had died in prison before their trials took place. Surprisingly, there was very little protest to the enshrinement of these war criminals. A professor of religion at Kokugakuin University, a Shinto-supported university in Tokyo, defended the action, commenting that it was natural to enshrine them since they died for the service of Japan and since their war-crime trials were conducted by foreigners.

The late 1970s were also marked by the return of Japan's self-confidence in its traditional values and institutions, a return that accompanied the country's growing economic success. This self-confidence has also contributed to the conservative and nationalistic mood. During the early postwar period Japan had embraced the universalistic pretensions of the new institutions established by the Allied Powers. The predominant opinion was that prewar nationalism, the emperor system, and State Shinto had led them astray. To the extent that Japanese institutions and values diverged from the Western pattern, they were regarded as somehow premodern, feudal, and "abnormal." If Japan was to recover and develop into a modern, democratic, and progressive industrial society, it was thought, Japanese traditional values and institutions had to be eliminated in favor of the liberal-democratic

A procession of local dignitaries and political leaders pay a visit to a Gokoku Jinja. Kagawa Prefecture.

principles of the West.

By the late 1970s, however, the Japanese were seeing themselves and the world in terms that were quite different from those of the early postwar period. The nation's traditional values—in some respects the very ones that had been rejected in 1945—were now acclaimed as providing Japan with a unique advantage in building an advanced industrial society. Such comments were made not only by Japan analysts, but, perhaps more importantly to the Japanese, by foreign observers.

This surge of self-confidence has been evidenced by the veritable flood of "success literature" that has inundated the bookstores with volumes on the reasons for Japan's economic success, all emphasizing the unique characteristics of the Japanese people and their culture. Japan outstripped the economic performance of other advanced industrial countries, goes the usual explanation, because its historically formed institutions have fostered greater productivity.

Japan's economic success and its consequent pride in its social values and institutions pushed the people further toward the right. KOMIYA (1979) estimated that until the mid-1960s eighty percent of the opinion leaders were of the progressive persuasion, but that in 1978 the situation reversed, with eighty percent then belonging to the central or conservative portions of the political spectrum. In view of this, however, a rather paradoxical social process was simultaneously taking place. YAMAZAKI (1984) argues that the 1970s was the only period in Japan's modern history in which the nation was totally without an aggressive national goal; the image and power of the state had shrunk in the consciousness of the Japanese people for the first time since the Meiji Restoration in 1868. Though the state had by no means lost its role as a functioning political system, it suffered a rapid diminution in the perception of the individual Japanese citizen.

During the hundred-year process of modernization and industrialization that began with the Meiji Restoration, the image of the state was a powerful force in determining national attitudes. Such national slogans as "Catch up with the West," "Build a strong army," "Increase production," "Develop Japan into a trading nation," and "Raise the gross national product" became ingrained in the minds of the citizens. Japan's development into an economic giant, for example, was closely linked to the income-doubling national program launched in 1960. At no other time in Japanese history had the aims of the state and the individual been so closely identified as during the 1960s.

The increasing "individualization" of the Japanese people and secularization of Japanese culture that accompanied the country's growing economic affluence during the 1960s weakened Japan's ability to take aggressive national collective action during the 1970s. The state lost its fascination for the people and no longer provided moral incentives in their individual lives. The state, in short, ceased to be a "combat group" working toward a major objective. KATSUDA (1981) observed that the liberal social order of the 1960s lost sight of a concept of the state to which citizens owe their loyalty.

EDUCATIONAL REFORM AND THE NEW NATIONALISM

In the 1980s the Japanese government, concerned with its weakness, sought means to remedy the situation. One initiative was educational reform, taken after the ruling LDP won a substantial majority in the 1980 general election. A consensus had begun to emerge regarding the direction education should take, particularly with regard to social studies and history. Hence in June 1980 Tanaka Tatsuo, the Minister of Education, openly criticized social studies textbooks for ignoring Japanese historical heroes who had given their lives for their country. The following month Okuno Seisuke, the Minister of Justice, charged that the textbooks then in use failed to teach patriotism.

On 29 October 1980, the LDP formed a textbook committee to study the possible need for the revision of school texts, especially those in social studies. According to the committee's proposal, textbook revision should be promoted along with constitutional reform and an increase in military spending. The party members contended that textbooks carried a left-wing bias despite having passed through an authorization process. They charged that textbooks, by discussing only the shortcomings of capitalist economies, in effect glorified socialism; that little space was devoted to the importance of sound morals; that the importance of national defense was ignored; and that the constitutionality of Japan's Self-Defense Forces was questioned. The reason for these biases, they claimed, was that the Japan Teachers' Union, supported by the Socialist and the Communist Parties, put pressure on local boards of education to use only left-leaning texts. Consequently, these Diet members maintained, textbook publishers—engaged in a fierce competition for sales—commissioned only left-wing scholars as authors.

From 1890 to 1945 the Imperial Rescript on Education, following Confucian teachings, defined the purpose of education as promoting loyalty to one's parents and the emperor. Under the imperial system, education was controlled directly by the Ministry of Education. The present constitution, in contrast, does not allow the government a monopoly on education—the education system is supposed to be administered by laws approved by democratic process in the Diet. Textbooks for use in elementary and secondary schools are screened by the Ministry of Education; known as the authorization procedure, this screening is justified on the basis of insuring a standard level of excellence in all schools throughout the country.

One of the most conspicuous critics of the postwar educational system and its values has been the sociologist Shimizu Ikutarō, himself a convert from the progressive camp. In his book *Sengo o utagau* [Doubts about the postwar period],

SHIMIZU censures postwar education as wholly divorced from the life of the people and concludes that the values of the 1890 Imperial Rescript on Education are still valid and appropriate for the present (1980a: 98). He sees the philosophy underlying the progressive postwar reforms as similar to Enlightenment thought: the two share, in his opinion, a contempt for history and a worship of science and reason. They also hold a similar faith in the fundamental goodness of human nature, believing that if institutions are reformed human behavior will change. Shimizu feels, in contrast, that institutions must be rooted in the lives of the common people, and for this reason he rejects the universalist, non-Japanese nature of the postwar system. Because of Shimizu's prominence, his thesis has provided strong theoretical justification for the government's efforts to reform education.

Shimizu also wrote a sensational book, *Nippon yo, kokka tare* [Japan, become a state!]. He claims that by relinquishing its military power and its right to defend its interests Japan ceased to be a state, and became simply a society whose essence is economic activity (SHIMIZU 1980b). He proposed a revision of the constitution that would allow Japan to be armed as a nation should be, so that the country could regain its identity as a nation-state.

The efforts of the LDP and the government to strengthen nationalism and restore traditional moral education increased after Prime Minister Nakasone Yasuhiro, an ardent nationalist, came to power in 1982. Nakasone declared in 1985 that the postwar era of Japanese history was over: forty years after the war's end, a new era, unassociated with the humiliating defeat, had to begin. All institutions, especially those imposed upon Japan after its defeat, must undergo a total reevaluation. The goals of Nakasone's "new nationalism" stressed Japan's historical achievements, the reestablishment of the Japanese identity, and the exploration of its cultural roots. To implement these goals Nakasone formed the Provisional Council on Education Reform. Judging by its early draft proposals, the commission—whose members are, for the most part, conservative and nationalistic—is clearly looking for ways to strengthen traditional values and moral education.

Prime Minister Nakasone and the members of his cabinet paid a formal visit to Yasukuni Shrine on 15 August 1985.

This visit, on the date of Japan's World War II surrender, marked the first time a Japanese head of the government had visited the shrine in an official capacity since the end of World War II. The official visit served to exacerbate fears of a resurgent State Shinto and a new militarism. Although the prime minister tried to put the worries to rest, the symbolic move aroused condemnation both at home and abroad. China, for example, attacked the visit as an attempt to "reverse the verdict on Japanese militarism, which was long ago condemned to the dustbin of history."

According to the *Japan Christian Activity News* (15 August 1985), Nakasone made a revealing speech when he was president of Takushoku University. Entitled "Yasukuni Shrine as the Japanese Spiritual Home," the speech had been given over seventeen years before, when the bill to nationalize Yasukuni Shrine was first presented to the Diet. The speech, the main themes of which Nakasone has repeated on many occasions, indicates his attitude towards the shrine to this day:

> Those enshrined in the Yasukuni Shinto Shrine include believers of many faiths: Tenri-kyō, Konkō-kyō, Christianity, Shinto, Sōka Gakkai, and Zen. They include all who died in the war effort, from the lowest soldiers to the top generals. I believe that this type of Japanese spiritual ground is necessary. When the prime minister goes to the USA, for example, he offers a wreath at Arlington Cemetery. However, when a prime minister or president comes to Japan, where does he present a wreath? We do not have such a place. Can we then call our country a state?

Regarding the place of Yasukuni Shrine in the nation and the reason that the shrine should be administered by the state, Nakasone said:

> Of course, Yasukuni Shrine must be separate from the Shinto religion. I believe that Shinto ceremonies, like those for purification (or ground-breaking), are not necessarily Shinto in a religious sense. Ground-purification ceremonies are performed by a Shinto priest for the construction of a Christian church. I believe this ceremony is simply a Japanese custom. In order that Yasukuni Shrine be separate from the Shinto religion, it should be nationalized. We should resurrect the symbol of Yasukuni Shrine as the Japanese spiritual ground where we can pay our respects to those who died for the sake of the country. This is done through the commemoration and

enshrinement of their spirits. By placing the shrine under a special legal body, it would thus come under the umbrella of the state. As long as the state exists in Japan, we should have a place where foreign dignitaries can formally attend a worship service with the Emperor of Japan. Otherwise, Japan cannot be called a state.

Given the political success and status of the prime minister, this speech may very well sum up the feelings of many Japanese citizens toward the revitalization movement.

CONCLUSION

There are two clearly discernible aspects of the movement to revitalize Japanese civil religion. First, the movement's principal organizers and participants are LDP members and government leaders who have been the political and economic elite of Japan for the last two-and-a-half decades. Second, whenever government leaders take up such national religio-political issues as the nationalization of Yasukuni Shrine and the moral education of children, other related issues inevitably emerge. These include the restoration of the emperor system as the center of the state, the promotion of national defense efforts, anti-Communism, the revision of the peace constitution, and the reform of education, particularly in the areas of social studies and history—issues closely associated with the framework of Japanese civil religion.

The image and concept of the state has been an immeasurably powerful force in molding the attitude and commitments of the Japanese people in their efforts to create a modern industrialized state. As COLEMAN (1970) observed, Japan was a prime example of state sponsorship of civil religion in the period of modernization. This has only started to change since the early 1970s, as indicated in this paper.

When Japan surrendered to the Allied Powers in 1945, it was forced to abandon its civil religion that had been molded during the nationalistic and ultranationalistic periods. In the process the Japanese lost something much deeper: the ancient worldview that formed the source of their identity and sense of destiny. Thus the Japanese were sojourners in their own country for the first time in their long history, and they looked desperately for something to believe in. A variety of new religious movements rose and flourished.

Nevertheless, it is my view that the fundamental metaphysics of the Japanese, i.e., their archaic and optimistic cosmological view of human existence, remained intact to a significant degree. Evidence for this view can be seen in Shinto communal rites and festivities, and in the fundamental conception of reality held by most Japanese. The traditional cosmology and religious values that help shape the Japanese cultural identity and upon which Japanese civil religion was constructed have survived without much alteration to the present day.

Japan was able to rebound from the ashes of defeat and commit itself to building a new "democratic" nation-state because it retained its traditional cosmology and religious values. To be sure, the national symbols of postwar Japan have become worldly and universalistic, and the country has vigorously pursued the goals of secularization and democratization. Yet the traditional values and institutions have facilitated the actual process of nation-building, enabling the Japanese leadership to obtain enormous commitments from the citizens in the 1960s despite the obviously secular nature of the national goals.

Weissbrod (1983) suggests that societies whose social identity is based on religious core values tend to have greater difficulty in establishing substitute secular values on which to form a new identity. Furthermore, she argues that members of such societies are likely to undergo a crisis of identity if such a substitution is made, and to search for a renewed religion-based identity. In the brief period since 1945, Japan has attempted to formulate a secular substitute for its traditional religious values and identity, but reactions to the effect have already set in.

Japan is now in the process of reexamining the concept of nationality that the victors in World War II imposed upon it more than forty years ago. On the one hand, many constitutional scholars insist that, despite its questionable origins, the new peace constitution has lasted forty years and has been assimilated into Japanese culture—that, in short, it has been "Japanized." For them, the present constitution, although imposed by General Douglas MacArthur, represents peace, democracy, and a vision of the future. On the other hand, popular sentiment and opinion, backed by the ruling political party, increasingly support the revision of the constitution.

Many political leaders claim that Japan cannot be a free, sovereign nation, the master of its own fate, without the "right of belligerency." The outcome of this debate will have important implications for the future social order of Japan as well as its religio-political consciousness.

NOTE

* This essay first appeared in *Sociological Analysis* 48/4: 328–41 (1988). Reprinted by permission. K. Peter Takayama is Professor of Sociology in the Department of Sociology and Social Work, Memphis State University, Memphis, Tennessee.

[1] This court decision was reached almost twelve years after the time a local assemblyman filed suit against the Tsu City mayor. In 1965 Shinto priests performed a ground-breaking ceremony for a new city gymnasium, and for this service were paid in funds from the city budget. The assemblyman objected to having the priests paid out of public funds, believing that the constitutional guarantee of separation of religion and state had been violated. It was the Supreme Court's decision that the Shinto ceremony had been a commonly accepted practice in Japan for hundreds of years. The Court, reversing an earlier decision by the Nagoya High Court, expressed the final legal opinion that a Shinto ground-breaking ceremony should be understood as a traditional cultural custom rather than as a religious activity. Ground-breaking ceremonies are nothing extraordinary to the Japanese, but the court case gained national attention since until 1965 nobody had questioned something as ordinary as a ground-breaking ceremony.

Yasukuni-Jinja and Folk Religion

The Problem of Vengeful Spirits

Klaus ANTONI

O N 15 AUGUST 1985, the fortieth anniversary of the end of the Pacific War, then Prime Minister Nakasone Yasuhiro paid his respects to the country's war dead at Yasukuni Shrine in Tokyo. As the first official visit by a Japanese head of government since Japan's surrender, this gave rise to much discussion even in the Western press. We were told that Yasukuni, the shrine for the war dead, was a symbol of Japanese militarism and that therefore official visits imply a vindication of that former political system. But what is not understood in the West are the deeper roots of the problem.

The issue centers mainly on the question of whether the shrine is a mere *memorial,* to be compared to the Tombs of the Unknown Soldier in Western countries, or if it is a real *shrine* in the sense of a definite religious place, a holy site of the Shinto religion.

The political and ideological dimensions of this discussion are obvious. If the shrine is *not* a religious place, as it is declared by a strong and influential faction of the Association of Shinto Shrines (*Jinja Honchō*) then it could easily be taken under governmental control again, as it was until the end of the war. Those opposed to the official recognition of Yasukuni foresee a revival of so-called State Shinto, the allegedly nonreligious state cult from the Meiji period up to the end of the war, where the Shinto shrines were mere ceremonial stages for the celebration of folk "customs" in accordance with the fundamentals of *kokutai* thought (see below). Therefore the political dimension of the discussion is for the most part an extension of its religious aspect.

THE OFFICIAL CONCEPT OF THE YASUKUNI DEITIES

Originally founded under the name of Shōkonsha (shrine for calling the spirits of the dead) in Kyoto, the shrine was trans- 招魂社

ferred to Tokyo and its name changed to Yasukuni-jinja in June 1879.[1] The spirits of all those who had died in the fighting leading up to the Meiji Restoration—formally established in 1868—were transferred to Yasukuni from their previous places of enshrinement.

靖国 The name of the shrine, "Yasukuni," was bestowed by Emperor Meiji, who wrote the following in an address to the spirits deified there:

> With a loyal and honest heart you have passed away, not worrying about your homes, not minding your own lives. Founded on these great and highly heroic deeds, our Great Empire is to rule as a peaceful land (*yasukuni*); so We renamed (this shrine) Yasukuni-jinja, "Shrine of the Peaceful Land" and made it an Imperial Shrine of Special Status (*bekkaku-kanpeisha*). We vow to make sacrifices of paper and silk (*mitegura*) and of laudatory congratulations, and, from now on forever, to worship and admire you.[2]

From that time on the spirits of all soldiers killed in the wars of Japan were enshrined on Kudan hill in Tokyo, the location of Yasukuni Shrine. For the soldiers and their families it became a source of deep pride that even the emperor paid his respects at the shrine and worshiped the divinities there, who were in fact the spirits of ordinary people.[3]

国体の本義 The programmatic script on the essentials of *kokutai* (nationalist) ideology, the *Kokutai no hongi* (1937), states:

> The Emperor's deeds that remain with us are so many as to defy enumeration when we cite such things as how he enshrines as deities in Yasukuni shrine those loyal subjects that have sacrificed their lives for the nation since about the time of the Restoration, lauding their meritorious deeds without regard to standing or position, and how he poured out his great august heart in giving relief in times of natural calamities. (MONBUSHŌ 1937: 31; GAUNTLETT and HALL 1949: 77)

Everyone who died for the Empire in a war was deified and became a protecting god for the country, therefore the name of Yasukuni, "Peaceful Country." Moreover, this point was understood as an expression of imperial gratitude to the people, and served as a means of strengthening the new dynastic idea in post-Tokugawa times.

Since the Yasukuni shrine was founded during the Meiji period, it first of all has to be explained in the context of the ideological and religious worldview of this epoch. However, it is apparent that for a deeper understanding we must take religious ideas into consideration, which have their origins outside the sphere of this particular problem.

One of the specific traits of Meiji thought was the total dis-avowal of Buddhist ideas. But in fact we do find an historical parallel in Buddhism itself, which in turn further supports our understanding of the Yasukuni Shrine.

The term *yasukuni* may be read *ankoku* in Sino-Japanese pronunciation. We learn from history that in medieval times there existed so-called Ankoku-ji, temples whose names were written with the characters *an-koku*, "Peaceful Land." These characters were used also by Emperor Meiji to clarify the functions of the Yasukuni Shrine.

安国寺

The Ankoku temples were founded in the early fourteenth century by the first Ashikaga shogun Takauji and his brother Tadayoshi, following the advice of the famous Rinzai Zen master Musō Kokushi. One of the motives for founding these temples was to elevate the Rinzai faction of Zen into a position superior to that of the other Buddhist schools of the country.[4] It was further intended to strengthen the power of the Ashikaga Bakufu, since the temples were administrated by the Ashikaga family. But the system was not successful, and after the death of Takauji nearly all the Ankoku-ji temples disappeared. The political aspect of the temples' foundation appears to be predominant, but the religious dimension should not be neglected.

A parallel can be drawn between the systems of the medieval Ankoku-ji temples on the one hand and of the modern Yasukuni Shrine and its provincial Gokoku shrines[5] on the other. The Ankoku-ji also were established in favor of the souls of fallen warriors, especially for the war dead of the Genkō-era (1331–1333) battles.[6]

George SANSOM (1981: 372) writes on the motives of Takauji:

He wanted to have in every province an emblem of the spread of his influence over all Japan. But also he hoped to create good feeling by his pious enterprise, which was meant to comfort the spirits of those who had perished in his campaigns, both friends and foes.

In an analysis of Buddhist temple names Dietrich SECKEL (1985) establishes a system of fourteen categories. His tenth category is of importance in our context. It contains temple names that deal with 1) the peace of the country, and 2) the protection of the country and the emperor.

SECKEL states that "pacification" (*chin*) and "peace" (*an*) are "just two aspects of the same thing" (1985: 204); so, along with Ankoku-ji, "temples for the peace of the country," we find names such as Chinkoku-ji, "temples for the pacification of the country." He adds,

鎮国寺

> The meanings of "calming" and pacification" are combined in the term *chin-an*, which then bifurcates, so to speak, into the two temple names of Chinkoku-ji and Ankoku-ji. The terms *chin*, *shizumeru* (to calm, to pacify), and *mamoru* (to protect) play a role also in Shinto: the cult of the gods (kami) is for a good part understood as the "pacification" of evil or dangerous powers and as a prevention against unauspicious influence. *Chinkon-sai* is the feast "to pacify" the souls of the dead that have become kami. (SECKEL 1985: 205)

It is clear that the connection between the two spheres of the Buddhist Ankoku-ji and the Shintoist Yasukuni shrine is deeper than a mere similarity based on the analogy of names; it is founded on similarities in the field of a religious conception.

From the viewpoint of pure historical comparison we could hardly find a greater contrast than the one that exists between these two areas. Ashikaga Takauji and the Northern Court of the Nanboku era in Japanese history were regarded as totally negative factors in history, at least according to the imperial historiography in the *Dainihon-shi* [History of great Japan] of the Mito school. Furthermore, Takauji was a follower of Musō Kokushi and therefore a patron of Buddhism. Despite all these differences between the medieval Ankoku temples and the Yasukuni shrine in historical, intellectual, and religious meaning, we face a nearly identical underlying religious idea: all are places intended to give the country peace through the deification of the fallen warriors of former wars.

As was pointed out above, the idea of the *pacification* of the souls of the dead plays a basic role within this idea. So it is crucial to investigate whether this aspect is of importance for understanding the Yasukuni Shrine problem.

THE HERETICAL INTERPRETATION

The Yasukuni problem was treated by several authors in academic discussion within the last years. Special mention should be made of the works of ŌE Shinobu (1984), MURAKAMI Shigeyoshi (1974), and Ernst LOKOWANDT (1978 and 1981). These authors demonstrated that the problem under consideration has its foundation in the history and the ideological background of the shrine.

A new, we might say heretical, definition of the Yasukuni gods, which even produced an academic incident in recent times, is discussed by certain authors (SHIMAGAWA 1985; ŌE 1984: 115–20). Here the emphasis for understanding the real nature of the Yasukuni gods is put not on the orthodox aspects of imperial gratitude and protection of the country, but rather on the state of mind of the soldiers themselves. Their will to live was crushed and their deaths seemed without meaning, leaving their spirits full of hatred and frustration. Therefore, SHIMAGAWA (1985: 19) states, in the very moment of their deaths they had become bitterly hating, vengeful gods—*onryō-gami*—a term very well known in the history of Japanese religion.

Onryō or *goryō*, the "vengeful spirits of the dead," are a 怨霊 御霊
specimen of deity whose cult flourished especially in the Heian period of Japanese history (794–1185). The first incident of a *goryōe*, a ceremony for the pacification of these 御霊会
vengeful spirits that were regarded as a great danger for the community of the living, is reported from the year 863. The most prominent *goryō* deity in history is Tenman-tenjin, the deified spirit of Sugawara Michizane, famous statesman and opponent of the Fujiwara family. His case shows all of the important elements of the historical *goryō* cult. A man of high social position dies an unnatural death caused either by a personal enemy or through political intrigue. His spirit is thus full of hate and bitterness.[7]

The monk Jien writes in his historical work *Gukanshō*, dating from about 1219:

> The main point about a vengeful soul is that it bears a deep grudge and makes those who caused the grudge objects of its revenge even while the resentful person is still alive. When the vengeful soul is seeking to destroy the objects of its resentment,...the state is thrown into disorder by the slanders and lies it generates. The destruction of the people is brought about

in exactly the same way. And if the vengeful soul is unable to obtain its revenge while in this visible world, it will do so from the realm of the invisible. (BROWN and ISHIDA 1979: 220–21)

In medieval times the belief in vengeful souls (goryō-shinkō) flourished among the ordinary people as well. As HORI Ichirō (1968: 21) points out, it was mainly spread by Nenbutsu priests (hijiri), who taught the salvific value of chanting the name of Amida Buddha. In this belief, the mental state at the very moment of death was regarded as essential for the future fate of the soul. Everybody bearing a grudge in his heart while dying would become an onryō, while the others enjoyed rebirth in Amida's paradise. "Sometimes," HORI states, "Nenbutsu-hijiri advanced in the midst of battlefields to offer Nenbutsu to the spirits of those who had fallen, as well as to give dying soldiers assurance of salvation by Amida Butsu, urging them pray Nenbutsu" (1968: 123). This also provides the mental basis for interpreting the Yasukuni gods as onryō.

But there exists another item to be taken into consideration: the concept of goryō is an extremely individualistic one. The individual hatred and bitterness, the individual fear, do determine the fate of soul in the afterlife. But in the case of the Yasukuni Shrine it is a fact that the souls of all the war dead are enshrined as deities without regard to their former lives and the individual circumstances of their deaths.

THE CONCEPT OF "BAD DEATH"

Do we therefore have to reject the onryō concept of the Yasukuni gods as a whole? I do not think so. We know that the traditional Japanese attitude toward death was extremely negative and timorous. The living feared pollution by death, as we can see for the first time in the myths surrounding Izanagi and Izanami.[8] Especially feared were the spirits of persons who died unnatural and premature deaths, or who died far from home as strangers.

With this belief we arrive at a conceptual and general instead of an individual view of the horrible fate of the soul that is widespread among many societies, especially among the peoples of Southeast Asia. As for the concept of premature and unnatural death, there exists the technical term of "bad death" in comparative religion.[9] This term describes a

聖

specific view of the dead, based on fear and horror on the side of the living. In this worldview, premature and abnormal ways of death are regarded as being the same by definition, since to suffer early death means that the deceased cannot live his full life to its natural end. Only unnatural causes can be responsible for such a sad and dangerous fate. For the spirit of the departed this kind of death results in not being able to enter the afterlife, that is, the other side and next stage of human existence, because it was not able to go through all the stages of life (cf. JENSEN 1960: 366).

The human being is taught through several rites of passage during the course of his or her life all the knowledge that the spirit of the dead needs to know in order to pass the interrogation at the entrance to the next world. One who dies too early cannot pass this examination; he will fall into a state of loneliness and must wander around homeless in the realm between the two worlds of the living and the dead, always trying to lure living people into his own horrible state of existence (see SELL 1955).

As stated before, within this idea the manner of death is important in determining the fate of the spirit of the dead. Therefore it is of great significance for the problem under consideration that among the different ways of unnatural deaths there are two that are always mentioned: the death of the childbearing mother—she becomes a very dangerous ghost—and the death of the warrior.[10]

From the Toradja of Sulawesi (Celebes), for example, we hear that the soul of a fallen warrior becomes a wicked ghost, called a *bolinde*, which tries to frighten and kill living people (SELL 1955: 178). On the islands of Solor and Adonare the war dead are hung on a pole outside the village like slaughtered pigs; only after four days will they be buried (SELL 1955: 232–33).

Several reports tell us how human communities try to protect themselves against the evil influences of the ghosts of dead warriors. In eastern Indonesia, on the island of Halmahera, the Galela build little shrines, called "soul huts," for the spirits of the dead in the vicinity of the house of the bereaved family. The ghosts, being homeless and lonesome, are thought to be most dangerous to the members of their own families. Through this kind of ceremony, the community tries to catch the troubled soul and thus make the ghost harmless.

On the island of Samoa in Polynesia, people try to pacify and comfort the soul by catching it. After they have done so, it is said, nobody has to fear the ghost any longer (SELL 1955: 39).

We learn from the examples shown here that in this kind of archaic worldview the dead warrior is anything but a hero; instead he becomes a "bad dead," one who is feared especially by his own relatives. They try to calm and pacify the spirit—as in the Indonesian case—by erecting a *shrine* for the soul. According to this conception the emotions of fear and horror lead to the worship of the dead warrior.

YASUKUNI SHRINE AND THE "BAD DEATH" OF THE SOLDIER

Since ancient times the motif of calming, pacifying, and appeasing evil powers—especially souls—has been a prominent aspect of Shinto religion. We hear, for example, about the *Mitamashizume-matsuri Chinkon-sai*, the "Feast of Pacification of Spirits," which is mentioned in the *Engishiki* of the tenth century. This ceremony had "as its purpose to prolong the life of the sovereign and pacify or soothe the ancestral spirits" (BOCK 1970, 1: 94–97).

延喜式

Not much is recorded about the beliefs of the ordinary people of that time, probably because the writers of noble birth had little interest in the religious feelings of peasants and fishermen. But through folklore research we have information and descriptions about the fear of human ghosts, especially of those who recently died unnatural deaths.

In folk belief, one who died from natural causes is said to become a *hotoke*, a "Buddha." But those who die too early— especially the young and unmarried—will become "wandering spirits" who are perilous to the living. An impressive table showing the correlation between the manner of death and the future fate of the soul is given by Robert J. SMITH (1974: 55), who shows that all young people and unmarried adults dying abnormal deaths become "wandering spirits."

無縁仏
餓鬼

These spirits are called *muen-botoke*, "Buddhas without affiliation," or *gaki*, "hungry ghosts," originally a term for those who dwell in the second of the ten Buddhist worlds, suffering from eternal hunger and thirst. "From long ago," YANAGITA Kunio wrote, "people of Japan have had a dread of meeting such homeless spirits" (1970: 94).

In the folk belief of Okinawa, too, we find similar concepts of death. One who dies a violent death is said to become a *majimung* spirit, which is extremely perilous to the living. It is able to materialize in any form and is satisfied only when it catches the soul of a living being (LEBRA 1966: 29–30).

In the early modern period of Japanese history, that is to say the Meiji era (late nineteenth century), it is quite conceivable that a people who held such views toward the "wandering soul" would feel especially sensitive about fallen soldiers, the largest group of young and mostly unmarried dead, many of whom died far from home. They were ideal examples of those who died a premature "bad death."

This surely is a concept identical to the idea of "bad death" described above. Folk belief preserves the conceptual fear of the "bad death" that is quite different from the individualistic view of *goryō-shinkō*. Not because of personal hatred or frustration, but because of a specific manner and/or time of death, the soul becomes a harmful ghost.

CONCLUSION

As we have seen above, the violent death of a warrior is widely regarded as a distinct kind of "bad death." It is obvious, in my opinion, that in Japan the fear of such ghosts existed since early times, given the existence of the Chinkoku-ji and Ankoku-ji temples. Their religious basis was not a specifically Buddhist one, but rested rather on archaic religious emotions and fears, which had their roots outside of Buddhism.

Seen from this standpoint we arrive at far-reaching conclusions. It is known that Japanese society from the Meiji to the early Shōwa period was based on an ideological system called "familism." The Confucian ethical maxims of *chū*, 忠 "loyalty," and *kō*, "filial piety," were blended into the ideal of 孝 the Japanese nation, which itself was regarded as an actual family with the emperor as its head.

This view of the *kokutai*, the "national body," "national polity," or "national entity" of Japan, was elaborated mainly by the philosophers of the Mito school of late Tokugawa Japan. It was the Mito scholar Aizawa Seishisai (1782–1863) who first introduced the term to the theoretical debate on the Japanese state in his work *Shinron* [A new discourse], in the year 1825. Here *kokutai* does not mean the "body" of any nation in general, but definitely and exclusively the specific characteristics of the Japanese nation only.

Although the heterogeneous elements of *kokutai* thought—
the Confucian concepts of loyalty and filial piety, and the
神国 Kokugaku idea of Japan as a "land of the gods" (*shinkoku*)—
were known to the philosophical world of Japan since long
before, it was the ideologists of the Imperial Restoration who
developed a form of *kokutai* based on the idea of the uniqueness of the Japanese nation.

In the Meiji period this became the official concept of the
state. Japan was regarded as a great family. Since all Japanese
citizens were thought to be descendants of the mythical
ancestors with the Imperial line as their head—an idea based
on Japanese mythology and elaborated by the Kokugaku scholar Hirata Atsutane—the result was a concept of the Japanese
nation as a real family, not merely a family-like body.

The famous Imperial Rescript on Education, dated 30
October 1890, states (official translation):

> Know ye, Our Subjects:
>
> Our Imperial Ancestors have founded Our Empire on a basis
> broad and everlasting and have deeply and firmly implanted
> virtue; Our subjects ever united in loyalty and filial piety have
> from generation to generation illustrated the beauty thereof.
> This is the glory of the fundamental character of Our Empire....
>
> The Way here set forth is indeed the teaching bequeathed
> by Our Imperial Ancestors, to be observed alike by Their
> Descendants and the subjects, infallible for all ages and true in
> all places. It is Our wish to lay it to heart in all reverence, in
> common with you, Our subjects, that We may thus attain to the
> same virtue.

Wilbur M. FRIDELL (1970: 829) writes on the family state
ideology of the late Meiji years:

> Filial piety practiced in the individual family became, without
> change, loyalty to the comprehensive or national family. The
> traditional patterns and values of the individual family must
> be strengthened and maintained,...for it was the individual
> family system which supported the comprehensive (national)
> family system and thereby preserved *kokutai*.

But this concept of *kokutai* contains a specific risk within
the context discussed here. If one single family has to fear the
souls of members who died from unnatural causes, so, of
course, the nation as a whole (as the "family of families") has
to fear the totality of members who die such bad deaths. To

calm and pacify them, and—we remember the East Indonesian case—to make them harmless, a shrine has to be erected and specific ceremonies have to be undertaken. In these the religious fears of the ordinary people, based on the folk belief in evil ghosts, can be calmed.

In Tokugawa times the cult of the heroic warrior was associated with the bushi class. After the Restoration everybody, regardless of status and social position, could serve in the army. This, in my opinion, created a political need to change the fear of wandering spirits into a feeling of pride in the heroism of the war dead.

That this is not mere speculation is shown by the words of the Imperial Rescript presented by Emperor Meiji on the occasion of founding the Kyoto Shōkonsha, dated 10 May 1868. Much is said in this rescript about imperial gratitude and the loyalty of the dead; but in one short sentence the other—the horrible—side of heroism becomes visible. In this sentence it is said that the shrine is also erected with the intention of soothing and pacifying the souls of the dead.[12]

Even in the ongoing discussion on the status of the Yasukuni Shrine this aspect can be clearly seen in documents related to the shrine. In a bill dated June 1969, which was introduced to achieve governmental control over the shrine by denying its religious nature, we find, among the stated aims of the Yasukuni Shrine, the orthodox view that it serves to express the admiration of the entire people for those who sacrificed themselves for the sake of the country. But it is also stated that the shrine shall pacify and appease them. Ceremonies and feasts, says the text, shall be conducted in order to pacify the spirits of the fallen soldiers.

From this it is clear that the country in fact becomes a *yasukuni*, a "peaceful land," because the warriors as "bad dead" are no longer a threat and danger to it. In this view the country is protected *from* instead of being protected *by* the spirits of the fallen warriors.

NOTES

* This article first appeared in *Asian Folklore Studies* 47 (1988): 123–36. Reprinted by permission. Klaus Antoni is Professor of Japanology at Trier University, Germany.

1 Cf. the documents in MURAKAMI 1974: 107; LOKOWANDT 1978: 328–29, No. D 94; KAWADA 1982: 66–67.

² Translation based on the Japanese original of the address (MURAKAMI 1974: 109). The translation given by the shrine office differs in several ways: "You have given your lives for your country. You sacrificed yourselves to make the country peaceful. This shrine was established to invocate your spirits. We call the Shrine the Yasukuni (to make the country peaceful) Shrine. We are sure to continue to offer prayers forever for the sake of your spirits" (YASUKUNI JINJA SHAMUSHO 1975: 1).

³ HOLTOM (1963, 5) illustrates this point by discussing the case of a liberal university professor who, in the year 1938, asked publicly whether a man of clearly bad character could become a deity of the shrine too. He was attacked for this by official sources: "He was accused of having insulted the national structure and of having heaped indignity on the sacred spirits of the warrior dead and the holy cause in which they had given their lives.... The sacred quality of the divine emperor attaches to a Japanese the supreme command of an emperor who can do nothing wrong.... 'No matter how much of a wrongdoer, no matter how evil, a Japanese subject may have been, when once he has taken his stand on the field of battle, all his past sins are entirely atoned for and they become as nothing'."

⁴ Most of the Ankoku temples were not newly built—they merely received new names and were incorporated into the new system. It is said that the first Ankoku-ji was the former Kumeta temple in Izumi Province, which was renamed in 1338. See MATSUNAGA 1974–76, vol. II: 223–27; AKAMATSU and YAMPOLSKY 1977, 313–15.

⁵ Parallel to Yasukuni-jinja, the national shrine for the war dead, there exists in every prefecture a prefectural shrine for the war dead under the name of Gokoku-jinja (Shrine for the protection of the country). These shrines were until 1939 registered as regional Shōkonsha. See LOKOWANDT 1978: 96, n. 351; KAWADA 1982: 68.

⁶ Cf. AKAMATSU and YAMPOLSKY 1977, 314; MATSUNAGA 1974–1976, II: 226.

⁷ Two descriptive works were published in recent years regarding the historical goryō complex, TUBIELEWICZ 1980 and PLUTSCHOW 1983. Here the fate of Sugawara Michizane and other prominent figures, such as Prince Sawara, is discussed in detail.

⁸ According to Japanese mythology, Izanagi-no-mikoto purified himself after his visit to the land of the dead (see CHAMBERLAIN 1982, 44–49).

⁹ The term "bad death" is a direct translation of the German "der schlimme Tod," which is a technical term in the field of the history of religions. In 1955 Hans Joachim Sell published his great work on this concept of death among the Indonesian peoples.

¹⁰ SELL (1955: 3) lists, among others, the following categories of dead persons: women who die during childbirth, fallen warriors, dead children, murdered persons, and victims of accidental death, suicide, and execution.

PART 3

Traditional Religious Institutions

Introduction to Part 3
Traditional Religious Institutions:
Decline and Continuity

Paul L. SWANSON

THE IMPACT OF industrialization and urbanization on traditional religious patterns and institutions is a significant factor in contemporary Japan. Demographic changes—mainly shifts in population from rural to urban areas—have contributed to a decline in village shrines and festivals and a weakening of the extended family and its connection to the traditional family temple. On the other hand, there has been the creation of new religious forms in urban areas, such as religious practices in the workplace and the creation of new *matsuri* (festivals) in urban and suburban areas such as New Towns. There have also been changes in the most "basic" of religious observances, such as the patterns of *hatsumōde* (first New Year visit to a shrine)—each year record numbers of visitors flock to famous urban sites such as Meiji Shrine in Tokyo or Heian Shrine in Kyoto, but fewer and fewer people visit small local shrines. Annual observances (*nenjūgyōji*), including rites of passage like *shichi-go-san* (shrine visits for children at the ages of 3, 5, and 7), and *o-bon*, the summer festival for the ancestors, show healthy participation. Newly evolved forms of institutional participation include having the family car "blessed" or "dedicated" at a local shrine, with the accompanying receipt of a talisman for traffic safety, and the annual flocking of students to shrines and temples to pray for success in the school entrance examinations (*gōkaku kigan*).

祭

初詣

年中行事
七五三
御盆

合格祈願

We can also note mixtures of continuity and discontinuity in institutional religion. For example, the Pure Land Shinshū tradition—still the largest Buddhist organization in Japan—is struggling with issues of modernization as well as questions concerning the role of the still-powerful traditional hierarchy. We also have the "created" or "invented" tradition of the imperial enthronement ceremony—a discontinuity with what actually occurred through most of Japanese history, but presented by the Imperial Agency as the preservation of tradition.

Thus we see that claims of a decline in traditional and institutional religion must be qualified. Certainly fewer people define themselves in terms of affiliation with a religious institution, but it is also true that religious institutions are adapting in various ways in an effort to meet the needs of a changing clientele. The studies in this section present a few "snapshots" of the role of traditional religion and religious institutions in contemporary Japan.

Ian Reader's essay shows that in spite of some decline and change, the role of the family in Buddhism is still significant. In other words, Buddhism is most often a "family affair," and also most often focusses on dealing with the death process, performing mortuary rituals, and providing the context for venerating ancestors. Reader focusses on the Sōtō Zen school, but it is safe to say that his comments and conclusions are representational of what occurs in any of the traditional mainstream Buddhist sects.

One of the important traditional roles of religion in Japan has been to foster community spirit and loyalty, and what used to be a village affair has now often been taken over by the company. With the popular image of busy robots and efficient computerized production lines, readers may wonder what could be more removed from "religion" than a Japanese factory. In fact, however, the workplace in Japan abounds with continuities (and discontinuities) with the past, from small shrines on factory shelves and department-store roofs, to company-sponsored religious rituals and activities. **David Lewis**'s brief look at the religious practices of one Japanese factory illustrates this situation. One may also mention the increasing incidence of company graves replacing that of the family graves at the temple. At Mt. Kōya, the center of Shingon Buddhism and historically a famous place for graves, at least one major Japanese company has a grave where a visitor can deposit his or her *meishi* (business card), and eventually receive in return a thank-you card acknowledging the visit.

The system of religious and emotional support provided by the family and rural communities in times of trouble has weakened. In turn, the burden of facing such problems increasingly falls on the individual, especially young parents and the elderly. The study of *mizuko kuyō* by **Hoshino Eiki** 水子供養 and **Takeda Dōshō** analyzes the religious implications of abortion and the rituals performed to assuage the problems that arise from this situation. The study also mentions the wider practice of *kuyō* (memorial services) for various subjects such as dolls and pets. **Fleur Wöss** takes a look at *pokkuri-dera*, temples where elderly people pray for a painless and quick death. The selection shows that death and dying is still a major part of religious beliefs and practices in Japan. While in a sense this shows a continuity with the past, it also reveals that new religious forms have been chosen to deal with these old and familiar problems.

Religious specialists are not totally absent from the present scene, though monastic institutions are certainly waning in popularity. **Paula Arai** shows that, despite a decline in the number of traditional Buddhist nuns in Japan, and though most of them are elderly, there is positive change and development in the sense that nuns have achieved a higher status than in the past.

Once again, the situation of traditional religious institutions in Japan is too complex to address completely in these short readings. Additional details on these subjects, and alternative perspectives, can be found in the readings suggested below.

FURTHER SUGGESTED READINGS

FOARD, James. "The boundaries of compassion: Buddhism and national tradition in Japanese pilgrimage." *Journal of Asian Studies* 16/2: 231–51, 1981.

INOUE Nobutaka, ed. *Matsuri: Festival and Rite in Japanese Life.* Contemporary Papers on Japanese Religion, vol. 1. Translated by Norman Havens. Tokyo: Institute for Japanese Culture and Classics, Kokugakuin University, 1988.

ISHII Kenji. "The secularization of religion in the city." *Japanese Journal of Religious Studies* 13/2–3: 193–209, 1986.

LAFLEUR, William. *Liquid Life: Abortion and Buddhism in Japan.* Princeton: Princeton University Press, 1992.

MORIOKA Kiyomi. *Religion in Changing Japanese Society.* Tokyo: University of Tokyo Press, 1975.

_____. "Ancestor worship in contemporary Japan: Continuity and change." In *Religion and the Family in East Asia*, George A.

DeVos and Takao Sofue, eds. Los Angeles: University of California Press, 1986.

NEWELL, William H. ed. *Ancestors*. Hawthorne, NY: Mouton de Gruyter, 1976.

SASAKI Shōten. "Shinshū and folk religion: Toward a post-modern Shinshū 'theology'." *Bulletin of the Nanzan Institute for Religion & Culture* 12: 13–35, 1988.

SMITH, Bardwell. "Buddhism and abortion in contemporary Japan: *Mizuko kuyō* and the confrontation with death." *Japanese Journal of Religious Studies* 15/1: 3–34, 1988.

SMITH, Robert J. *Ancestor Worship in Contemporary Japan*. Stanford: Stanford University Press, 1974.

SONODA Minoru. "The traditional festival in urban society." *Japanese Journal of Religious Studies* 2/2–3: 103–36, 1975.

Buddhism as a Religion of the Family

Contemporary Images in Sōtō Zen

Ian READER

ALTHOUGH MUCH HAS BEEN written about Zen Buddhism—probably more, in English, than about any other facet of religion in Japan—this has invariably focused on philosophical and theoretical aspects or, usually in a more popular vein, on the dramatic and often bizarre nature of encounters between Zen teachers and pupils. In contrast, very little has been written about Zen Buddhism in its present context in Japan, about Zen Buddhist religious organizations, or about the ways in which temples with a Zen Buddhist affiliation relate to people in Japanese society.[1] There is little that enables us to know that Zen Buddhism is not just a somewhat abstruse or deeply philosophical means towards the attainment of a lofty enlightenment beyond the grasp of all but a few, but also has been, and continues to be, a living, broad-based religious structure that also deals with, and caters to, the needs of a wider populace.

Despite the images of austere monasticism and penetrating philosophy implicit in most of the works about Zen Buddhism, it has not always been much different from other branches of Buddhism in Japan. Zen Buddhist temples are active in dealing with the death process, in performing mortuary rituals and in providing a basis and situation through which people may venerate their family ancestors in much the same way as temples of all other branches of Japanese Buddhism. Zen priests have, since the latter part of the nineteenth century, like most other Buddhist priests in Japan, usually married, raised families, and lived lives less focused on meditation and monastic principles than on performing funeral and other religious rituals for the laity. In all, only about thirty of the fifteen thousand temples belonging to the Sōtō Zen sect (the single largest Zen Buddhist organization in Japan) are primarily monastic or meditation-orientated.

Moreover, the priesthood is more hereditary than vocational: a very high proportion of Sōtō priests have inherited their temple and the priesthood from their fathers who were priests before them. The large majority of priests marry and many also do other work to supplement the income they receive as priests.[2]

In other words, in its Japanese context, Zen Buddhism has a broad basis and function, encompassing aspects of social as well as religious structure. It has developed in Japan as a mainstream religion, exhibiting not just the universalisms implied in Zen doctrine and meditation, but also the particularisms of the Japanese religious environment and world. One aim of this article is to draw attention to these more overtly Japanese elements as seen through the eyes of one contemporary Zen Buddhist sect, Sōtō Zen. This will, I hope, help to provide a broader picture of Zen Buddhism than is generally gathered from the literature at hand.

Another purpose is to provide an outline and picture of the major orientations of Japanese Buddhism in general. As I have already stated, Zen Buddhism in its institutionalized forms has been, and is, part of the religious mainstream establishment in Japan, and many of the concerns manifested in the publications and pronouncements of the Sōtō Zen organization can be found elsewhere in Japanese Buddhism and, indeed, in other Japanese religious movements as well. As such, looking at some of the themes currently of importance to the Sōtō Zen sect, besides giving insights into the nature and character of Zen Buddhism in Japan, will provide a window onto the overall world of Japanese Buddhism and the environment in which it exists and functions today.

The documentary focus of this inquiry is to be found in the large amount of publications of all sorts, but especially short books, pamphlets, and leaflets, produced at and issued by the Tokyo headquarters of the Sōtō Zen sect and sent out to its temples, priests, and affiliated members throughout Japan. Although this corpus of literature is large and diverse in nature, there are some common themes and images that recur enough to make them stand out as particularly worthy of note.[3] The theme I intend to examine here is the use made of imagery revolving around the concept of the family. This is of note because of the important role that the family and household as a unit has played in the world of Japanese religion in general and Buddhism in particular, and through it we shall be able to see the degree to which adherence to traditional values is important to organized Zen Buddhism. It is also of interest to look at the extended use made of family imagery precisely because the family as an institution stands in antithesis to the monastic ideals of Buddhism that lie at the heart of Zen's development. Indeed, the literal meaning of the Japanese word for becoming a monk, *shukke*, is "to leave one's home."

出家

Before embarking on a discussion of these issues and of the ways in which such imagery appears in Sōtō literature, it will be necessary to give a brief outline of the position of established Buddhism in Japan today. This will make it clear why the family/household as a unit is so important to Japanese Buddhism and why it thus appears as a major theme in the religious writings of Buddhist organizations such as Sōtō.

BUDDHISM IN JAPAN: MAJOR STRUCTURAL THEMES

Although Buddhism first appeared in Japan in the sixth century AD, it was primarily, in its early centuries in Japan, a religion of the court and the elite. It was not until the thirteenth century and after that it made any great advance into the mass society of the rural peasantry or the growing urban artisan classes.[4] When it did so, one of the major means by which it was popularized and brought into the sphere of peasant life was through asserting that it could offer the peasantry a more efficacious means of hope and solace in death than could be found in the traditional folk religious structure. By assimilating traditional folk beliefs about the influence of the souls of dead members of the lineage on the living, Buddhism took on the role of guiding, through the performance of rituals and the use of Buddhist prayers and incantations, the souls of the dead to the ancestral world, from which they would guard and protect the living.[5]

In time Buddhist temples became major repositories of memorials to family ancestors and the site of family graves. Eventually, too, households acquired their own Buddhist altars (*butsudan*) at which the ancestors were also venerated, and to which the Buddhist priest would be asked to come to offer prayers at regular intervals. As such, the Buddhist temple and priesthood became important for handling the problem of death, for caring for the dead, and for bringing the

仏壇

---

living and the dead, the household and its ancestors, together in a unity. To this extent the role of Buddhism came to be seen by the populace as a whole to be primarily ritualistic and social, concerned with the processes of death and of upholding the extended family and household, which was traditionally seen in Japan as a fusion of the living and the watchful, protective spirits of the dead.

It should perhaps also be noted that the household/family lineage (Japanese: *ie*) has long been the primary element in Japanese social structure: people were (and still are, to a great degree) defined by group, especially *ie*, rather than as individuals. Affiliation to a temple (and hence, to a Buddhist sect) was through the household: there was little overt conception of personal, chosen individual faith, especially after the formalization of this temple-household system.

This occurred during the Tokugawa (1600–1868) era, when laws were passed forcing all households to belong formally to a Buddhist temple and sect. All funerals had to be performed at the Buddhist temple to which one's household was affiliated, a rule that extended to Shinto priests who, although permitted to carry out Shinto rites and services, had to die as Buddhists. The fees received from funerals and the series of rites that were required to transform the dead soul into a full ancestor formed the basis of the Buddhist temple's economy, a function they still have to this day. The household-temple system (*danka seido*) was primarily designed as a means of making sure that people did not follow the forbidden religion of Christianity (the Buddhist temples were required to enforce an oath on each household which was vehemently anti-Christian) and as a means of social control and regulation (the temples becoming transformed into something akin to local government offices), and has formed the basis of relationships between the Japanese and Buddhist temples and sects ever since.[6]

檀家制度

Although the *danka seido* as an obligatory system was abolished in 1871, its influence still continues to this day. Many people and households have transferred their religious affiliations elsewhere, or have simply let them lapse, but large numbers still follow the course of tradition and maintain an affiliation to the temple where their ancestors worshipped and are venerated. To a very great extent this accounts for the large numbers of people who count themselves (or are counted) as Buddhists in Japan: the latest religious yearbook published by the Ministry of Cultural Affairs shows that 92,064,760 people were classified as Buddhist in 1986.[7] A preliminary look at the figures, then, would suggest that traditional Buddhism in Japan remains strong, numbering approximately 80 percent of the population.

This apparent strength is, however, rather misleading. Often affiliation is because of tradition and inertia, with belief and active involvement a secondary concern, or no concern at all. Because contact with Buddhism is via a household relationship, and for many Japanese conditioned very largely through the still socially necessary process of dealing with death through a particular medium, very large numbers of people do not see themselves as Buddhists in terms of belief but in terms of circumstance. Japanese people are liable to state that they have no religious belief or interest, while maintaining in the same breath that they (or, more precisely, their households) are Buddhist. One university professor I know, when asked what sect of Buddhism he belonged to, replied "I do not know. No one in our household has died yet." Generally people tend to use such terms as "our household belongs to the ... sect" rather than talk in personal terms. Clearly, to a great extent, Buddhism is, for a large number of people, more an adjunct to the social system than anything else.

The numerical strength of Buddhism is thrown into further perspective when it is realized that Buddhist organizations, in reporting membership numbers, count not individuals but affiliated households and then multiply the number by the average family size. This in itself shows clearly the degree to which the household as a unit is important to organized Buddhism in Japan as well as the lack of focus on individuals. The inflated figures are really a distorted outline of the true depth of support that Buddhist organizations can call upon. The Sōtō Zen sect, probably the most analytically frank of all Buddhist organizations in Japan, has in recent years been conducting surveys of those formally affiliated to it, and has come up with many disarming figures to show the shallowness of commitment of those classified as members. For example, it had an "official" membership, in 1987, of 6,885,575 members.[8] An in-depth survey carried out by the sect in 1985, however, reports that, while there were 1,491,138 households affiliated to sect temples, only 287,135 people could be classified as active believers or participants in temple activities.[9]

If the vast discrepancy between official and real support were not indicative enough of the soft center of Buddhism's position, another survey carried out by the sect emphasizes the point. Many people who belonged to Sōtō temples appeared to be remarkably ill-informed of the teachings of Sōtō, while very few professed any interest in Zen meditation (theoretically the basis of Zen Buddhism).[10] When asked why they went to temples, 77.8 percent stated it was for reasons connected with funerals and mortuary rites, 7.8 percent went for "spiritual reasons," and the rest did not respond. Again, in response to a question seeking to ascertain the times they would visit a priest, only 5.2 percent indicated that they would do so in order to learn about Buddhist thought or to seek advice with their problems; 61 percent said it would be to request a ritual connected with death and the ancestors.[11] While interest in ancestors and the rites surrounding them was strong, interest in and knowledge of Sōtō teaching itself was strikingly weak. Indeed, over 43 percent of those surveyed did not know the name of the sect of the temple they were affiliated to, while over 90 percent could not name either of the Japanese founding figures of Sōtō Zen, even though both of them feature prominently in Sōtō literature.[12]

Buddhism stands in a rather precariously fragile position in many ways in Japan. Cemented into the social system yet to a great degree religiously sterile, its putative members are conditioned to feel that it is little more than a means of dealing with ancestors and death. Even this is not always the case, for urbanization in particular has loosened the links between the people and their temples. As people have moved into the cities, rural Buddhist temples (and Sōtō was always essentially a rural movement) have seen their members disappear. Moreover, modern developments such as more secularized burials, along with the extraordinary growth of new religious movements in the cities, many of which are beginning to supplant traditional Buddhism by offering their own funeral and mortuary rites and services and by providing their own ways of venerating the ancestors, have clearly eroded the support of older, established religious structures such as Buddhism.

However, all this does not necessarily mean that the established Buddhist orders lack vigor or ideas. As we have seen, much of the information about the fragilities of Sōtō Buddhism's relationship to its members comes from research financed and carried out by the sect itself. In fact, the sect has responded to the problems of indifference and lack of solid support in many ways, and, in the following section, I shall shed some light on how, through the written word and skillful use of images, the Sōtō Zen organization has been trying to counteract these problems.

RETAINING LOYALTIES: THE HAPPY FAMILY

In former times, no doubt, Buddhist priests worked hard to win converts to their faith: but such times are long past, and nowadays all their efforts are devoted to keeping the loyalty of the parishioners whose families have worshipped at their particular temples for generations.[13]

These words are spoken by the priest of a Pure Land Buddhist temple at the center of *The Buddha Tree*, a novel written by the ex-priest Niwa Fumio in the mid-1950s. Despite the difference in sect and era, the implications of his words ring true for Sōtō Zen Buddhism (and, indeed for all established Buddhism in Japan) today. As will become clear, much of Sōtō's activity, especially in terms of its written material, is very clearly aimed at retaining the loyalties of those with long-standing generational links to Sōtō temples.[14]

When one considers the overriding importance of the traditional bond that existed between temples and the households affiliated to them, a bond especially cemented through a connection to past generations, it is hardly surprising to find that a major theme running through the attempts of Sōtō Zen to retain the loyalties of its traditional membership revolves around the intertwined themes of tradition, heredity, and the family as an enduring symbol. The Japanese sociologist of religion Morioka Kiyomi has noted the general tendency of Buddhism in Japan to focus in its teachings on the importance and role of the family, with Buddhist sermons almost invariably focusing on family roles (MORIOKA 1975: 99). Sōtō is certainly no exception here; indeed, it quite probably uses such themes with greater dexterity and subtlety than most. From its Tokyo headquarters it issues a steady stream of literature of all sorts, largely short booklets and leaflets but occasionally longer works as well, all of which transmit the messages and outlooks of the organization. Apart from an occasional exception, such as an annual magazine aimed at young urbanites that is sold at book shops, all such publications are distributed through the nationwide network of Sōtō temples to priests and, through them, to those who come to Sōtō temples.

Since the large majority of those who visit temples do so for reasons connected with Buddhism's social role in relation to the household, especially at the various times in the yearly calendrical cycle when the ancestors are honored, it is not surprising that much of this literature revolves around such themes as inherited tradition, ancestral legacies, and the importance of the family. It should be stressed at this juncture that not all Sōtō publications are so focused: there are some that are more clearly centered on such aspects as meditation and Buddhist practice. Nonetheless, these form a minority, just as those involved with Sōtō who meditate are in a minority (READER 1986: 26–27). For the most part, exhortations to a moral family life and observance of customs and traditions predominate.

A poster displayed prominently outside a Sōtō temple I passed in the village of Nishijō in Nagano, a mountainous area in central Japan, bore the words:

The prosperity of the family comes from worshipping the ancestors; let us meet them serenely before the statue of Buddha.[15]

The handwritten poster was presumably the work of the temple priest (although Sōtō itself has produced printed posters with very similar wording), but it mirrors themes that are predominant in contemporary Sōtō writing, and reflects the type of thinking that the sect encourages its priests to develop. A volume produced by the sect for its priesthood and their families, *Jitei no sho* [Book for a temple family], provides guidelines to priests on how they should conduct themselves and their temples so as to be a role model for others. The importance of family life is repeatedly stressed: the priest and his family should provide a working example to all around them of the ideal and harmonious family centered on the priest/father of the family, who has the active role of performing rituals and going out to talk about Buddhism. The wife should dutifully serve him, staying at home looking after the children and their educational needs, as well as being on hand to help around the temple, making tea for visitors, and generally keeping it spotlessly clean. The children, too, should help out here.[16] This type of idealized home structure closely mirrors the traditional, conservative ideal in Japan: it is frequently stressed by other religious groups as well and is a constant theme amongst those who feel that the growing fragmentation of traditional social values and roles is leading to unrest and social problems.[17]

This process of idealizing the family in religious terms is carried further by a companion guidebook for Sōtō sect members, *Sōtōshū danshinto hikkei* [Handbook for Sōtō sect followers], which provides advice and teachings about Sōtō for the ordinary member just as the *Jitei no sho* does for priests. A large proportion of its one hundred and twenty-two pages centers on family life, ways of venerating the ancestors, and ceremonies connected with the death process. The family is defined as being a living continuum of the ancestors, the current generation, and those who are to come in future; the temple is the place that unites all these ages as it is the resting place of the ancestors.[18]

A long section at the end of the book, under the title *Shinkō no seikatsu* [A life of faith], centers on ideal modes of family life: belief is clearly equated with the correct etiquette of the traditional family, with much emphasis being placed on correct table manners and other such aspects of daily life. Harmonious family life, which includes praying to the ancestors both at one's home *butsudan* and in the temple, becomes the basic model of a religious life. The ancestors are to be venerated, as they have not only given life to the present generation but have also united them with the Buddhist tradition that flows to the present generation through the bloodstream of their ancestors. This tradition, which is depicted as peaceful and harmonious, is upheld through a direct relationship to the temple and, through that, to Buddha.[19] It is a theme that occurs frequently elsewhere in Sōtō writing as well.

Inherent in the tradition that has been inherited from one's ancestors (and mirroring the implicit obligation of those in the *ie* to assure its continuation in the future) is the duty to pass it on, to rear children, to love them, and to bring them up as dutiful people who will love and obey their parents in life and after death. Naturally, this involves making sure one's children become good and dutiful supporters of the temple and sect. The action of being a good parent becomes, in such terms, a Buddhist practice in itself:

> Parental love that thinks of the child is in itself the compassionate mind of Buddha.[20]

Here (a point that will be developed further later on) the relationship between the parent and child is made analogous to that between the parents and the great teachers of Sōtō Zen Buddhism: in this case, the teachers stand as parents, the parents/sect members as children.

Often there is a particular focus on the mother (invariably depicted as kind, gentle, and, as with the ideal priest's wife in the *Jitei no sho*, humble) in her relationship with her children. Frequently idealized as a model of selfless love and compassion, the ideal mother looks after the home, dutifully cleans the family *butsudan,* and (this is important) instills Buddhist actions into her children. A series of posters produced by the sect in recent years depicts such a mother guiding her children in prayer; the accompanying captions carry such imprecations as "Let us live joining our hands together in prayer." Some years ago another Sōtō poster, designed to be displayed on notice boards outside Sōtō temples, read:

> If the mother worships, the child worships.[21]

The family as an idealized unit, then, forms a basic part of ordinary Sōtō teaching, as do past generations, the ancestors who formerly visited Sōtō temples. The importance of maintaining a correct relationship with the ancestors, which will involve the family with the temple and sect, is a recurrent theme that intertwines with the idealization of the family structure. Many explanatory publications are devoted to explaining how one should care for the ancestors. For example, the leaflet *O-butsudan no matsurikata* [How to worship at the family Buddhist altar] explains just that: to worship correctly and regularly will, one is informed, bring good results such as the development of "Buddha mind" (*busshin*). Parents are shown how to train their children to do so, thus ensuring that the roots of traditional Buddhism will be implanted in the next generation. The leaflet further ties in Sōtō teaching to the traditional structure of ancestor veneration by suggesting that one should have a memorial also to the Buddha, and to the two Japanese monks who are seen as the founders of the Sōtō tradition in Japan, Dōgen and Keizan, in the *butsudan*. Thus, followers are encouraged to extend the process of venerating their ancestors to worshipping figures from the established Buddhist pantheon and, at the same time, towards incorporating those figures as ancestors in their own right.[22]

The close links between the ancestors and Buddhism as it has evolved in Japan are perhaps nowhere more clearly expressed than in a short booklet *Sōtōshū no nenjūgyōji* [Yearly events in the Sōtō sect] published by the sect as a guide to yearly observances, rituals, and other such events. In it is a section entitled *Shinkōjūkun* [The ten articles of faith], which was designed as a basic set of principles for the ordinary Sōtō sect member. Most of the articles center on the etiquette of behavior in dealing with the ancestors (one should regularly clean the *butsudan* and pray to the ancestors) and in affirming the importance of the temple in this. The mortuary tablets commemorating the ancestors should be enshrined at the temple and family members should visit the temple regularly to pay their respects and to report important events in family life to the ancestors enshrined there. Of the ten articles, nine deal with the family in both its living and extended dimensions and only one, the tenth, makes any mention of such Zen practices as meditation.[23]

In a series of comments on these articles in the Sōtō almanac for 1982 the importance of the temple and its priest in such matters is brought to the fore in such a way as to imply that family fortune and unity are inextricably bound up with one's ties to Buddhism. For instance, it comments on the sixth of these articles (which entreats members to have their children taken to the temple for a naming ceremony after birth and then to report the birth to the ancestors at the temple) as follows:

> To have one's children named by the priest who has for long looked after and guarded one's ancestors at the temple is a great blessing. Such children will surely grow up to be healthy and bright.

As the children grow up the temple connection continues to be of importance:

On entering school or coming of age one will first wish to go to the temple to purify one's mind and renew one's vow of hard work and thanks at the grave of the ancestors.[24]

In such ways family, ancestors, temple, and sect are interwoven into a unity of identification and belonging, each component part presented as interdependent and vital to the growth and prosperity of the others. The articles of belief offered to those associated with Sōtō temples thus reflect the powerful importance of the household-temple relationship to established Buddhism, as well as show the ways in which it is used to provide a means by which formally affiliated members may be persuaded to feel more closely involved with the temple.

Images of the harmonious family whose life is upheld and enriched by its connection to a Sōtō Zen temple extend further still to the point where the sect itself is transformed in image into an extended happy family. As has been mentioned earlier, Sōtō encourages its members to venerate the Buddha, Dōgen, and Keizan, as well as family ancestors, in the *butsudan*. In fact, it has produced a small hanging scroll depicting Buddha, Dōgen, and Keizan suitable for enshrinement in a *butsudan* for this very purpose. Dōgen and Keizan are formally referred to by Sōtō as the *ryōso*, the two (or joint) founders: the ideogram *so* means not just founder but also ancestor. Thus these two monks from the past stand as sect ancestors, part of the common heritage of all Sōtō members.

両祖

Moreover, each is assigned a role function as ancestor. Dōgen, the austere thirteenth-century monk who went to China, encountered the Sōtō tradition there, and brought it to Japan, was a strict and at times uncompromising meditator and thinker who extolled the virtues of monasticism and adherence to strict Buddhist precepts. Keizan, also a dedicated meditator and ascetic, was instrumental in developing, in the late thirteenth and early fourteenth centuries, Dōgen's Zen teaching to make it more compatible with the Japanese religious environment.

It was with Keizan and his successors that Sōtō Zen became fused with popular folk religious ideas, developed its funeral associations, and became a large and important religious movement—previously it had been little more than a monastic backwater. Dōgen is regarded by the sect as the original implanter of the seeds of Sōtō in Japan, and Keizan is

RELIGION AND SOCIETY IN MODERN JAPAN

revered as the one who nurtured these seeds and brought them to fruition. Their respective roles thus ideally translate in terms of imagery into father and mother roles.

Espousing the idea that Sōtō itself can be seen as a family, the Sōtō priest Fujimoto Kōhō writes that "if Dōgen is seen as the father, Keizan is the mother,"[25] an image used in many other Sōtō pamphlets besides. At times, reflecting the traditional image of family roles in Japan, which depict the father as stern, the arbiter of family conduct and law, and the mother as gentle and warm, the nurturer of children and mediator of the father's strictness, Dōgen becomes the "strict father" and Keizan the "gentle mother."[26]

The Buddha also is referred to in ancestral terms, as the ultimate source of the lineage: all are children of the Buddha, and to become a formal member of the sect is to become heir to his blood lineage, to enter the bloodstream of Buddhism.[27] This analogy of the bloodstream has also been used elsewhere, in the *Danshinto hikkei*, to unite the present generation to Buddhism through the ancestors. Buddha, ancestors, and the present generation are thus joined in familial unity.

There is a religious motive behind this continued use of family images, besides the obvious economic one of ensuring the continued loyalty of the household to the temple. As the leaflet *Anata no bodaiji* [Your family temple] puts it:

We wish to make you, as well as being an affiliated member of the family temple, into a believer at that temple.[28]

The pamphlets and publications designed to create a sense of empathy in the minds of formally affiliated members are designed to create the conditions whereby they will translate that sense of empathy and belonging into something deeper. Formal commitment through the inertial processes of the Japanese socio-religious system may help keep the sect financially alive but it does not provide the sect with any true religious dynamic or, in the long run, any committed followers. Naturally, those involved in running what is, despite the formalistic aspects of Japanese Buddhism, still a religious organization are keen to encourage belief and active religious participation in their members.

One way of doing this, it is felt, is to encourage people to develop a real awareness of, and commitment to, basic Buddhist principles. This is done by deepening the empathetic bonds people feel towards their family temples and by persuading them to make a more binding formal commitment to Buddhist principles. This involves a formal lay Buddhist orientation: preceptual ordination as a believer had become instituted as the ideal for lay followers. It is considered to be the equivalent, for the lay person, of the strict monastic practices of meditation for the monk, and equally enlightening. Preceptual ordination involves a commitment of faith in Sōtō Buddhist principles, active support of the temple and sect, and vows of morally correct behavior. Long used in Sōtō as a means of inducting people into a deeper relationship with Buddhism (indeed it was used by Dōgen and was a major theme in Keizan's expansion of Sōtō), this action has particularly in the last hundred years been elevated by Sōtō into a vital area of religious action.[29]

Through preceptual commitment comes knowledge of the true nature of Buddhism and a realization of the peace and contentedness that all people seek. It thus offers a means of countering the troubles of modern society and a way of reorienting that society. The ideals and beliefs expressed through it offer a means of upholding the principles of happy family life. Through it they become models for further social peace, as is expressed in these words, taken from the Sōtō leaflet *Anata no bodaiji*:

> We must build the family and society on the practice, vows, and beliefs founded in taking the precepts.[30]

The importance of the family for the continuing well-being of Buddhism in Japan stems from the historical relationship between the *ie* and the temple. As has been shown in this section, Sōtō Zen, in seeking to consolidate its position and to secure its foundations in the modern age, makes great play of this relationship. By focusing on idealized images of the family and tradition it seeks both to preserve and deepen the links that bind people to Buddhism. There can be no clearer recognition of the dynamics underpinning established Buddhism in Japan, or, indeed, of the importance of the household and family in social and religious terms in Japan, than the attention that has been paid to it in recent years in the writings emanating from the Sōtō Zen Buddhist sect.

CONCLUSIONS

The extensive uses made by one Buddhist organization of images and themes about the family manifest a variety of interlocking concerns and provide us with a number of messages not just about that organization but about the general state and nature of Buddhism in Japan in general. That the deep-seated traditional ties that have bound people to Buddhist temples in ages past are so clearly reaffirmed shows that the *danka seido*, for all the problems it has faced and despite the numerous factors that have served to undermine it, continues to be of vital importance for the continued prosperity of established Buddhism in Japan. So, too, does the continuing interrelationship of Buddhism and the ancestors. One can see, also, the degree to which the family and household itself has been, and remains, an important factor in the Japanese religious world, a religious unit and principle in itself.

In addition to the concept of the family per se, the stylized images that bind it to tradition speak volumes about the strength and appeal of the notion of tradition itself as a quasi-religious ideal. In reality this is not so much a reaffirmation of tradition as it is a creation and idealization of the notion of the past. The image of the past is a creation distinct from its reality: in terms of the household-temple relationship things were not necessarily as harmonious as they are depicted in Sōtō imagery. Tokugawa laws made people join temples and enforced their participation in Buddhist rituals. The ancestors whose blood lineage has transmitted Buddhism and a temple relationship to current Sōtō members may not necessarily have particularly desired to have that relationship: draconian laws insisted, at times on penalty of death, that they did so.

However, the recourse to traditional images does not require factual accuracy—the importance lies in the nuances created by the image. The concern with tradition and, more pertinently, with ideas of what tradition represents, is to a great degree related, in Japan, to definitions of Japanese identity set in contrast to the growing modernization of Japanese society. Modernization is equated with Westernization and implies, in these terms, the loss of cultural identity. Accordingly, the use of idealized images of tradition seeks to reassert and re-create cultural identity and, when linked to religious themes, to redefine a sense of Japanese religious awareness.

The extensive use of traditionalism in terms of family images used by Sōtō indicates the extent to which the idea of tradition as a cultural and religious principle is important in contemporary Japan. It also shows the degree to which Buddhism in general, as well as Sōtō in particular, is inextricably tied to a particularized social and cultural environment in Japan. Although Zen Buddhism (and Buddhism in general) espouses universal principles, in Japan it has, especially in institutional terms, become deeply rooted in the localized structure of society and in the environment conditioned by the existing religious beliefs and social customs of the Japanese. Any universal religion has localizing/particularizing tendencies when it encounters different cultures, and Zen Buddhism has been no exception. Indeed, when one looks at the overall ways in which Zen Buddhism has evolved and exists in Japan as an actual entity, rather than as a theory, one is struck by the intensely Japanese, as opposed to universal, ambiance it has acquired.

In Sōtō's concern with ancestors and Japanese tradition one can see a clear example of the indigenization of Buddhism, of its transmigration, at least in its Zen guise, from being primarily monastic and meditative into being a religion of the household. As I have implied, the legacies of the household system have tended to stultify Buddhism in Japan in the present day, limiting its effectiveness as an active religious principle. However, this does not mean that the Buddhist tradition is dead. The fact that major Buddhist organizations such as Sōtō can recognize their problems and can take inventive steps towards restoring their strength and recreating the image of Buddhism is indicative of its continuing depths. There are indications, indeed, that Sōtō Zen, at least, in its declared attempts to shift the focus of its membership from formal affiliation to commitment via belief in Buddhist principles, is making some steps towards using its grounding as an indigenized and localized structure as a means of reasserting the universal, with Japanese themes and spheres of concern used as a means of reintegrating the localized structure of Buddhism into its more universal dimensions. That the family both as a reality and as an ideal remains a pivotal point in this process is testimony to the continuing importance and centrality of the household past and present to Zen and all other forms of Japanese Buddhism.

NOTES

* This article first appeared as "Images in Sōtō Zen: Buddhism as a religion of the family in contemporary Japan," in *The Scottish Journal of Religious Studies* (1989) 10/1: 5–21. Reprinted by permission. Ian Reader is Lecturer in Contemporary Japanese Studies at the Scottish Centre for Japanese Studies of the University of Stirling.

1 Some attention has been paid in English to the study of the institutional structure and nature of Buddhism in Japan in earlier ages, especially by Martin COLLCUTT (1981), Neil MCMULLIN (1984), and William BODIFORD (1993). There is virtually nothing, however, on the contemporary situation. Outside of sectarian studies there has been very little in Japanese either.

2 Sōtōshū Shūmuchō (head office of the Sōtō Zen Buddhist sect; SSSMC), ed., *Sōtōshū shūsei sōgō chōsa hōkokusho*, Tokyo, 1987, pp. 24–26, shows that over eighty percent of Sōtō priests have inherited their temples and that in over eighty percent of cases temple priests are married. Some years ago a leading official of the sect suggested that over eighty percent of its priests had other jobs (Tanaka Ryōsan in SSSMC, ed., *Genshoku kenshū* vol. 2, Tokyo: SSSMC, 1981, p. 102, although the 1987 survey suggests a lower figure somewhere around the forty percent mark (p. 37).

3 I have discussed other themes in contemporary Sōtō thought and action elsewhere (see READER 1985 and 1987).

4 In fact it was for long forbidden to give Buddhist teachings to the masses. Buddhism was seen by the elite as being its own special preserve and the key to power and privilege. Nonetheless, there was a growing tendency for religious ascetics to spread the word of Buddhism to the populace at large from around the eighth century onwards. It was not until the thirteenth century, however, that it became a real mass movement.

5 This orientation, focusing on the souls of the dead as fixed entities, appears to be somewhat antithetical to traditional Buddhist thought, which holds that everything is impermanent and that there are no such things as "souls." Certainly this is a case of Buddhism being modified to fit into a more generally Japanese religious environment. However, there is little in Japanese Buddhist literature that deals with this apparent conflict or seeks to account for the seeming contradiction. On the expansion and popularization of Zen, especially with regard to the use of charms and amulets, see Bernard FAURE (1987).

6 In English the most accessible discussions of the *danka seido* are K. MARCURE 1985 and MORIOKA 1975: 89–113.

[7] Bunkachō (Ministry of Cultural Affairs), ed., *Shūkyō nenkan*, Tokyo: Gyōsei, 1987, pp. 44–45.

[8] Ibid., p. 77.

[9] SSSMC, ed., *Sōtōshū shūsei sōgō chōsa hōkokusho*, p. ii.

[10] This issue has been discussed in greater depth in READER 1986.

[11] SSI (Sōtōshū shūseichōsa iinkai), ed., *Shūkyōshūdan no ashita e no kadai*, Tokyo: SSSMC, 1984, survey section, pp. 23–27.

[12] Ibid., p. 18 and p. 39.

[13] F. Niwa, *The Buddha Tree* (trans. K. Strong), Tokyo: Tuttle, 1976, p. 214.

[14] Various Sōtō officials have stated that this is the general intent of the sect: see Reader 1985, pp. 39–42.

[15] The original was of course in Japanese, as are all other quotations from Sōtō literature discussed in this article.

[16] SSSMC, ed., *Jitei no sho*, Tokyo: SSSMC, 1980, pp.33–46.

[17] In READER 1987. I have expanded on this theme. On the importance of traditional family values in the newer Buddhist-oriented religious movements, see Helen HARDACRE 1984, especially pp. 98–127.

[18] SSSMC, ed., *Sōtōshū danshinto hikkei*, Tokyo: SSSMC, 1976, pp. 56–57.

[19] Ibid., pp. 93–122.

[20] SSSMC, ed., *Sōtōshū danshinto hikkei*, p. 105.

[21] This poster was displayed outside Kōzen-ji, a Sōtō temple in Hakodate in Hokkaido, Japan, in August 1981. The others mentioned are currently distributed by the sect and can also be obtained at its head office in Tokyo.

[22] SSSMC, ed., *O-butsudan no matsurikata* (no date or pagination); this, and the other leaflets cited in this article, were collected from Sōtō temples in 1981–1982 and during the period 1985–1988. The leaflet cited here was first seen in 1981, but is still available at sect temples and offices.

[23] SSSMC, ed., *Sōtōshū no nenjūgyōji*, Tokyo: SSSMC, 1981, p. 4.

[24] SSSMC, ed., *Sōtōshū hōreki*, Tokyo: SSSMC, 1981, pp. 28–29.

[25] Fujimoto Kōhō, *Gasshō no sekai*, Tokyo: SSSMC, 1977, p. 2.

[26] SSSMC, ed., *O-butsudan no matsurikata*.

[27] This theme frequently occurs in Sōtō publications, especially, it seems, in the short pamphlets and leaflets referred to above. Examples of such usage can be found in SSSMC, ed., *Kaeriyuku hotoke wa tada no rengedai* and *Toshi ni ichido no o-kyakusama*, both issued c. 1981.

[28] SSSMC, ed., *Anata no bodaiji* (no date or pagination, but issued c. 1981).

[29] On this point and the reasoning behind it see READER 1985, pp. 32–41.

[30] SSSMC, ed., *Anata no bodaiji* (n. 28, above).

Religious Rites in a Japanese Factory

by David C. Lewis

ELIGIOUS RITES in Japanese factories have been mentioned in passing by several writers (e.g., ROHLEN 1974, ABEGGLEN 1975), but there has been no systematic investigation of this potentially very fruitful area of research. The present paper focuses on rites in a large synthetic fibers factory in a provincial city with a population of over 230,000 in the Kansai region of Japan. The factory was built in 1926 to 1927 and originally employed about 10,000 people, a figure that has been reduced to about 4,000 nowadays through increased mechanization. It is the largest and oldest plant among the thirteen factories in Japan belonging to a firm that I shall call by the pseudonym Nissen. This company derives about 70 percent of its revenue from the production of synthetic fibers such as nylon but in recent years has expanded into other spheres of industry, including the production of video tapes, optical products, plastics, pharmaceuticals, and even the construction of lightweight durable panelling for the American space shuttle.[1]

Virtually all the religious rites at this factory revolve around the theme of *safety*. A few also include aspects such as the removal of pollution or prayers for the firm's continuing prosperity. However, this emphasis on safety is by no means confined to the religious sphere. It would appear from the few references to safety in DORE's comparisons between two British and two Japanese factories (1973: 23–4, 189, 244–45) that safety is generally more emphasized in Japanese than in British factory life. It might be that this reflects a greater degree of danger in the Japanese workplace, as suggested by KAMATA's account of conditions in a Toyota factory (1982), but in the introduction to Kamata's book Ronald Dore suggests that Toyota may be quite exceptional. Kamata's account, dating from the pre–oil shock days, may also reflect an extreme situation at Toyota, since overall statistics for deaths from industrial accidents show relatively little difference among Japan, Western Europe, and the U.S.A. Nevertheless, at an ideological level there appears to be a consistently greater emphasis on safety in Japanese firms, as evidenced by practices such as the conspicuous use of "Safety First" slogans in Japanese factories generally, and by the conspicuous placement of large notice boards around the plant in the Nissen factory, each consisting of graphs showing how many days had elapsed since a major accident had last occurred in the factory. In the same firm there is a motto that at present says "Safety First, Quality Second, Production Third." Before the 1972 oil crisis the last two items were reversed, but the motto has always included the phrase "Safety First." Similarly, each morning the workers in each department look up to a notice on the wall of their workplace on which is written a "Safety Eulogy" or "Safety Chant" (*anzen shō*), and all recite the words in unison. The text differs a little from one department to another, but the following example from a department in the research unit is probably fairly typical:

IN PRAISE OF SAFETY
May today be happy all day through
Just as yesterday was too.
Happiness and safety go hand in hand.
So may safety always pervade our orderly work
In the workplace to which we devote ourselves.
Safety. Safety. Safety.

One other example comes from the "General Affairs" administrative department, where each morning all the workers recite together:

Not forgetting to smile the whole day long
Today also, by keeping the rules, let there be no disaster.

Other aspects of this concern with safety could be cited, ranging from special safety days in the factory twice a month, when all workers wear "Green Cross" safety armbands, to the awarding of trophies to departments having an unbroken safety record for five or seven years, but the general pattern is clear and sets the context in which religious rites for safety are performed.

GENERAL RELIGIOUS RITES

The religious rites in this Nissen factory fall into two principal categories, namely those that occur at traditionally fixed occasions in the ritual year and those that are more specific to this company or factory. Rites in the first category include those performed at the New Year or on the first Day of the Horse after *setsubun*, the *hatsu-uma sai*, both of which 節分 初午祭 appear to have equivalents or parallels in a number of other firms. My information is based on conversations with, and questionnaire replies from, employees in other firms, but there is scope for more extensive research on this topic in the future in order to examine variations by industry, size of firm, and so on. It also appears that other firms have specific rites that are not performed at Nissen. An example is the practice reported to me by a section manager in a pharmaceuticals firm. Twice a year at *higan*, when Buddhist ancestral rites are 彼岸 performed, some employees in that firm participate in a ceremony to give thanks or pray for the spirits of the dead animals used in vivisection for experimental purposes.

The following rites at Nissen are among those in the more general category that have parallels or variants elsewhere:

1. On New Year's Day the top three managers in this factory go together, unaccompanied by their wives because it is company business, to three different shrines in the city, where they pray for the safety of the employees in their factory and give substantial financial donations from the company. (They also have lunch together in a prestigious hotel at company expense and are provided with a company car and chauffeur for the occasion.) They then pray together at each of the five shrines on the hillside behind the factory for which the company has responsibility. These small shrines do not have any permanent priesthood but are used at certain times of the year by the firm for religious rites, for most of which a Shinto priest from a local shrine near the factory comes to officiate at the rites.

2. On the first working day of the new year all the department managers (*buchō*) and higher executives in the factory, plus members of the factory's safety committee, assemble at the principal Nissen shrine for the "New Year Safety prayers." It is a brief ceremony, at the beginning of which the General Affairs section manager announces, "Now we are

going to pray for the safety and prosperity of our factory this year" and then all in unison bow twice towards the altar area, clap their hands once, and then bow once more. The ceremony is then declared over and all the men gradually disperse.

3. On the first Day of the Horse after *setsubun*, in early February, is the *hatsu-uma sai*, a rite that has continued in this industrial setting from the agricultural background of traditional Japan. On this day the god of the mountain (*yama no kami*) is said to descend from the hills to become the god of the rice paddy (*ta no kami*). Thus this rite has its origins in invoking the deity's protection and blessings in order to ensure material prosperity through an abundant crop. However, the general attitude to this and virtually all the other rites at Nissen among those who take part is that the religious rites are to pray for safety at work, a few also mentioning prosperity as another, apparently subsidiary, purpose in their prayers. This *hatsu-uma* rite also has a parallel in the autumn, when the god of the rice field returns to become the god of the mountain; this *shū-uma sai* has at Nissen become amalgamated with another autumnal rite held at Inari shrines, the *o-hitaki sai*, which at Nissen is a parallel and identical rite to the *hatsu-uma sai*.

For these rites at Nissen a Shinto priest from a local shrine is hired to perform the ceremony, which consists of a ritual purification (*o-harai*) followed by prayers and the offering of sacred *sakaki* leaves on the offering dais (which had been specially prepared with offerings of fruits, vegetables, *tai* fish, rice wine, rice cakes, and other items) by representatives of different sections in the factory. Those who present their offerings, accompanied by the usual bows and claps, are first the Shinto priest, then the plant manager, then the leader of the company union, followed by a representative for the male bachelor's dormitory, the Nissen "women's division" representative, the male and female representatives of the company housing for married employees and finally the Nissen "catering manager." Technically he is not a Nissen employee but rather the head of a catering firm that has a permanent contract for running the firm's canteens. However, his family also owns the Shinto shrine just behind the main Nissen shrine. After the ceremony all the participants go to this shrine owned by the catering manager to perform a brief rite. They then go on to a third little shrine at the top of the hill behind

山の神

田の神

御火焚祭

お祓い

RELIGION AND SOCIETY IN MODERN JAPAN

these other two, an old shrine dedicated to a god of silk production, for which Nissen has taken over de facto responsibility, and there perform an even briefer ceremony before all disperse back to their offices.

4. Around the time of the Bon ceremony in August, when the ancestors are said to return to this world for a short time, Nissen hires a Buddhist priest to perform a *segaki* rite for 施餓鬼 feeding the souls of the "hungry ghosts" on the mountainside where the company shrines are located just behind the factory. The area was the site of a battle in the year AD 672, and later it was used as a samurai training ground. Also on the hillside are a few *kofun*, burial mounds dating from the preliterate period that remain unidentified in terms of who was buried there. The whole area therefore contains the spirits of many potentially harmful or vindictive spirits. These are thought to be either embodied in or guarded by the wild animals in the area. Therefore at the *segaki* rite the Buddhist priest prays for the spirits of the dead and then he and a man who represents the Nissen company for the event distribute around the hillside the various offerings of fruit, rice wine, and rice cakes for the wild animals to eat.

5. At the end of the working year a "Major Purification" (*ō-harai shiki*) for the top management in the factory is performed. This is also officiated over by the local Shinto priest, and the climax of the rite consists of the priest taking out two strips of cotton cloth, each about twelve to eighteen inches long, which he had previously folded into two lengthwise. Taking a pair of scissors, he makes small incisions along the folded edges of the cloth, enough to represent each of the participants in the ceremony with perhaps a few extra incisions to ensure there would be a sufficient number. The strips of cloth are then laid over two wooden offering stands that are carried around the participants by two assistants from the General Affairs section, who offer them in turn to each participant. As each manager takes the cloth he blows onto it and then rips it from the incision to about halfway down the width of the cloth. The symbolism of this act is that the sin and pollution of the previous year are transferred onto the cloth, which is then taken away by the priest and later burnt at the shrine. Although animal sacrifice is not practised among the Japanese, it is interesting that this rite contains very similar imagery of sin and pollution removed by a

scapegoat-type substitute, which is subsequently ritually destroyed.

お守り
お札

6. Another practice at Nissen that is probably common to many firms is the purchase each year of safety charms (*o-mamori*) at company expense for all the firm's vehicles. Similarly, protective charms (*o-fuda*) are placed in all the buildings and most offices around the factory.

地鎮祭

7. Whenever new plants are installed or buildings set up at the factory, a *jichinsai* ("ground-breaking" ceremony) is performed to appease the local deity.

RITES SPECIFIC TO NISSEN

While the rites discussed above are at fixed occasions in the ritual year and have parallels elsewhere, it is likely that the details of the *segaki* rite and of the end-of-year purification are more specific to Nissen, just as the details of the additional shrines visited during the *hatsu-uma* rite are specific to this factory too. Other rites are much more specific to this particular company, but some, such as the ceremony on the anniversary of the founding of the firm, are likely to have parallels elsewhere in which the details are considerably different. The Nissen rites specific to this firm can be further subdivided into those that are local versions of common types of rites elsewhere (such as the ceremonies connected with the anniversary of the founding of the firm) and those that have been initiated at Nissen subsequent to the occurrence of specific disasters in the factory. Three rites falling into the first subdivision are:

例祭

1. The festival for the god of the mountain (*yama no kami reisai*), which honors the tutelary deity of the hillside behind the factory. This is said to be a female deity whose traditional speciality was bestowing children on childless couples, but she is said to listen only to the prayers of men and not of women. Therefore at this rite all the participants are male, including a specifically male representative of the neighborhood council for the Nissen company housing, in contrast to the male and female representatives for that area at the *hatsu-uma* rite. Representatives from other local neighborhood associations also take part, each of them male, each of whom offers *sakaki* and performs the normal Shinto prayer of bowing twice, clapping his hands twice, and then bowing once

more. Other parts of the rite consist of purification rituals performed by the priest, prayers recited by the priest, and bows towards the offering dais at various intervals when the General Affairs section manager tells them to do so by his command of "*Rei!*" Each delegate is given a gift afterwards from the company, Nissen employees receiving a bag of satsuma tangerines, and the visitors receiving in addition a specially wrapped box of bean-curd cakes.

2. In January of each year a Shinto priest comes to perform the ritual opening of the company's martial arts hall for the coming year. Members of the Nissen *jūdō*, *kendō*, and *kyūdō* teams all participate, as well as some employees' children who are learning these martial arts. The company boat team is also represented. The ceremony consists of prayers, bows, and the offering of *sakaki* branches by representatives of the different teams. The highlight consists of cutting a rice cake made in the traditional "mirror" style resembling the curved mirrors of the Heian era. This is said to symbolize the splitting of the so-called "observing self" described by Ruth BENEDICT (1946: 288–89) whereby the aim of the martial arts is to achieve such perfect unison between thought and deed that one no longer reflects on what one is doing. All participants are also given a gift of two rice cakes as they leave after the end of the ceremony.

3. On 16 April of each year, the anniversary of the founding of Nissen, all the former and present directors of the firm assemble at the main company shrine behind this factory, the company president and some other top executives coming from the head office in Tokyo. They all have a party the previous night at a prestigious hotel in Kyoto, where the senior executives stay overnight. The following morning they attend the ceremony at the company's oldest factory, where the shrine is located. The shrine is dedicated to the fox god Inari, the patron of merchants and traders, though originally an agricultural god. It is to this deity that the Nissen officials address their prayers for safety and prosperity. A convoy of company cars conveys the visitors from the factory to the shrine on the hillside, where in a specially erected pavilion they receive their name badges and await the others. Two Shinto priests perform this ceremony: the usual one and another senior priest from an important local shrine. As far as I could tell the rite followed essentially the same kind of

pattern as the other Nissen rites. After ritual purifications of the priests (performed only at this rite with two priests), the offering stand, and the participants, the rite consisted of prayers and perhaps offerings by delegates. I was permitted only to observe the beginning of the ceremony and after that was requested to wait in the pavilion. It seemed that my presence was too irregular for the junior officials responsible for the rites to take the risk of jeopardizing their promotion prospects if the top management from Tokyo were to disapprove of a foreigner observing this company ritual. After the rite they were conveyed back to the plant by a convoy of company cars, where after refreshments they attended a nonreligious ceremony for honoring those department managers with good production figures or other outstanding achievements.

The three rites described already as specific to Nissen are all Shinto. Other rites specific to this firm, which were initiated following disasters in the factory, are largely Buddhist. They are viewed in the same way by the participants, however, because they are seen as prayers for safety. Whereas the Shinto rites are performed on traditional occasions as precautionary rituals to invoke the gods' blessings, the Buddhist rites are directed to specific known departed spirits who are potentially vindictive if not appeased. The *segaki* rite described already is another Buddhist rite of a similar type. These rites are as follows:

1. On 13 January 1955, fire broke out in one of the dormitories for single men and destroyed the building. Although there were no casualties from the fire, the plant manager at the time decided to initiate an annual pilgrimage to a temple of the fire god Fudō, about an hour's journey from the factory and at the top of a nearby mountain. On the first day in the year designated for the worship of Fudō, the *hatsu-Fudō*, the 初不動 top management of this factory, of an associated factory that was built on the site of the burnt-down dormitory, and of another nearby Nissen factory, accompanied by union representatives, go in company cars to this temple to pray. Afterwards they have lunch together, provided by the temple but paid for by the firm, and return to their work in the factory by mid-afternoon. Each year new safety plaques (*fuda*) to protect buildings from fire are bought from this temple and installed in all buildings in the factory where there are ovens or other uses for fire.

2. On 1 April 1973, another large fire broke out in the factory. This one was attributed to the company's neglect of the spirits of the warriors who had died in the battle in that area in AD 672 and who had not received a proper burial, since they had perished in the swamps. That battle had taken place on 22 July, so on that date all the department managers and other senior management in the factory assemble for a rite conducted by a Buddhist priest, during which all line up to burn incense in the same way as is done at a Buddhist funeral. Every other month on the 15th of that month, simply because it is a convenient date in the middle of the month, the Buddhist priest also performs the prayers by chanting sūtras and lighting incense. For those other eleven months in the year one man from the General Affairs department is the only one who represents the company. He is the one in charge of the practical arrangements for the rites and is the same person who represents the firm at the *segaki* rite. The whole rite lasts for about twenty minutes, after which the priest leaves straightaway in his car, having already been given his fee at the beginning.

3. When the factory was built in 1926 to 1927, several British, German, and Italian engineers were seconded from firms such as Courtaulds in order to help build the plant. One of these, an Italian engineer named Minelli, committed suicide in the factory on 17 February 1927 and was buried in a public graveyard in Kyoto. He left behind a wife in Italy but no children, though he was 44 years old at the time of his death. By Japanese Buddhist standards he had no one to perform his ancestral rites for him. They are aware that Minelli was a Roman Catholic, but they continue to this day to visit his grave at Bon and on the anniversary of his death each year. The grave is cleaned on the previous day by the man responsible for the "donkey work" in these rites, but on the official day for the grave visit the three top managers of the factory (or their deputies if they are otherwise engaged) travel in a chauffeur-driven company car into Kyoto, light incense, pour water over the gravestone, and bow towards it with their hands together in the same way as for a Buddhist grave rite. Those in the top management positions today never knew Minelli and they perform the ritual as part of their jobs and as a token of respect to one who was a kind of "ancestor" in their company and had helped to found it. However, it is not

unlikely that one of the original motivations behind the firm's instituting this annual ritual is the idea that a man who committed suicide in their factory and had no descendants might become a vindictive *muenbotoke* or unattached spirit. As such the principle of safety would require the firm to assume responsibility for his grave rites because there was no one else to do so.

火の神様   4. At least one office in the factory contains a Shinto godshelf that is dedicated to the god of fire (*hi no kamisama*) because there was a fire in that building in 1967. They bow to it, change the water, and offer fresh *sakaki* leaves there twice a month (on the 1st and 15th). This was one example that I happened to notice, but there are many other offices I never visited, and it is likely that other offices would have similar practices.

5. When the film department in the factory began to experience a serious accident rate, the department manager decided that he and his section managers should go to the company's Inari shrine on the first workday of each month in order to pray for safety. Nevertheless, the accident rate in their department continued to be high, and an inconsistency between their prayers and their experiences became obvious one day when they returned from the shrine to find that one of their men had cut off his finger on a machine. It might be that this experience influenced the film *buchō* two years later when I asked him about his attitudes to the rites in the factory, because he at first replied that the prayers are "half efficacious" but then added that they have "no technical effect," only affecting one's state of mind and feelings rather than having any technical effect.

OBSERVATIONS

It is apparent that professed belief in the effectiveness of these rites has nothing to do with participation in them. Most participants say that they take part only out of obligation to the company because it is part of their job. However, when their attitudes are correlated with their positions in the firm these men seem more willing to express doubt or scepticism about the rites the higher they are in the company. The plant manager, for example, says that although his public image is that he believes, in so far as he has to take part in the rites, privately he denies any belief in the efficacy of the rites at all.

	Position in Company		
TABLE 1 ATTITUDES TO COMPANY RITES	High	Middle	Low
"Rites have no effect"	5	1	
"Spiritual but not technological effect"	2		
"Effect only on one's feelings"	2	2	
"Gods do protect and the rite has some effect"		4	2

His General Affairs department manager says that he thinks the rites have no effect, that there are too many of them, and that some of them ought to be abandoned as a waste of time. However, a little lower in the hierarchy of that same department the personnel section manager says that if any of the rites were to be neglected "something bad might happen to the fortunes of the company," so it is "safer" to continue the rites. Generally, as shown by Table 1, those lower down are more likely to express in some way more belief in the rites, as compared to those higher up, even though I tried to interview people on their own away from pressures or influences from colleagues that might lead them to give an "official" reply. It may be that even in such circumstances they were unwilling to express doubts, whereas those higher up had less to lose by doing so. Another factor accounting for this tendency may be that the senior executives had been involved with the rites longer and had experienced times when their prayers seemed not to have worked. The film department manager is a prime example of such a process.

Finally, it should be pointed out that the participants are largely managers, especially department managers or the factory manager, so that most of those lower down the company hierarchy do not even know of the existence of most of these rites. This is indicated by Tables 2 and 3, based on a questionnaire among residents of the company housing estate, which show how the higher management were more likely to reply to a question about religious rites at work, whereas many of those further down either left the question unanswered or else "scraped the barrel" by mentioning the fact that some residents go to the company shrine at New Year (because they can walk and thereby avoid driving after drinking) or by referring to the firm's relatively nonreligious

TABLE 2

RELIGIOUS RITES REPORTED ACCORDING TO STATUS IN THE COMPANY
Multiple answers are included

	Dept. Manager (buchō)	Section Manager (kachō)	Chief Clerk (kakarichō)	Fore-man (shunin)	Blue-collar worker
Personal shrine visit at New Year					1
Christmas Party			1	3	
Jizō Bon		2	1	1	
Jichinsai for new installation or building	2	4	2	3	1
"Anniversary of Company" prayers*				2	
Sakurano Inari worship		2	6		
Prayers for safety*	1	1	2	2	1
New Year prayers for safety	1	1		2	
O-hitaki	1				
End of Year "Major Purification"	1	2	1		
Yama no kami reisai	1				

* For each of these the following category is more specific and is most likely referring to the same event, but those lower down the hierarchy tend not to know the official names of the rites or of the company shrine.

Christmas party or the local Jizō festival in the summer, which is regarded mainly as a form of entertainment for the children. A few had participated in *jichinsai* rites for the installation of a new plant in their department or the erection of a new building in the factory, but it is only the higher management and a few others such as safety committee members, union representatives, or neighborhood association representatives who know about or participate in the more "serious" kinds of religious rites associated with their place of work.

The other exceptional participant in the rites is the "catering manager," who is involved in the *hatsu-uma* and *o-hitaki* rites because he inherited responsibility for one of the shrines on the hillside. His grandfather had become responsible for the shrine, which also became their family property, when a nearby castle was destroyed at the time of the Meiji Restoration. The shrine had been in the direction of the "devil door" (*kimon*) of the castle and protected it from supernatural attacks. After the castle fell to more natural

鬼門

TABLE 3

RESPONSE BY HOUSEHOLDS TO QUESTIONS ON RELIGIOUS RITES IN THE
COMPANY, COMPARED WITH REPRESENTATION IN SAMPLE AS A WHOLE

Wives' replies are included in two households
where the husband did not fill in a questionnaire

	# of house-holds in each group	% of total house-holds	# of households responding	% of households responding
Department Managers	5	2.0%	2	40.0%
Section Managers	22	8.7%	9	40.9%
Chief Clerks	94	37.1%	12	12.8%
Foremen	101	39.9%	13	12.9%
Blue-collar workers	31	12.3%	3	9.7%
Totals	253		39	

attackers, the catering manager's grandfather took over the shrine for reasons unknown to the grandson. However, this man, whom I shall call Yoshioka-san, also claims to be an amateur medium and says that it is hereditary. He describes his revelations from the spirit world as "mental flashes" and describes how he believes the spirits revealed to him in a dream what he should name his eldest son. On another occasion he went on a holiday to Guam, where he visited some wartime trenches in which Japanese soldiers had been killed. There, as was his habit, he began to recite Buddhist sūtras. On his return to Japan the spirits revealed to him that by his action he had enabled the spirits of twelve dead soldiers to return to Japan with him. His influence on the religious life of this company is important to note, because his reputation as a medium has led his colleagues in the factory and in other Nissen plants to consult him about various matters. One went to Yoshioka-san about a stomach problem and was told to go and pray to a particular Buddhist idol in the vicinity. The factory managers of the Nissen plants in Ishikawa and Ibaraki prefectures both consulted Yoshioka-san at different times about the proposed installation of Shinto shrines (*yorishiro* 依り代 or *yashiro*) in their factories, and if a tree is blown over or tilted 社 in the company shrine's precincts it is Yoshioka-san who is consulted in order to ascertain the will of the gods about whether to cut it down or straighten it again. In such ways it is likely that the occult influences of this man have made Nissen exceptional in certain ways to initiate more rites than might have been the case otherwise. The representativeness or otherwise of this case study can only be determined by further empirical studies.

CONCLUSIONS

Three theoretical comments may be made on the basis of the above data:

1. *Safety* as a theme is conspicuous in both religious and nonreligious contexts in Japanese factory life, permeating both aspects so that they become mutually complementary rather than contradictory.

2. *Secularization* hypotheses predicated on an assumption that the nonreligious aspects of industrial society are essentially antagonistic or contradictory to religiosity break down in the light of this kind of data from Japan. Rather than declining in an urban industrial context, it is clear that in Japan religious rites have not only survived but may have even increased in both number and variety through factors such as fires and other disasters in the industrial context.

3. *Scepticism* about the efficacy of the rites is nevertheless present, at least privately among some participants. They perform the rites out of a sense of obligation or duty, as part of their work, and they perform the roles of "vicars" as vicarious representatives of their department, union, or neighborhood association in relation to the deity. However, when most of those supposed to be represented before the gods know nothing or next to nothing about even the existence of most of these rites, and those who represent are often sceptical about the efficacy of the rites themselves, it would seem to be difficult or impossible to apply a Durkheimian type of sociological analysis to such a situation.

NOTE

* This article first appeared in the *Japanese Journal of Religious Studies* 13/4: 261–75, 1986. David C. Lewis is an honorary Research Associate at the Mongolia and Inner Asian Studies Unit, University of Cambridge.

1 My research on this firm was conducted during two periods of anthropological fieldwork from 1981 to 1982 and 1983 to 1984, during the second of which I was able to observe and conduct interviews about the religious rites conducted in the plant.

Mizuko Kuyō and Abortion in Contemporary Japan

HOSHINO Eiki
TAKEDA Dōshō

*I*T IS DIFFICULT to recall exactly when weekly magazines and T.V. programs began to take up and sensationalize the theme of a curse associated with *mizuko*, that is, aborted or stillborn children. It is manifestly clear that the pain and sorrow of losing a child is most directly realized by the would-be mother. It is also undeniable that losing a child through abortion is unavoidable for many mothers, because of a variety of circumstances. However, to prey on people's suffering and weakness by advertising that you can remove such a curse, or at least alleviate its effects, such as guilt feeling, strikes one as a pernicious business. Nevertheless, there are a large number of people who respond to these solicitations. Why are these memorials or offerings for aborted or stillborn children (*mizuko kuyō*) so popular in Japan today, 水子供養 and what is it about them that appeals to contemporary Japanese?

There are some who believe that the large number of abortions carried out in Japan today, and the increasing demand for *mizuko kuyō*, are due to the deluge of sexual information and the shameless profusion of the so-called sex industry, and that abortion is most common among the younger population. However, as we shall see in more detail later, the available data does not support this theory. Instead, this trend is closely connected with the religious views of the Japanese people, especially their concept of the spirits of the dead, and in this sense *mizuko kuyō* is an important topic for those interested in Japanese religion. In this article we will examine *mizuko kuyō* and the related subject of memorials for pets (*petto kuyō*) from the perspective of religious studies. Since the subject encompasses a number of sensitive issues, we will first take a step back and examine the background of this situation.

A typical newspaper leaflet advertising *mizuko kuyō,* urging the reader to properly pacify the spirits of aborted children for a fee of ¥10,000($90.00)/spirit.

THE JAPANESE CONCEPT OF THE SPIRITS OF THE DEAD

As we have already mentioned, *mizuko kuyō* is closely connected with the Japanese concept of the spirits of the dead. While we cannot fully discuss this topic here, it is the accepted opinion of most scholars that the animistic nature of Japanese religion is an important factor in this concept. We do not intend to discuss here whether animism is the belief that attributes a soul or spirit even to inorganic entities, as defined by the 19th-century anthropologist TYLOR (1958, ch. ten), or the belief that attributes some more general "power," including some soul or spirit, even to inorganic entities. Here we are referring to an animism in the later broader sense of attributing an ambiguous "power" to certain objects.

Traditional Eastern religions such as Hinduism in India or Mahāyāna Buddhism, unlike the monotheism of Christianity or Islam, have an emphatic "animistic" coloring, with strong polytheistic or pantheistic tendencies. The particularly polytheistic Japanese myths are well known, but in this article we are interested more in the relation of *mizuko kuyō* to Japanese Buddhism. On this point NAKAMURA Hajime says:

For the Japanese of old, even the grasses and trees had a spirit (*seishin*), and it was generally believed that these inanimate objects could become enlightened and thus be saved. In other words, the idea that even "non-sentient" (*hijō*) objects could attain Buddhahood, based on the Tendai concept of the ultimate reality of all existences (*shohō jissō*), was very strong in Japan....

精神

非情

諸法実相

The idea of attributing a spirit to even grasses and trees can be found in Indian Buddhism.... However, according to many Indian philosophies, living beings attain liberation through knowledge, and the idea that grasses and trees could attain enlightenment was not developed. (1961: 18)

Ꮢis idea was traditionally expressed through such phrases "the grasses, trees, and land all without exception attain Ꮟddhahood" (*sōmoku kokudo shikkai jōbutsu*) and "the ᴐuntains and rivers and grasses and trees all have the Ꮟddha nature" (*sansen sōmoku shitsu'u busshō*). Even nonᏁtient entities such as grasses and trees or mountains and ʳers can attain Buddhahood; how much more so can senᴉnt beings. This is the ultimate expression of the Buddhist ᶥief that "all sentient beings have the buddha nature." Of ᴜrse this "buddha nature" is not, Buddhologically speakᴣ, equivalent to the spirit that is pacified through *mizuko* ʲyō, because at least this spirit is the spirit of the dead. ᴐwever, it is very doubtful that this academic distinction ᴉs regarded as important by the general populace.

草木国土悉皆成仏

山川草木悉有仏性

The fact that the framework for allowing this sort of develᴏment was provided by Buddhism does not mean that ᴜddhism generally handled the memorials for the spirits of ᴇ dead, as it does today, from an early historical period. It is ᴉll known that from the time before the introduction of ᴜddhism the Japanese felt an intense aversion toward ʳpses or anything associated with death, and that there ᴇre many taboos associated with death. Death was a central ᴇm in the list of defilements. Neither Shinto nor other eleᴇnts of folk religion allowed contact with the bodies of the ʲad, whether they were those of human beings or animals, ᶁ even today anything associated with death is taboo to a ᴉnto shrine. No one in mourning can participate in a shrine ʲremony.

In the case of contemporary Japan, one can get the impresʲn that Buddhism has acquired exclusive rights for handling matters associated with the dead. Some may think that this was always the case for Buddhism in Japan, but this opinion is mistaken. It is now believed that the common people in Japan around the seventh century did not bury their dead in graves but rather discarded corpses by the side of the road (SHIMODE 1972: 14). During the mid-Heian period a story was told of Fujiwara no Tadahira (880–949), the head of the northern branch (*hokke*) of the Fujiwara family, who once visited his father Mototsune's (826–891) grave and mentioned that the graves of his grandfather-in-law Yoshifusa (804–872) and his ancestor Uchimaro were also nearby, but that he himself was not sure exactly where they were. At the time Fujiwara Tadahira was at the peak of his powers, one who held posts such as the *dajō daijin* and *kanpaku*. Even a man of his high position was not sure of the location of the family graves. It is clear, then, that even members of high society were not particularly zealous in honoring their ancestors (TAKATORI and HASHIMOTO 1969: 29).

It was not until the late Kamakura and Muromachi periods (13th–14th centuries) that Buddhism began to play a role among the common people in providing funeral and memorial services. According to Takeda, most of the ordinary temples in Japan were either founded or restored after A.D. 1501. Even those that claim to have been "restored" have no clear records before this time, and it is safe to say that there were no permanent resident priests in these temples before the time of their "restoration" (TAKEDA 1971, Chapters 1–4). If it is true that Buddhist priests did not settle down in village temples around Japan until the sixteenth century, it must have been from this time that Japanese in general began to perform funeral services and to diligently observe memorial rites for their ancestors. It was on this basis that the Edo shogunate found it easy to establish the family temple system 寺請制度 (*terauke seido*). The relationship between Buddhism and the general populace, supported by the central pillar of funeral services and ancestral rites, has thus continued to this day, despite such anti-Buddhist government policies as the forceful 神仏分離 separation of Shinto and Buddhist elements (*shinbutsu bunri*) after the Meiji Restoration (late nineteenth century). The Meiji constitution, based on the patrilineal system, has passed into history, and there was talk for a while after the Pacific War that under the new democratic constitution such ancestral rites would disappear, taking with them the Buddhism that depends on such activity to survive. However, this prediction has not materialized, and even today there is no sign that the Japanese concern for their ancestral spirits has diminished.

SPIRITS AND THEIR MEMORIALS

Buddhism in Japan today is so closely affiliated with ancestral rites that it is often called "funeral Buddhism" (*sōshiki bukkyō*). That does not mean that all spirits of the dead are treated in the same way. Two good examples are the spirits of the *mizuko* and the spirits of dead children. *Mizuko* refers to children who die shortly after birth and fetuses who are stillborn (including both natural miscarriages and "artificial" abortions). "Children" refers to those of seven years of age or younger. 葬式仏教

The spirits of the *mizuko* and dead children were, in traditional Japanese society, not treated the same as the spirits of dead adults. Chiba and Ōtsu have written extensively about the differences in funerary rites for these different subjects. It was not only the funerary rites that were different. In general, graves were not built for *mizuko* or children and there were no memorial services held especially for them. In some parts of the country, however, there were separate graveyards for children, called *kobaka*. One can also find such customs as the placing of sardines or some other fish in the mouth or in the casket of the *mizuko* or child before burial. According to CHIBA and ŌTSU, however, the purpose of this practice was to prevent the *mizuko* or child from "attaining Buddhahood" after death and to allow them to be reborn in this world (1983: 20–24, 137–42).

In any case, it is undeniable that throughout Japan the spirits of dead children and *mizuko* were handled differently than the spirits of adults. One example of this point is the practice of having the village *nenbutsu* association (*nenbutsu kō*) perform a funeral service for a dead child rather than calling a Buddhist priest from the temple. It is also not unusual to place the "ancestral" tablets of the dead children and *mizuko* under, rather than on, the shelves of the *shōryōdana* during *o-bon*. The offerings to these spirits are also placed under, rather than on, this ancestral shelf. 念仏講

精霊棚

FIGURE 1		
TYPES OF SPIRITS		
human spirit	*uenrei*	has a direct descendant who performs ancestral rites
	muenrei	has no direct descendant to perform ancestral rites, e.g., people who suffer an unnatural death, *mizuko*, or stillborn children
spirit of sentient being	animal spirit	domesticated or work animal, laboratory animal, hunted game, pet
	fish spirit	fish caught or farmed for consumption
	others	insect or bug
spirit of a non-sentient being		needle, doll, and so on

We have mentioned above how in Japanese Buddhism not only sentient beings but also non-sentient beings possess the buddha nature. The custom of offering memorials for inanimate objects such as dolls or needles, or for victims of one's profession such as eels or whales, reveals the Japanese belief that such beings, whether animal or inanimate, have some sort of "spirit" (*reikon*) or "soul" (*tamashii*). Figure 1 is an attempt to categorize "spirits" on the basis of such memorial rites (or, more specifically, as the objects of memorial rites performed under the aegis of Japanese Buddhism).

霊魂

Uenrei, the spirit of one who has some relations left in this world to perform the ancestral rites, is the normal, most common type of human spirit. Having lived a full life, this spirit has descendants who after its death will perform the proper rites. It will thus become an ancestral spirit who protects its descendants. As YANAGITA Kunio has shown in his work *About Our Ancestors* (1970), this is the "normal" ancestral spirit of the Japanese.

有縁霊

The *muenrei* (spirit with no relations) is the opposite of the *uenrei*. It has no direct descendants to perform rites for it. It was believed that as a result, this kind of spirit could become vindictive (*onryō*) and bring about misfortune to those still living in this world. However, as we mentioned above, the *muenrei* of those who died as adults and those of children and *mizuko* were traditionally handled differently.

無縁霊

怨霊

The spirits of animals were traditionally handled through special memorial ceremonies for animals. In such cases, the animals being memorialized were invariably those that had performed some useful service for human beings. Examples would include memorials for cows and horses by farmers or horse traders; memorials for fish, porpoises, or whales by fishermen or whalers; or mounds (*senbikizuka*) built by professional hunters in honor of their game. Each of these involved certain ceremonies to be performed by a Buddhist priest, and often included the establishment of a memorial tower or mound. 千匹塚

Companies and research facilities use a large number of guinea pigs and other small animals for scientific experiments. Many companies perform a regular memorial ceremony, usually once a year, in honor of these animals. There are many towers built as memorials to animals in the famous graveyard on Mt. Kōya, the headquarters of the Shingon school.

In contrast to the longer tradition of memorializing all these animals, memorial services for pets is a recent phenomenon. These pets do not perform a useful service to their owners in the traditional sense. They are not work animals. In the past, dogs performed various services, such as that of a watchdog, and cats were kept to catch mice and thus to a certain degree were "economic animals." Modern pets, however, play a different role. The recent use of the English loan word "*petto*" for pets signifies the change in status for these animals from a traditional, economically useful role, to that of a "humanized" role as a member of the family. In fact, "*petto*" has become a Japanese word and the traditional word for "pet" in Japanese is already obsolete.

Memorial services for fish are commonly performed by fishermen. A fishing village almost certainly has a stone memorial tower or monument dedicated to the fish that have been captured and killed. The more traditional Buddhist ceremony of releasing captured birds or fish (*hōjō-e*) is closely related to this practice. 放生会

The memorial tower for white ants on Mt. Kōya is the most famous example of memorials for insects or other bugs. This tower was built by a major company involved in the extermination of white ants. For most people these white ants are harmful vermin, but for exterminators it is possible to say that they are a source of business and thus are indirectly beneficial entities.

Memorial services for needles and dolls have been performed at places such as Sensō-ji since the Edo period. This type of memorial, such as the one for needles, is often sponsored by those involved in the production of such materials or by professionals who use them in their work.

RECENT TRENDS

As we mentioned in the introduction, the topic of *mizuko kuyō* and the curse associated with *mizuko* is brought up almost weekly in the mass media. Advertisements in newspapers and weekly magazines by temples performing *mizuko kuyō*, and those distributed through the mail, reach a peak around the *higan* periods of the spring and fall equinox, when the Japanese traditionally visit the ancestral graves. The practice of *mizuko kuyō* is best represented by the building of *mizuko* Jizō (Skt. Kṣitigarbha) statues. The large numbers and energetic activity of those involved in using Jizō include temples specializing in *mizuko kuyō*, such as Shiunzan Jizō-ji; the numerous temples of various Buddhist sects that have traditionally performed *mizuko kuyō* as one of many activities; and the Benten-shū movement that encourages performing *mizuko kuyō* by building an enormous Jizō tower. Recently more and more Buddhist temples are building new *mizuko* Jizō statues and encouraging *mizuko kuyō*. There are also many new religions that, without encouraging people to build *mizuko* Jizō statues, offer spiritual comfort and nullify the guilt and curse associated with the spirit of a *mizuko*.

In light of this religious situation, one has reason to suspect that it is not merely the promiscuous sexual habits of the younger generation leading to increased abortions that accounts for the recent popularity of *mizuko kuyō*. There is no doubt that *mizuko kuyō* is closely related to the Japanese concept of spirits. We will now clarify the contemporary situation with regard to *mizuko kuyō* by comparing it to the infanticide (*mabiki*) and abortions practiced during the Edo period (16th–19th centuries).

間引き

The first point that must be clarified concerns the subject who practices *mizuko kuyō*. Let us take a look at the statistics on abortion compiled by the government under the Eugenics Protection Act. These statistics are based on official reports submitted by doctors, and it is suspected that the actual num-

Chart 1. Annual Abortions by Age Group — 1955, 1960, 1965–1991

Year	Total	Under 20	20–24	25–29	30–34	35–39	40–44	45–49	Over 50	Unknown
1955	1,170,143	14,475	181,522	309,195	315,788	225,152	109,652	13,027	268	1,064
1960	1,063,256	14,697	168,626	304,100	278,978	205,361	80,716	9,650	253	875
1965	843,248	13,303	142,038	235,458	230,352	145,583	68,515	6,611	237	1,151
1966	808,378	15,452	136,143	226,063	220,153	141,002	61,602	6,537	211	1,215
1967	747,490	15,269	124,801	199,450	204,257	138,570	57,367	6,391	177	1,208
1968	757,389	15,668	133,206	203,004	202,307	139,320	56,495	6,030	182	1,177
1969	744,451	14,943	137,354	201,821	192,913	135,269	54,793	6,105	166	1,087
1970	732,033	14,314	141,355	192,866	187,142	134,464	54,101	6,656	162	973
1971	739,674	14,474	152,653	184,507	186,447	138,073	56,379	6,024	197	920
1972	732,653	14,001	148,943	181,291	186,379	137,432	57,801	5,668	153	985
1973	700,532	13,065	134,053	177,748	179,887	131,010	57,658	5,985	151	975
1974	679,837	12,261	119,592	177,639	181,644	125,097	56,737	5,816	127	924
1975	671,597	12,123	111,468	184,281	177,452	123,060	56,634	5,596	208	775
1976	664,106	13,042	108,187	190,876	168,720	121,427	55,598	5,386	155	715
1977	641,242	13,484	99,123	175,803	165,923	123,832	56,573	5,774	157	573
1978	618,044	15,232	94,616	159,926	167,894	120,744	53,431	5,614	169	418
1979	613,676	17,084	94,062	145,012	173,976	125,973	51,521	5,228	124	696
1980	598,084	19,048	90,337	131,826	177,506	123,277	50,280	5,215	132	463
1981	596,569	22,079	90,525	123,825	185,099	118,528	50,724	5,246	141	402
1982	590,299	24,478	90,257	113,945	181,148	121,809	53,133	5,095	127	307
1983	568,363	25,843	89,235	103,597	165,680	126,215	52,862	4,539	104	288
1984	568,916	28,020	90,293	101,304	155,376	135,629	53,571	4,366	117	240
1985	550,127	28,038	88,733	95,195	142,474	139,594	51,302	4,434	94	263
1986	527,900	28,424	84,931	90,479	130,218	141,675	47,299	4,511	121	242
1987	497,756	27,542	81,178	86,633	117,866	131,514	48,262	4,408	105	248
1988	486,146	28,596	82,585	83,734	110,868	123,387	52,477	4,241	83	175
1989	466,876	29,675	83,931	79,579	103,459	111,373	54,409	4,237	72	141
1990	456,797	32,431	86,367	79,205	98,232	101,705	54,924	3,753	58	122
1991	436,299	33,286	88,217	75,446	90,803	92,676	52,203	3,538	44	86

| CHART 2 | | | | | | |
| TRENDS IN THE % OF ABORTIONS BY AGE GROUP | | | | | | |
Under 20	20–24	25–29	30–34	35–39	40–44	45–49
1955 1.2	15.5	26.4	27.0	19.2	9.4	1.1
1960 1.4	15.9	28.6	26.2	19.3	7.6	0.9
1965 1.6	16.8	27.9	27.3	17.3	8.1	0.8
1970 2.0	**19.3**	26.3	25.6	18.4	7.4	0.9
1975 1.8	16.6	**27.4**	26.4	18.3	8.4	0.8
1980 3.2	15.1	22.0	**29.7**	20.6	8.4	0.9
1985 5.1	16.1	17.3	25.9	**25.4**	9.3	0.8
1990 7.1	18.9	17.3	21.5	22.3	**12.0**	0.8
1991 7.6	20.2	17.3	20.8	21.2	12.0	0.8

ber of abortions may be close to twice the reported figures. We are not concerned here with the exact totals, but rather with the percentages and trends according to age groups. Also, it is safe to assume that the age group that experiences the most abortions would be most active in performing *mizuko kuyō*.

Chart 1 shows the total number of abortions according to age group and Chart 2 shows the percentage of total abortions according to the same age groups. Chart 3 shows the actual number of abortions per thousand women within each of these age groups.

A quick glance at Chart 1 shows that in the years for which we have statistics, i.e., from 1955 to 1991, the total number of abortions shows a steady decline, from almost 1,200,000 in 1955 down to less than 440,000 in 1991. The only exception is the age group of those under 20, which shows a slow but steady annual increase. Chart 2 shows that peak percentages reached by each age group follow a set pattern: peaks are reached by the age group of 20–24 in 1970 at 19.3%; by those 25–29 in 1975 at 27.4%; by those 30–34 in 1980 at 29.7%; by those 35–39 in 1985 at 25.4%; and by those 40–44 in 1990 at 12.0%. This five-year trend reflects the advancing wave of the baby-boomers, resulting in an inflated figure for that time period. In other words, as the members of the baby-boomer generation reach a certain age, their larger numbers are reflected as a peak percentage, resulting in a temporary reversal of the general trend toward a reduced number of abortions.

	Total	−20	20–24	25–29	30–34	35–39	40–44	45–49

CHART 3
NUMBER OF ABORTIONS ACCORDING TO AGE GROUP
(PER THOUSAND PEOPLE)

	Total	−20	20–24	25–29	30–34	35–39	40–44	45–49
1955	50.2	3.4	43.1	80.8	95.1	80.5	41.8	5.8
1960	42.0	3.2	40.2	73.9	74.0	62.7	29.4	3.8
1965	30.2	2.5	31.1	56.0	56.0	38.8	21.2	2.5
1970	24.8	3.2	26.4	42.2	44.7	32.9	14.7	2.1
1975	22.1	3.1	24.7	34.3	38.4	29.2	13.8	1.5
1976	21.8	3.4	25.2	33.8	38.5	28.3	13.4	1.4
1977	21.1	3.5	24.2	32.3	36.4	28.2	13.5	1.5
1978	20.3	3.9	23.8	31.2	34.9	26.8	12.7	1.4
1979	20.1	4.3	23.8	30.5	34.5	26.8	12.4	1.3
1980	19.5	4.7	23.3	29.3	33.2	26.8	12.0	1.3
1981	19.5	5.5	23.5	28.9	32.8	27.1	11.9	1.3
1982	19.3	6.0	23.2	27.9	33.3	26.8	12.2	1.2
1983	18.5	6.1	22.8	26.1	32.7	26.3	11.8	1.1
1984	18.5	6.5	22.9	25.8	32.7	26.9	11.5	1.1
1985	17.8	6.4	22.0	24.6	31.5	26.2	11.2	1.1
1986	17.1	6.1	21.3	23.5	30.4	25.2	10.9	1.1
1987	16.0	5.8	19.8	22.4	28.9	24.3	10.7	1.0
1988	15.6	5.9	19.6	21.6	28.0	24.1	11.0	1.0
1989	14.9	6.1	19.5	20.4	26.4	23.5	10.8	0.9
1990	14.5	6.6	19.8	19.7	25.4	22.7	10.3	0.8
1991	13.9	6.9	19.1	19.1	23.7	21.7	9.3	0.8

With regard to the age group most likely to be involved with *mizuko kuyō*, it is significant that ever since the statistics have been gathered in 1955, the age group that almost invariably has the highest number of abortions is that of women between the ages of 30 and 34. The age group 35–39 has usually been the third highest group, until it took the top spot in 1986 (due to the wave of baby-boomers). As we can see from Chart 2, the second highest group of those 25–29 fell to third place in 1985 (in 1982 according to Chart 1), and then was overtaken by the even younger group of those 20–24 in 1989 and is now ranked fourth.

Thus the trends that one can see from these statistics are, on the one hand, the increasing age of those who are having abortions, and on the other hand, the gradual increase in the number of abortions by those in the youngest age group under 20 years of age. As for the theory that abortions have increased among young people due to their sexual promiscuity, we can see that the number of abortions by those under twenty years of age has indeed shown a steady increase. However, in terms of percentages of total numbers of abortions, this age group cannot be considered the major group of those having abortions. This conclusion is also supported by Chart 3. This chart shows the number of abortions per one thousand women of that age group, and the fact that the age group 30–34 has the highest figures, followed by that of the age group 35–40, has not changed since the statistics began to be compiled in 1955. A significant difference from Charts 1 and 2 that can be noted from the statistics in Chart 3 is that there has been a steady decline in the number of abortions per population in all but the under-20 age group. It can be seen that women in their thirties have always been the age group demanding the most abortions. Thus it is women approximately 30 years of age, the majority of which are probably married women with children, that forms the dominant group of women who have abortions.

ABORTIONS IN TRADITIONAL AND CONTEMPORARY JAPAN

We have seen that the majority of abortions in Japan are performed on married women. The same could be said of infanticide and abortions during the Edo period. Let us then analyze the differences between the circumstances of married women in traditional society and those in modern society, where the basic unit is the nuclear family:

1. *Pregnancy.* In traditional society one lived in a closed, communal society. The fact of pregnancy soon became common public knowledge. In contrast, in the contemporary situation pregnancy is an individual or family affair and not a matter of public concern.

2. *Performance of abortion.* In traditional society abortion was performed with what now seem very crude and unreliable methods, often placing the mother in danger of losing her life (see ONSHIZAIDAN AIIKUKAI 1975). Today, under the Eugenics Protection Act, anyone can freely choose to have a safe abortion. The medical techniques have advanced to the point where it is not even necessary to be hospitalized. Therefore, the most important point is that it is possible to keep the fact secret.

3. *Reasons for abortions.* In traditional society infanticide and abortion were common but the reason for this was poverty, and to some extent an act of rebellion by the agricultural class against the feudal order. It is said that this practice was an important factor contributing to stagnation in population growth during this time. CHIBA and ŌTSU argue, in contrast, that infanticide was not a common practice but was resorted to only in times of famine or other crisis (1983: 14–110). In either case, infanticide and abortion were silently accepted and justified by society only in times of natural calamity or as an unavoidable means of survival.

In modern times abortion is a result of "a strong emphasis on birth control or a general heightening of a preference for fewer children" (MURAMATSU 1983: 14). BROOKS writes of "those persons who seem to abort their children because of self-centered materialistic aspirations" (1981: 133). It is a fact that there is no poverty in Japan today (compared with that of the past), and even though people have more than enough of the necessities of life, they constantly seek to improve their economic condition. Since any more than the minimum number of children would hinder this quest, it is commonly believed that many people immediately choose to have an abortion as soon as pregnancy is discovered. In this sense, contemporary abortions are performed for individual reasons, and each must be justified by individuals.

4. *Responsibility for abortions.* It is clear that responsibility for abortions in traditional society was not merely that of the individual. Responsibility was shared by the community in general, or there may not have been any sense of responsibility at all. In contemporary Japan the responsibility must be borne in secret completely by the individual. This is the basis for a feeling of indebtedness, which will be discussed in more detail later.

5. *The concept of the spirits of children.* According to CHIBA and ŌTSU, in traditional society there were definite differences in funerary practices between those performed for adults and those for children. Since "the life of a newborn child was sent into this world from the spiritual realm of the kami (*shinrei*)" (1983: 37), a Buddhist funeral was denied 神霊 children, but prayers were added by relatives that they would be reborn in this world. CHIBA and ŌTSU extrapolate the idea that "since the spirit is something that is given by the kami, it

can be returned in case it is not needed at that time, and received again when it is required" (1983: 141–42). In contemporary Japan, however, there is no belief in a special or different kind of spirit belonging to children. At the risk of being misunderstood, it could be said that children have now been included in the same group as that of adults. The next point is related to this one.

6. *Naming of children.* In traditional society, as mentioned above, children who died under the age of seven were not buried in a grave, and thus lost any further direct connection with the village or temple. This indicates that these children had not yet become full-fledged members of the group or society (CHIBA and ŌTSU 1983: 167), and that, according to the concept of spirits expressed in section 5, they would have another chance to be reborn and join that society. The particular characteristic of these children, including aborted and stillborn children, was their namelessness. In contemporary Japan, on the other hand, children (including stillborn children) are buried with the same formal funeral ceremonies as adults, even though these are admittedly more toned down than a funeral for an adult. Usually posthumous Buddhist 戒名 法名 names (*kaimyō* or *hōmyō*) are given. A problem arises with aborted children. In general, funeral ceremonies are not performed for them and they are not given posthumous Buddhist names. However, the namelessness of *mizuko* is based on the fact that the abortion was carried out in secret, hidden from society in general. The fact still remains that for the person who aborted the child a life had been harbored in her body and that this life was rejected by her. The memory remains and cannot be easily dismissed. From the perspective of the Japanese concept of life and spirits, the aborted child in contemporary society should have a name.

ABORTION AND RELIGION

In light of the above analysis, there are clearly at least two definite differences between the two societies. These are the differences, first, in the social system, and, second, in the concept of spirits with regard to children. Both of these differences are well illustrated by the attitude taken by these two kinds of societies toward abortion.

The traditional, local community, with its strong inter-personal relationships and restrictive local mores, had a concept of spirits that distinguished between those of adults and those of children. Therefore infanticide and abortion could be justified to some extent among the community as a whole. To that extent the responsibility was also shared by the community, and an individual did not have to bear the burden alone. In addition, the belief that the child could be reborn spared the individual and community from suffering guilt for having performed infanticide or abortion. There is also the fact that the life expectancy of children in general was very uncertain at this time, and the death of a child was easier to accept.

Contemporary society, on the other hand, has evolved, along with increasing industrialization and urbanization, more and more toward being centered around small families and the nuclear family. Now abortions are carried out in a milieu wherein the spirits of adults and children are not distinguished, and so the aborted child is considered a living entity entitled to life. In such a society the individual seeks to have an abortion alone and in secret, and thus must also bear the responsibility alone and in secret. It is in this situation that a conscientious person will suffer self-recrimination and a feeling of indebtedness. As ONO has written, "Instead of the offering of a memorial for all spirits (in the traditional local community) in which the unhappiness and suffering of others, and one's own distress, is shared, could it not be said that the popularity of *mizuko kuyō* is an individualization of suffering?" (1982: 25).

Given this structure of contemporary society, the causes for the popularity of *mizuko kuyō* become clear. As Brooks has pointed out, behind this increasing popularity are the "conflicting feelings" of those who undergo abortions. On the one hand there is the feeling that abortion goes against the principle of respect for life. On the other hand is the belief that spirits of *mizuko* who are not memorialized are potentially dangerous, i.e., there is a fear of suffering from a "curse" (BROOKS 1981: 133–37). Abortion in contemporary Japan is not unavoidable or necessitated by natural calamity, but is carried out by individual will in the midst of material prosperity, against a child whose probability of dying before reaching maturity is otherwise extremely low, and who has become "humanized" in contemporary society. This results in a feeling of indebtedness and self-recrimination and a search for a cause and effect relationship that finds the reason for one's happiness or unhappiness in the fact of an abortion. In addition, anxiety of a possible curse from an aborted baby, based on this feeling of indebtedness, comes from the aforementioned development that children are now considered as being in the same category as adults (the "humanization" of children). In traditional society the spirits of the children were not considered as possible purveyors of a curse, whereas in contemporary society the spirits of children are treated the same as the spirits of adults, and thus have the potential for casting a curse.

We can thus say that the purpose of contemporary *mizuko kuyō* is one of providing comfort from the feeling of indebtedness and anxiety that comes from a fear of this curse. Examples to illustrate this point are easily found, such as the writings of Hashimoto Tetsuma of the Shiunzan Jozō-ji on the transformation of such curses to worldly benefits through performing memorial services, notes such as *omoidegusa* (unpublished reminisces) by pilgrims to Jikishi-an in Kyoto, or the pamphlet *Yasuragi* (Comfort) published by the Benten-shū. For one concrete example, let us look at one of the unpublished notes known as *omoidegusa*:

> After having one miscarriage and aborting one child, we were blessed with two children—one boy and one girl—and I am now living happily with both my husband and aunt.
>
> However, I feel heartbroken when I think of that child (which I aborted) and think of what it would be like if the child was alive.
>
> I am now thirty-six years old, and I think that many different experiences, though some are very sorrowful and painful, help one to grow and mature.
>
> I also had a romantic relationship [when I was young] which ended with me crying the night away, but this experience has made me stronger. I want to tell young people to face life resolutely, and not be disheartened.
>
> I look forward to continuing self-improvement.

Finally, a few words on *mizuko kuyō* and the practice of religion in general in contemporary Japan. MORIOKA categorizes the relationships between contemporary people and religious institutions as follows:

1 Temporary (*ichijiteki*) relationship. A relationship that does not continue steadily for a long period, but is a temporary relationship based on a short-term need. 一時的

2 Surface (*hyōmenteki*) relationship. A merely outward or superficial relationship that does not penetrate to the deepest dimension of the personality. 表面的

3 Beneficial (*kōriteki*) relationship. A relationship based on worldly benefits (*genze riyaku*). 功利的 現世利益

4 Liberated (*kaihōteki*) relationship. A relationship that is not restrictive but is liberated from the narrow confines of the traditional family temple relationship (1980: 93). 解放的

These relationships to religious institutions that Morioka points out as indicative of a society based on the nuclear family in this age of urbanization are very pertinent to *mizuko kuyō*. For example, *mizuko kuyō* is in almost all cases a temporary relationship. There is no formal funeral, and any follow-up services are done at the discretion and convenience of the individual. It is a superficial, surface relationship, because it ends as soon as one is set free from any possible curse and is thus comforted. It is a mutually "beneficial" relationship for the same reason. It is a "liberated" relationship because in most cases the person seeking to offer a memorial service does not go to the family temple but to a place with which one has little or no previous connections. We can conclude that *mizuko kuyō* fits right into the pattern defined by Morioka as typical for contemporary religious activity in Japan.

MEMORIALS FOR PETS AND DOLLS

Finally, some comments concerning memorial services for pets and dolls. As we mentioned at the beginning, memorials for animals and tools that are beneficial to human society have traditionally been the objects of "memorial" services. This practice continues today, in a sense, in the form of memorial services for pets and dolls. Of course, memorial services for useful animals, such as farm animals, and tools used in one's work, also continue as before.

The belief that animals and even inanimate objects possess some form of "spirit" or "soul" is as common among the Japanese today as it was in the past. How does this relate to the current cases of memorial services for pets and dolls? We

A memorial for dolls near Ōsu Kannon temple in Nagoya.

believe that memorial services carried out in contemporary Japan for pets and dolls are fundamentally different from those carried out in the past for animals. On the one hand the belief in the presence of spirits in these objects is the same. This is illustrated by the following story printed in the 9 September 1984 edition of the *Asahi shinbun*. The residents of Urawa City in Saitama Prefecture had submitted a petition to the city government that the dead bodies of animals not be disposed of and burned with regular waste material, and the city was considering the construction of a separate furnace specifically for the cremation of pets. According to our finding, about twenty of the cities in a certain suburban area of Tokyo do not at the present time burn the bodies of pets along with the garbage, but have commissioned the handling of such pets to a certain private dog-and-cat cemetery. It is clear that even government agencies in Japan are not comfortable with the idea of handling the bodies of pets as just so much garbage. The idea that "all sentient beings possess the buddha nature" is alive and well in modern Japan, but a fundamental difference has arisen in contemporary society concerning the place of animals. The basic unit for society today is the nuclear family, and these families have fewer members. Since there are fewer children, those children have fewer brothers and sisters, and often animals—pets—have become substitutes. In the case of older couples, animals become substitutes for children. The fact that animals are becoming "humanized" is reflected in the way their sphere of life is widening into areas formerly reserved only for human beings, such as their being considered a member of the family, and in the growing number of magnificent cemeteries and family columbariums run by pet professionals specifically for dogs, cats, or other pets after they die. This trend cannot be explained merely by the lack of space in the city to continue the practices of traditional society, or in the countryside, where pets were privately buried in one's garden or backyard.

The same can be said for the memorial services for dolls. Since ancient times dolls were considered vehicles for spirit possession, and often services were held to send the doll's "spirit" on to the next world, but in the present day we find a tendency to consider a doll as a member of the family, just as "animals" became "pets." The same "humanization" has occurred.

These animals and dolls, which in traditional society were considered by the community and workers as objects that contributed to the welfare of human society, are in contemporary society considered the private possessions of individuals, and are gradually becoming "humanized." It is at this point that we find commonality with *mizuko kuyō*. The characteristic relationships between contemporary people and religion outlined by Morioka can be seen here in that the funeral services for these pets are conducted by the individual owner apart from the aegis of the family temple; the relationship is temporary, as seen in the typical contract with a pet cemetery for only three years; and so forth.

We can conclude with the comment that, although memorials for animals and tools by communities and professional groups continue as in traditional society, these kinds of memorials have split into two streams. The fact that memorials are now for pets and not merely "animals" is the most conspicuous aspect of such memorials in contemporary Japan.

NOTE

* This article was translated from the Japanese by Paul L. Swanson. It appeared originally as "Indebtedness and comfort: The undercurrents of *mizuko kuyō* in contemporary Japan" in the *Japanese Journal of Religious Studies* 14/4 (December 1987): 305–20. The contents and statistics were updated for inclusion in this volume.

HOSHINO Eiki is Associate Professor at Taishō University in Tokyo, and head priest of Fukuzō-in, a Shingon Buddhist temple. TAKEDA Dōshō is Lecturer at Taishō University and a priest of Ryūsen-ji, a Jōdo Buddhist temple in Tokyo.

Pokkuri-Temples and Aging

Rituals for Approaching Death

Fleur Wöss

O DIE OR NOT TO DIE—that is *not* the question. Do what we will, death is an inescapable accompaniment of life. The question of *how* we will die is one that all of us think about from time to time, however; not so much while we are young, with death a distant reality hidden by our future hopes and plans, but increasingly so as our remaining time grows short and the end of life confronts us. Interests gradually shift from the occupational to the personal, especially after retirement and the completion of child-raising duties. Declining health and the deaths of relatives and friends bring the old face-to-face with the possibility of long-term illness and suffering, and lend immediacy to the question of how they themselves will die. Such concerns are reflected in the following poem by Nonagase Masao, which depicts a comfortable life and death:[1]

Longing for the western capital

My teacher in Kyoto
lived in a house in the woods
What has he been doing lately?

When you eat, eat amply
When you sleep, sleep leisurely
When you die, die suddenly.

This is a "saying of Yamato," handed down from times past
My teacher wrote it for me once
My teacher, Master Shinyoto
I follow the saying when I eat and sleep
But how about when I die?

Ample eating, leisurely sleeping, and sudden death (*kuu toki nya tappuri, neru toki nya yukkuri, shinu toki nya pokkuri*)—these are the components of a happy life. What concerns us here is the aspect of "sudden death."

Pokkuri shinu is an expression meaning "to die suddenly, peacefully, and without long suffering." Although the desire for a peaceful death is universal, in Japan it has given rise to special places where people pray to die in this way. These places are the so-called *pokkuri-dera*, temples where prayers for an easy death are, it is believed, likely to be granted. What makes the temples worthy of discussion is the enormous popularity they have attained in recent years, especially among the old. This essay examines the background of this popularity and analyzes the possible factors responsible for its development.

The mass popularity of the *pokkuri*-temples accompanied a growing interest in the problems connected with aging. In 1972 Ariyoshi Sawako published a novel entitled *Kōkotsu no hito* [A man in ecstasy] that dealt with the issues of senility and old age. The book became an immediate best seller, with over a million copies sold within six months. The mass media picked up on the new topic, producing numerous features on euthanasia, old people's homes, and *pokkuri-dera*. Television programs about the temples brought them wide exposure and publicity, turning many that were once impoverished into prosperous financial enterprises. Colorful festivals once or twice a year that drew tens of thousands of visitors to even small temples allowed television reporters to link the curious with the tragic. Sensational incidents involving old people were widely discussed, such as the story of an old couple who visited a *pokkuri*-temple in Shikoku, then drowned themselves in the Inland Sea.

Although *pokkuri*-temples are found in every part of the country, the most popular are concentrated in the Nara and Kyoto regions. Some have a long history as *pokkuri-dera*, others only recently acquired their reputations for easing death. Most of the "traditional" *pokkuri*-temples are associated with a particular holy person who, it is believed, experienced a peaceful death there. Such is the case of the most famous and often-visited of such temples, Kichiden-ji in Nara, located not far from Hōryu-ji. The temple is also called *koshimaki-dera*, because, it is said, the mother of the Pure Land Buddhist saint Genshin died peacefully there after having offered her *koshimaki* (kimono undergarment) to Amida Buddha.

Since Kichiden-ji has been discussed in detail by a number of Japanese scholars,[2] I will briefly introduce a less-known *pokkuri-dera* on the Izu Peninsula, one whose reputation was achieved rather recently due to the attention of the mass media.

ACTIVITIES AT A *POKKURI*-TEMPLE

On a hill in the interior of the Izu Peninsula, near the village of Yugashima, is a temple of the Zen sect named Kinryūzan Myōtoku-ji. It boasts an imposing main hall, but this is not what most visitors turn their attention to. The building that they consider most important is the smallest one on the precincts: the *tōsu*, or temple toilet. The tutelary deity of the structure is Ususama Myōō, a being whose reputation for warding off evil spirits and purifying the impure gained it a reputation for special powers of healing. The building is filled with natural stone and wood formations resembling male and female genitalia, donations from the temple's believers. At the entrance a huge stone phallus catches the visitor's eye; a signboard advises one to stroke it to guarantee the health and strength of the male members of one's family. The visitor is then urged to step over a hole (the former toilet), an act that is reputed to prevent abdominal diseases through the power of the deity Ususama. Before leaving the temple precincts most visitors buy a piece of underwear— available in all sizes and shapes—bearing a stamp with the figure of the Ususama Myōō; wearing is believed to guarantee the continuing effects of Ususama's powers.

明徳寺

Kinryūzan Myōtoku-ji was "discovered" in 1974 by reporters from NHK, the Japanese national broadcasting company. In a television program about *pokkuri-dera* they identified Myōtoku-ji as one of the many "fashionable" temples of this type, setting off the Myōtoku-ji's new and still-growing popularity. Most of the visitors that now flock there are actually on weekend trips to nearby hot springs, and stop by to pray for a healthy future. Even on the average weekday the temple can expect seven or eight busloads of visitors, and during the annual Ususama festival in August it is packed with tens of thousands of old people who gather to pray. The sale of underwear has brought unexpected profit and wealth to the temple and its family.

Efficacious underwear for sale at Myōtoku-ji.

How, then, is the belief in Ususama Myōō and his powers connected with our discussion of *pokkuri*-temples? The answer can be found in the type of requests that older visitors to the temple make of him. Let me quote several messages left by old women on *ema*, the small wooden plaques used by the Japanese to make their desires known to the deities:

> When my time has come to enter the other world I want to die easily and without long suffering.

> My daughter-in-law and I are on good terms. Yet I feel terrible when I think of how in the future she will probably have to help me with my bodily functions. When I come here [to pray that this will not happen] my mood brightens.

> Help me, that no one will have to help me with my bodily functions, that I will be free of suffering, and that I will be able to sleep well.

The Japanese phrase most often seen in these prayers is *shimo no sewa. Shimo*, "lower" or "below," indicates the private parts of the body, and *sewa* means "care." Hence the translation above, "to help with the bodily functions," usually in the case of an illness that does not permit the patient to go to the toilet properly. Being ill, helpless, and confined to bed are the things that the older visitors to the *pokkuri*-temples fear the most.

Hence, when elderly visitors request good health from Ususama, they are in effect asking that they live out their lives without burdening others, and, by implication, that they die without the kind of extended illness that would require extended care. It was this aspect of Ususama worship that caused the NHK reporters to present Myōtoku-ji as a *pokkuri-dera*.

OLD AGE IN JAPAN

Similar desires are expressed by all adherents of the *pokkuri*-temples. According to a recent survey, the reason offered by most worshippers at Kichiden-ji (93 percent) to explain their visits was, "I don't wish to become bedridden and burden other people." The second most common reason was, "I don't want to suffer with a prolonged illness like cancer" (18 percent). The tragedy behind these comments is obvious. These old people—the majority of visitors are aged fifty-six to seventy—do not wish to end their lives as a nuisance to others.

More than 80 percent of the *pokkuri*-temple adherents are women. Is turning to *pokkuri*-temples for comfort an approach that suits women more than men? Why do women in particular fear becoming bedridden and having to depend upon others? Are there other reasons behind the wish for a sudden and easy death? Is the popularity of the *pokkuri*-temples related to the worsening circumstances of the elderly in Japan? To find the answers to these questions we must focus on the present situation of old people—particularly women—in Japanese society today.

The average age of the Japanese population has risen steadily in recent years. John CAMPBELL, in his recent book on aging in Japan, summarizes the situation as follows:

> Although the basics are the same in Japan as elsewhere, the problems presented by Japanese old people are different in some secondary but important respects. First, Japan has had an unusually young population for its level of GNP throughout the postwar period, with only about 5 percent age 65 and over in the 1950s, 7 percent in 1970, 10 percent in 1985, and 12 percent in 1990. Many European countries were around the 15

percent level in the 1980s. Second, a combination of healthy habits and medical advances has given Japan the highest life expectancies in the world: 81.8 for women and 75.9 for men as of 1989. Third, mainly because the birth rate dropped sharply after the postwar baby boom and has stayed low, population aging is proceeding more rapidly than in any other advanced nation. From 1990 to 2000, the share of people 65 and other is estimated to rise from 11.9 percent to 16.3 percent. By 2020, Japan will have about the highest proportion of elderly in the world, almost 24 percent 65 and over.[3]

Paralleling the increase in Japanese life expectancy has been the loss of many of the traditional roles that once made old people feel wanted and needed.[4] The traditions they are capable of handing down no longer command respect. Their once-valued advice has lost its relevance in today's fast-changing society. Changes in the content of education have deprived them of their ability to teach the grandchildren. Electrical appliances often intimidate them, so that they are of little use even for housework.

Complicating the situation for women has been the change in patterns of child raising. With longer lives and fewer children, Japanese women—who have traditionally been expected by society to regard the bringing up of children as their central purpose in life—find themselves condemned to idleness for the final three or four decades of their lives. New careers seldom provide an outlet for their energies: there is little interesting work available for middle-aged women reentering the job market. No wonder that the number of women claiming to have no purpose in life increases after the age of forty. The number continues to rise as women grow older, with a sharp jump occurring after the age of sixty; among women over seventy, more than 60 percent find no purpose to their lives.[5]

Old people in general, and old women in particular, tend to spend their final years with the family of one of their children, preferably that of their oldest son. Even those who do not do so by choice are frequently left with no alternative by their financial situation.[6] The national pension system does not provide anything beyond a bare subsistence income, and widows are entitled to only half of their husband's pension. This is insufficient to maintain an independent household.

In traditional farming communities this presents few difficulties—the houses are large enough to accommodate old people without crowding, and the old fulfill an important role by helping with the farm work. In the urban communities where the large majority of Japanese now live, however, the presence of aged parents burdens their grown children in two important respects: they drain the family's finances at a time when the grandchildren's educational expenses require much of the available money, and they occupy precious space in the cramped residences. A common saying reflects the situation in the average urban home: *Toshiyori to butsudan wa okutokoro ga nai*—"There's no room for the aged and the Buddhist altar." Urban housing is designed for two-child nuclear families, and provides no space for such nonessentials as old people and Buddhist altars. The older generations—the aged parents and the ancestors enshrined in the altar—no longer have an important role in the life of the family.

The ideal arrangement, of course, would be to have either a single house large enough for the younger members to live separately from their elders or a second house within a five-minute walk, but these solutions are far beyond the means of the average family. With space so limited, some families resort to the practice of passing their parents from sibling to sibling. An eighty-seven-year-old woman at a *pokkuri*-temple mentioned that every six months she is sent to live in a different child's home. The situation creates difficulties for her in finding friends, and is hardly designed to make her feel welcome by the respective host families.

An added difficulty for elderly women is their relationship with the wife of their son. Raised at a time when obedience and strict submissiveness were expected of a daughter-in-law, many mothers-in-law feel cheated now that women of the younger generation claim the right to their own lives and opinions.

THE PLIGHT OF THE BEDRIDDEN

If a healthy old person is a burden to his family, how much more so an aged relative who is not even able to go to the toilet properly? The possibility of finding themselves in such a situation seems to be of greater concern to women, who are generally more conscious of the state of their health than are men. A bedridden person is not only financially dependent (as most old women are anyway) but also totally reliant on the help of family members. Caring for such people is still thought of as the sole responsibility of the patient's family— state institutions are so over-burdened that they can offer no help to anyone who still has a living relative, whether that relative is willing to care for the person or not.[7]

Since most old women live with their son's family, the nursing usually falls upon the daughter-in-law, who may be completely enslaved by the needs and whims of the bedridden person.[8] Old men in such a situation generally rely on their wives (who almost always outlive them), but in a recent survey not a single woman visitor at a *pokkuri*-temple thought of her husband as a potential caretaker if she should find herself confined to bed.

Women's greater awareness of the possibility of finding themselves in the complete care of one of their children—and their desire to avoid burdening them in such a way—does much to answer the question of why women adherents so outnumber men at the *pokkuri*-temples. When I asked visitors at Myōtoku-ji what they thought the reasons for the preponderance of women were, female adherents were almost unanimous in citing the desire of most women not to burden the members of their family (not a single male adherent offered this explanation). Japanese women are more sensitive to the question of dependency because it is a stronger element of their lives: as children they depend on their parents, as wives on their husbands, and as old women on their children. They also tend to be more concerned about family relationships, since most have been confined to the house for most of their lives. Moreover, they know from their own housekeeping experience how great a nuisance a bedridden person can be for the caretaker and for the family in general. A woman who becomes bedridden has not only lost her role and therefore her meaning in life—she is also keenly aware that she is adding considerably to the household chores.

All of this assumes, of course, that the old person has someone willing to care for her; for the increasing number of elderly who are not so fortunate the problems may be even greater. Thus the fear of solitude may rival the fear of dependency in driving women to the *pokkuri*-temples to pray for an easy death. More women than men find themselves alone in old age because of their higher life expectancy and because they tend to be younger than their spouses to begin with. Loss of their partner intensifies their estrangement from family and modern society. No longer is there someone around to share their everyday pleasures and worries; even children cannot provide the kind of understanding that a mate of the same age can. Many women find their purpose in life in caring for their husband; his death thus deprives them not only of companionship but of something to live for. The resulting psychological stress takes a physical toll as well: widows tend to have poorer health than women whose partner is still alive.

The number of people who live alone is particularly high among visitors to the *pokkuri*-temples. According to one survey, such people comprise 12.5 percent of all visitors, compared to 7 percent of the general population for women and 3 percent for men—a very high percentage indeed. Loneliness is thus particularly likely to be a problem among those who call at the temples. Even living with one's children, however, does not necessarily prevent a feeling of isolation. One old woman remarked in an interview, "I live with my son's family. My daughter-in-law is very sweet and does her best to comfort me, but somehow I feel like a guest." This woman walks two hours every day to a *pokkuri*-temple and two hours back.

The *pokkuri*-temples can provide spiritual consolation and companionship with people having similar problems. Sometimes one can see visitors on benches in the temple precinct, waiting for somebody to talk to.

A final reason should be mentioned for the preponderance of women at the *pokkuri*-temples: the religious factor. A certain amount of religious belief is necessary to undertake a journey to a temple—one must believe that it will be helpful to pray there. Women in general seem more inclined to feel this way. A survey among old people to find out how they use their pocket money has revealed that women over sixty spend the greatest amount on their grandchildren, followed by temple visits and offerings. Men in the same age group use most of their spending money on cigarettes; temple visits and offerings were in twelfth place.[9]

Religious faith provides the believer with the greatest treasure: hope. Old people whose future in the present world is short and bleak can look forward to a better life. Many of the *pokkuri*-temples belong to the Jōdo-shū or Jōdo Shinshū schools of Pure Land Buddhism; to pray there for an easy death implies at the same time a desire for quick rebirth in Amida's paradise, a future that must seem considerably brighter to most believers than the one remaining to them here on earth. This suggests another reason why so many believers pray for a quick death in case of incapacitating illness, even if they are well cared for by their family. What they desire is a better future.

POKKURI-TEMPLES AND SUICIDE

In view of the desire for sudden death among the worshippers at the *pokkuri*-temples, one question inevitably arises: How does prayer at *pokkuri*-temples relate to suicide?

The suicide rate in Japan is characterized by the growing number of suicides in higher age groups. Some 28 percent of all suicides in Japan are committed by people over sixty, with the highest rate found among those over eighty.[10] The suicide rate for women over seventy-five was far higher in Japan than in any other country covered by the WHO statistics for 1988 (the USA, France, the former West Germany, Italy, the former Czechoslovakia, Sweden, England, and Wales); the rate begins to climb steeply in relation to women of those nations around the age of 65.

Yoshizawa Isao, a specialist in the field of suicide, offers several reasons for the high suicide rate among old people in Japan. Illness, he says, is the principal factor in the overwhelming majority of cases, due to the unwanted dependency and the loss of life purpose that it brings about.[11] The second main motive is the loneliness resulting from widowhood and the hostility that old people frequently sense from the family. The third main reason is the financial difficulties that accompany the lack of a pension system sufficient to allow a decent and independent life.

Yoshizawa's conclusions were supported by research in Hokkaido, which also found illness to be the major precipitating factor in suicide among the old; 65 percent of all suicides could be explained on this basis.[12] Yoshizawa blames the poor state of social services in Japan for the high suicide rates: more facilities should be provided for the elderly sick, he feels, and help should not be limited to those without relatives.

Hence the conditions that lead to suicide—illness, dependency, loneliness, and financial difficulties—are the same as those that motivate worship at the *pokkuri*-temples. The difference between the two responses may be one of degree. The difficulties feared by the temple-goers are usually still in the future, and the possibility of future difficulty may not be a sufficient reason for suicide.

CONCLUSIONS

The general situation of old people in Japan throws much light on the recent rise in popularity of the *pokkuri*-temples. Old age is a time when people begin to worry about prolonged illness, suffering, and confinement to bed. They fear that if they live with their children they will burden them financially, occupy needed living space, and trouble the daughter-in-law. If they live by themselves, loneliness and isolation become problems. In either case the elderly lack a sense of self-worth and life purpose. Severe illness increases their problems, especially in Japan where the social welfare system does not provide enough facilities for the bedridden. Incapacitating illness leaves the old person with two unwelcome choices: either to encumber their family or to be left lonely and unwanted in an institution. Greater life expectancies mean that more and more people will have to face such problems in the future.

Another striking feature of the *pokkuri*-temple phenomenon is the large number of female adherents. Women live longer than men, are more concerned with their health, and are more exposed to loneliness. They tend to be more sensitive than men to the possibility of burdening their children, since Japanese men can generally rely upon their wives for care. Finally, women are more likely than men to turn to religion for comfort.

The main tragedy of old people today seems to be their loss of a meaningful role. Their visits to the *pokkuri*-temples may appear to express a wish to escape from life, but may it not be an attempt to find a new source of hope and meaning? Elderly people whose lives no longer provide a sense of purpose turn to the next life. Hence the *pokkuri*-temples may be seen as simply another expression of the universal human desire for a better future and a more meaningful life.

NOTES

* An earlier essay on this subject appeared as "Escape into Death, Old People and Their Wish to Die" in Gorden Daniels, ed., *Europe Interprets Japan*, Kent: Paul Norburg Publications, 1984, pp. 222–29. Fleur Wöss is a member of the Institut für Japanologie at the Universität Wien.

1 Nonagase Masao, "Rakusei kanjō," in *Yūhi no rōjin burūsu*, Tokyo: Kado Sōbō, 1981, pp. 78–79. Translation by author.

2 See, for example, Inoue Katsuya, "Pokkuri shinkō no haikei," *Jurisuto* 12, *Sōgō tokushū: Kōreika shakai to rōjin mondai* (1978), pp. 200–204; Inoue Katsuya, "Rōjin no shiseikan. 'Pokkuri ganbō' no shinriteki haikei," in Inoue Katsuya and Nagashima Kiichi, eds., *Rōnen shinrigaku*. Tokyo: Asakura Shoten, 1980, pp. 188–202.

3 See CAMPBELL 1992, p. 6.

4 See, for example, Tanaka Yoshirō, "The Plight of the Elderly," *Japan Quarterly* 26 (1979), p. 68.

5 Men lose their meaning and purpose in life after their fifty-fifth year, the time when most of them are forced to retire. See Fujin ni Kansuru Shomondai Chōsa Kaigi, ed., *Gendai Nihon josei no ishiki to kōdō*. Tokyo: Ōkurashō Insatsukyoku, 1974, p. 136.

6 They make up about 60 percent of the total elderly population, a figure which is going down at the rate of about 1 percent per year.

7 Not that being institutionalized is a welcome prospect to anyone. Although much less common in Japan than in the West, the institutionalization of the elderly is on the rise. The dying process now seldom occurs in the home: in 1947 only 9 percent of all deaths took place in institutions, while in 1977 the figure was 50 percent (55 percent in urban areas, 41 percent in the countryside). The percentage continues to rise. At present hospitals account for the majority of these "institutional" deaths, but it is predicted that the number occurring in old people's homes will increase in the future. Certain of the institutions for the elderly are so-called *sushiya-byōin*, private hospitals that welcome bedridden patients, assign a variety of diseases to them, and treat them accordingly. The more injections and special treatments they give for these supposed ailments, the more money they are able to extract from relatives and health insurance policies.

8 A vivid account of the difficulties a woman has to tackle when she cares for a bedridden person is the novel by Okifuji Noriko, *Onna ga shokuba o saru hi*, Tokyo: Shinchōsha, 1982.

9 See *Kōbe Jogakuin Daigaku ronshū* 21/1 (July 1974), pp. 62–63.

10 See Yoshizawa Isao, "Rōjin no jisatsu," in Ōhara Kenshirō, ed., *Gendai no jisatsu*, Tokyo: Shibundō, 1980, p. 136.

11 Yoshizawa, "Rojin no jisatsu," pp. 137–38.

12 Ōhara Kenshirō and Yoshizawa Isao, "Sōrōnenki no jisatsu," in Ōhara Kenshirō, ed., *Jisatsu no shinrigaku, seishin igaku* (vol. 3 of *Jisatsugaku*, 5 vols.), Tokyo: Shibundō, 1978, p. 80.

Sōtō Zen Nuns in Modern Japan
Keeping and Creating Tradition

Paula K. R. Arai

I N THE FALL OF 1987, as a travelling scholar of Buddhism, I sojourned to India. At this time I met Kitō Shunkō, an elderly Sōtō Zen nun returning to India for a final pilgrimage to the Mahābodhi Temple in Bodh Gaya. As we walked around the Bodhi Tree her face glowed with the wisdom of enlightenment. Compassion emanated forth from her every motion. Her laughter resounded with the peace found in understanding life and death. I knew after our first conversation under the bodhi tree that I wanted to learn as much as possible about her way of life. She was a living model of all that I had been studying. This nun embodied harmony in its richest form. What teachings have helped her gain such wisdom? How did she train to be so compassionate? Where is the spring of her ebullient laughter?

As we walked along the Nirange river where Śākyamuni once walked, a brilliantly pink sun rose into the sky. She wove stories of the years she spent in India building the Japanese Temple in Bodh Gaya with poetry by the Zen master Eihei Dōgen Zenji (1200–1253) and information about a nunnery, Aichi Senmon Nisōdō, in Nagoya, Japan. We laughed heartily as the image of meeting again in this nunnery worlds away flashed through our minds.

NUNS IN PERSPECTIVE

Nuns have been a vital and important facet of Buddhism since the original Sangha was formed during Śākyamuni Buddha's lifetime (c. 566–486 BCE). To date, however, nearly all scholarly research has focused primarily on the male monastic experience and history within the tradition. Recently, however, there has been increasing attention to nuns within the Buddhist tradition.

The first ordained Buddhist in Japan was a nun named

Zenshin-ni. She took the tonsure in 584 CE. Shortly thereafter, two women, Zenzō-ni and Ezen-ni, became her disciples.[1] In 588, they again made history by being the first Japanese to go abroad to study. They undertook the strenuous voyage to China in pursuit of a deeper understanding of the monastic regulations.[2] Another landmark in Japanese Buddhism is that the first Buddhist temple in Japan was an *amadera*,[3] Sakurai-ji, founded in 590.[4] Although these monumental moments in the development of Japanese Buddhist history illustrate the fact that nuns were a significant force in the introduction of Buddhism to Japan, their vital contribution has been relegated to rare footnotes and scarce publications.

尼寺

My exploration into the world of Japanese Buddhist nuns concentrates upon the Sōtō sect of Zen, for it is the largest and most organized sect of nuns in Japan. Presently there are about 1,000 Sōtō nuns, followed by approximately 400 Jōdo-shū nuns, and around 300 Rinzai Zen nuns.[5] The Sōtō-shū has the highest number of nunneries, three (Aichi Senmon Nisōdō, Niigata Senmon Nisōdō, and Toyama Senmon Nisōdō), compared to the Jōdo-shū, which has one (Yoshimizu Gakuen of Chion-in). The other sects do not have a special school for the sole purpose of training nuns.

My study of Sōtō Zen Buddhist nuns focuses on the foremost Sōtō nunnery in Japan, Aichi Senmon Nisōdō. This nunnery, the first autonomous school established for nuns, was founded in 1903 by four nuns during the Meiji years of rapid modernization. Since then Japan has spiraled to the peak of technological accomplishment. The quality of life at the nunnery, however, remains a living kernel of the traditional arts and values of Japanese culture.

The current abbess of Aichi Senmon Nisōdō, Aoyama Shundō, is a woman widely respected within the tradition by virtue of her spiritual excellence and her being among the first women to be granted an education at the Sōtō sect's Komazawa University. Her reputation extends into the broader Japanese society through her numerous books and articles written for the laity on topics including tea and zen and spiritual development. The international scholarly community is familiar with her work in religious dialogue. Therefore, under the leadership of Aoyama Sensei, Aichi Senmon Nisōdō is a vital resource for exploring the various facets of the dynamic life of nuns in Japan.

Through Kitō Sensei's introduction, I spent four months in training at the nunnery, from 1 September to 23 December 1989. My academic background in Japanese Buddhism, personal religious orientation, and Japanese cultural heritage (my mother is a native Japanese) enabled me to segue into the rhythm of life within the cloistered walls of the nunnery with a minimum of discordance. This phase of participant observation was a rare opportunity to examine at first hand the nuns' daily pattern of study and meditative discipline.

The daily schedule of the nunnery is similar to that of any standard Zen monastery, for they all use as their base Dōgen's *Eiheishingi*. Dōgen wrote these regulations in a thorough and meticulous fashion. It is designed to teach the disciples to act in accordance with the Dharma in each and every activity—to treat all life with respect, to purify the mind of illusions of self and other, good and bad, desire and dislike. The ideal behind this method is to make the regulations and ideals of the Sangha an internalized mode of living, rather than an external set of regulations to be obeyed. No actual system, of course, is as perfect as the ideal that can be articulated on

永平清規

4:00 a.m.	*shinrei* 振鈴, wake up
4:15	*zazen* 坐禅
5:00	*chōka-fugin* 朝課諷経, morning sūtra chanting
6:15	*seisō*, daily morning cleaning of nunnery
7:30	breakfast
8:00–12:00	time for classes, *samu* 作務 (working together—gardening, cleaning, preparation for events), or private study
12:00	lunch
12:30–3:00	classes, *samu*, or private study
3:00	tea
4:00	*banka* 晩課, evening sūtra chanting
4:30	*hattō sōji*, clean Worship Hall
5:30	*yakuseki* 薬石, dinner, which consists of the day's leftovers
6:00–8:00	private study in one's own room
8:15	*yaza* 夜坐, nightly *zazen*
9:00	*kaichin*, lights out

Morning and evening services at the Aichi Senmon Nisōdō.

paper. Nonetheless, the training at the nunnery seeks to free one from the delusions, desire, and ignorance that plague most sentient beings. Although modifications of some of the regulations have been permitted due to the changes in technology since Dōgen's time, the rhythm of life at the nunnery retains the spirit of Dōgen's ideal.

The key to finding peace in the midst of the strenuous schedule at the nunnery is to accept the fact that the present moment is important. What must be done, must be done. One just does what is necessary. To rebel against this reality only causes one to suffer. To contemplate "maybe" or "later" only means that one must fight against these wishes *and* keep pace with the others. Yet, to accept the task before you and to do it with your whole heart leads to joy and freedom. These are words that many acquainted with Zen practice are familiar with. I was, too. But in the midst of it, I found out just how true they are. When it is cold, it is cold. When your right knee hurts, it hurts. When the morning wake-up bell rings, you wake up. When the bell in the *zendō* is struck, you stand up. When the gong is struck, you go to eat. When the *samu* drum is beaten you go to work. It is as simple as that.

Preserving the traditional schedule, this nunnery allows the nuns to bathe, shave their heads, and do laundry on days that contain either a 4 or a 9. At times when the heat and humidity of Nagoya persisted, I dreamt of pouring the water for the flowers over my own wilting head. At these moments I felt the tenacity of tradition. Yet, it is precisely because the nuns do not waver on these details that they are genuine living bearers of the Zen tradition.[6]

The structure of the nunnery is organized around the various tasks that must be performed to make the nunnery function. They are divided according to the system that originated in Chinese Buddhist monasteries.[7] Since the nunnery is small, it presently functions with a minimum number of divisions, or *ryō*: *Ino-ryō*, *Chiden-ryō*, *Tenzo-ryō*, and *Anja-ryō*. The *Ino-ryō* is responsible for making decisions, informing everyone of events, and making sure everyone abides by the rules. The next in rank of importance is the *Chiden-ryō*. The primary function of those in this division is to take care of the worship hall, the ceremonies, and rituals. They also go out to *zaike* homes (laity) and chant sūtras upon request. This is one of the most common activities of nuns once they graduate from the nunnery, so their time in the *Chiden-ryō* is an invaluable opportunity for new nuns to learn the various rituals a nun is expected to perform. The *Tenzo-ryō* is one of the vital organs of the nunnery. The *tenzo* must prepare all the food for the nuns in a nutritious, economic, and aesthetic fashion. Here one learns how to prepare vegetarian dishes with creativity, for the *tenzo* must wisely use all the food donated to the temple without any waste. The *tenzo* has the power and responsibility of keeping the nuns healthy and happy. The final division has the sensitive responsibility of taking care of the guests of the nunnery. The *Anja-ryō* members learn how to be gracious to lay visitors, high *rōshi-sama* (Zen masters), and guests off the street. This interface with various sorts of people is a time for refining the art of understanding people's varying needs and feelings.

Responsibilities are rotated each semester, so that all the nuns can learn the various things that go into running a temple. Since their numbers are small, nuns tend to get a more thorough training than their male counterparts in large monasteries. Each nun usually has the chance to be in each division at least twice during the minimum two-year program. The small numbers also allow each nun to be responsible for more within each division. This makes them strong and competent members of the Buddhist clergy when they graduate.

Another dimension of the *ryō* system of organization is

that the nuns' rooms, the seating order in the *zendō*, the seating order at meals, and bathing order is determined by their *ryō*. The result is that the nuns in any given *ryō* must do everything together during their tenure in that *ryō*. It is an efficient and effective method for learning to cooperate with any kind of person that crosses your path. The situation is perhaps exacerbated now that the composition of communities of nuns has become more diverse. In earlier times the nuns were all about the same age and had similar backgrounds. The range of ages (presently 21–71) is the most striking source of tension and misunderstanding. Furthermore, the nuns come from previous experiences as diverse as having been the associate director of a company to being the daughter of a *yakuza* (Japanese mafia). All the nuns agree that human relations are the most difficult aspect of training.

THE EDUCATING OF ZEN NUNS

The nunnery offers elementary through advanced levels of training. The first rank, *yoka* (Preparatory Curriculum Degree), requires two years of training at the nunnery while completing a high-school education. Most women, however, enter with a high-school diploma, so they enter straight into the *honka* (Basic Curriculum Degree) training. During these two-year programs the nuns learn to chant the sūtras, perform the various necessary ceremonies and rituals, cook *shōjin ryōri* (Japanese vegetarian food), clean, sew religious garments, take tea and flower lessons, do zazen, and take a number of academically oriented courses on Buddhist texts. The third level of advancement is a two-to-three-year program for *kenkyūsei* (Research Curriculum Degree). This is considered the level where the nuns refine what they have learned in the previous years. Since many ceremonies and rituals only occur once a year, it requires many years to perfect and deeply understand the complicated ritual motions and profound meaning embodied in the various ceremonies. The highest level of training is called *tokusō*, the Advanced Curriculum Degree. Most nuns do not complete this training, for it is a long and challenging program. Although they are still in training themselves, they become responsible for the younger nuns' training. Completing this training qualifies them for becoming a high-level teacher.

精進料理

Among the required activities for all levels of nuns are taking courses in a number of Buddhist texts. *Rōshi* from other temples come to the nunnery to teach these courses. Among the texts studied is the *Gakudōyōjinshu* (*Points to Watch in Practicing the Way*) by Eihei Dōgen Zenji. It is vital for the nuns in training for it covers fundamental issues such as the necessity of arousing Bodhi-mind, the importance of finding a true teacher, and the basics of harmonizing body and mind. Keizan Jōkin Zenji's (1268–1325) text, *Zazen-yōjinki* (*Things to be Careful about Regarding Zazen*), is read with keen interest for, among numerous essential things, it instructs the new nuns on more mundane aspects of zazen, such as how to keep from getting sleepy (focus your mind on your hairline). It describes the kind of clothing suitable for zazen—not luxurious, not rags, comfortable—and cautions one to eat moderately lest one get sick. Breathing techniques are also described to help enable one to find harmony of body and mind. Dōgen's *Shōbōgenzō zuimonki*, recorded by Koun Ejō Zenji (1198–1280), is also scrutinized for it is a text that records original talks Dōgen gave to his disciples in training at Kōshō-ji. The main teaching of this text instructs the disciples how to see impermanence and egolessness. Although the majority of the nuns do not have the time, training, or inclination to analyze these texts philosophically, they understand the core of these texts with their bodies.

The educating of nuns also includes the study of Chinese poetry, or *kanshi*. Providing a foundation in reading Chinese, poetry enables nuns to gain a broader perspective and interpretation of Buddhism as it interplays with culture. Buddhist sermons, or *hōwa*, are also practiced, for the nuns will be expected to give sermons on various occasions throughout their career once they leave the cloistered walls of the nunnery. One of the favorite classes, *dōwa*, or children's stories, challenges the nuns to express their understanding of Buddhist teachings in a simple and creative way. The nuns take turns telling stories to one another, and the ones who listen enjoy reverting to childhood innocence and happy-go-luckiness.

Saihō—sewing Buddhist garments—is also an integral activity within the nunnery. All the nuns learn to sew all the garments necessary for a nun. This includes a *kesa*, *rakusu*, *zagu*, *koromo*, and *kimono*. Most nuns begin with sewing a *rakusu*. A *rakusu* is a miniature, symbolic version of a *kesa*.

漢詩

法話

童話

裁縫

Preparing for calligraphy practice.

Kesa are the only robes worn by the ordained in Theravādin countries, as it was in the days of early Buddhism. But as the Dharma moved to cooler climates and sundry cultures, the robes of monks and nuns also underwent appropriate transformations. The Chinese added the *koromo*, a long-sleeved robe, and the Japanese added another layer underneath, the *kimono*. Nuns and monks also began to include working, whether it be tilling fields, cooking meals, or cleaning floors, as an essential dimension of Buddhist practice. Since it was cumbersome to work with so many layers, the modified *kesa*, the *rakusu,* was developed. Zen nuns frequently sew *rakusu* for their beloved teachers and friends. The tiny stitches required for making a *rakusu* are seen as an expression of the commitment one has to the Dharma; thus, to offer a *rakusu* as a gift is a highly symbolic gesture. Once one masters the intricate pattern of a *rakusu*, one can advance to the complicated, but meaningful, project of sewing one's own *kesa*. This is usually preceded, however, by the sewing of the *zagu*, or kneeling mat, since it is a much less involved piece. Many of the nuns then go on to sew their own *koromo* or *kimono*, but this requires great amounts of time. During their tenure at the nunnery this is usually not reasonable. But all the nuns learn how to sew tiny stitches in straight lines. The Abbess, Aoyama Sensei, frequently reminds them that this is the same way one follows the path of Buddhism—taking tiny steps in a straight line (a line of pure concentration on the Dharma)—not an easy task.

At Aichi Senmon Nisōdō, along with the traditional Zen training that includes *zazen*, chanting sūtras, studying Buddhist texts, sewing, cooking, and cleaning, the nuns include flower arranging, calligraphy, and tea ceremony as integral elements of their training. Mastery of these contemplative arts is not an ornamental supplement to their training but is required for receiving the certificates of graduation the nunnery offers. The nuns take tea and flower lessons throughout their tenure in the nunnery. The teachers of these arts, of course, are also nuns. They teach not only the basic skills of the arts, but they also teach the philosophy, more commonly called *kokoro* (heart-mind) in these circles, that accompanies 心 these arts. These arts thus simultaneously train the body, mind, and heart. This philosophy is based upon the principle that the body, mind, and heart are one. One soon learns that to perform these arts with beauty requires a clean spirit that draws on the deepest resources of one's *kokoro*. To teach the hand to pour water into the tea bowl is to teach the heart the way of compassion and wisdom.

Goeika, or its Sōtō-shū version, *baika*, is becoming an 御詠歌 梅花 increasingly necessary art for the nuns to acquire. *Baika* is a recently developed form of singing songs based upon the scriptures. The singing is accompanied by a bell and chime that the singer strikes in rhythm with the melody. As in all Japanese arts, there is an elaborate and meticulous pattern of ritual-like motions that helps the singer enter into a contemplative and focused state appropriate for putting Buddhist scriptures to song. It has become an extremely popular activity for lay women particularly, so a nun graduating from the nunnery must be able to lead such groups. Some of the nuns choose to concentrate on this art, while others choose the tea ceremony or flower arranging.

These arts serve as vehicles for practice, but they are also necessary skills for performing the various activities in a temple. It is, however, perhaps no coincidence that the arts that the nuns practice are also the arts expected of a proper Japanese woman. The monks do not practice these traditional arts as the nuns do. Although at all temples flowers must be arranged and tea served to guests, monks usually consign these tasks to their wives, whereas nuns must do these activities on their own. Another aspect of the nuns' involvement in these traditional arts gives insight into the nuns' contribution to general Japanese society. Many of the nuns teach tea or flower lessons in their temples. The students are not necessarily Buddhists, but they are women interested in refining their skills and hearts. Teaching these traditional arts not only allows the nuns to make an impact upon the cultivation of Japanese women, it also serves as a means by which nuns may make an acceptable form of income. Most temples run 檀家 by nuns do not have parishioners, or *danka*, so they must find other means of support. An investigation into the role of the traditional arts in the lives of the nuns is a multifaceted issue. Through the traditional arts the nuns reveal the beauty of their spirit, their independence in running a temple, the sociological ramifications that impinge upon their lives, their contribution to preserving traditional culture in contemporary Japanese society, and their economic ingenuity.

BUDDHIST ACTIVITIES AND CEREMONIES AT THE NUNNERY

写経 There are various monthly activities held at the nunnery that help train the nuns in basic temple responsibilities. *Shakyō*, sūtra copying, is an activity, like all activities, primarily attended by lay women. The most commonly chanted sūtra in the nunnery is the *Heart Sūtra*, and so it is no surprise that this is the sūtra everyone copies. Another activity that is open to the public is the *Nichiyō-sanzenkai*. One Sunday each month is designated for allowing anyone to experience a day of Zen lifestyle. Women come from all over, near and far, to participate in this. Aoyama Sensei, the abbess, gives two talks during this day of zazen and zen-style eating. Most people find the day a little painful, but worth every bit. They keep coming back for more. This is another opportunity for the nuns to learn how to interact and help the laity. It is also a chance for the nuns to be reminded of their own progress, for they were once in the position of those whose legs ache and could not enjoy eating because there were too many details to remember during the meal.

摂心 *Sesshin* (intensive zazen sessions) are also open to the public, but they are mainly for the deepening of the nuns' training. These are held once a month, usually for three days. They also have a long *rōhatsu sesshin* in December and a five-day-long *sesshin* in February. These periods of concentrated practice become part of the rhythm of the lifestyle. Many nuns look forward to this time, because it means diminished interaction with others. Most of the life in the nunnery involves intense human relations, so it is a chance where nuns may rest from this more stressful aspect of life in the nunnery. Another activity at the nunnery is the holding of the Dharma Lineage ceremony. This is a ceremony where laity can receive the precepts and a *kaimyō,* or precept name, usually reserved for the deceased or the ordained. Most temples do not perform this elaborate ceremony, for it is demanding in terms of time, money, energy, complexity of ritual, and in seriousness. The nuns at this nunnery, therefore, are extremely fortunate to have the rare opportunity to learn the intricacies of this solemn ceremony. It places them in the important position of being able to assist with this ceremony when they graduate.

戒名

Ceremonies punctuate the life of a nun. The first ceremony that all experience is the *tokudoshiki.* This is the ceremony at which a woman shaves her head and dons the robes that will be a part of her life from that moment on. It becomes her new birthday. Many nuns enter directly into the nunnery after they have taken the Bodhisattva Vows.

得度式

The ceremony for entering the nunnery brims with commitment, excitement, and hope for the future. Yet, it is also a time of uncertainty and readjustment. Everyone is learning how to put on a *kesa,* how to chant sūtras, how to eat properly, and where to place their slippers. They must even learn to respond to their new Buddhist names. This year, 1990, was an especially joyous time, because for the first time in ten years the nunnery received ten new women at one time. The numbers of entering nuns has been steadily diminishing for the last few decades, but this year there was a turn in events. This brought joy, relief, and hope to all.

During their tenure in the nunnery the nuns will participate in and perform many ceremonies, but one of the most powerful and intimate is the ceremony to Ānanda. Ānanda is special to the nuns for he interceded to Śākyamuni on behalf of the first women who wanted to enter the Dharma. Through Ānanda's persuasion, Śākyamuni allowed the order of Buddhist nuns. Nuns have not forgotten Ānanda's act of compassion and wisdom.

The graduation ceremony is another moving moment in the life of the nuns. For some it means leaving the nunnery after five to seven years of training. Most, however, graduate after two years. In all cases, these years of training have inevitably been filled with a myriad of experiences, feelings, and insights into their own hearts. It is a noble life through which they persevered. They do not leave the same as they entered. Their hearts have been polished like stones in a tumbler, becoming rounder, smoother, and brighter with each motion of interaction with the other nuns, teachers, and laity affiliated with the nunnery.

LIBERATION AND TRANSFORMATION: RECENT CHANGES IN REGULATIONS

Secular and sacred realms have undergone unprecedented changes during this century. Nuns are fewer in number due to increased opportunities for women in the secular sphere, but advancements in official recognition of nuns have enabled them to take on new roles and responsibilities. Regulations authorized by the Sōtō-shū Shūmuchō[8] have moved in the direction of greater equality between monks and nuns. For most of Sōtō Zen history nuns were subordinated and not given opportunities for proper training or education. Therefore, they were also not allowed into positions of power or responsibility. They were expected to clean, cook, and sew for the monks. They watched the ceremonies from the sidelines, in between chores. Now the nuns have come into their own. The quirks of history have put them into the position of being the living holders of the traditional Zen lifestyle, precisely because they were expected to follow a stricter set of regulations in the past. The monks were given freedom after freedom, while the nuns were kept under close rein. Now the world of the nuns is a harbor for the traditional values and lifestyle of Zen. They generally continue the rhythm of life they learned in training at the nunnery, they remain celibate, and they do not have access to opportunities for making any sizeable amount of money.

In 1941 the Sōtō sect headquarters officially pronounced that nuns were only allowed to care for the lowest-ranking temples, called *heisōchi*. These were small temples with no parishioners. At that time the highest rank a nun could attain was lower than the lowest rank for monks. In 1953, however, all Buddhist sects in Japan underwent drastic modification. At this time the nuns were given more opportunities. They were officially permitted to become head priests (*jūshoku*) of *hōchi* temples, the middle-ranking temples in the system. In 1978 nuns were also allowed to attain the rank of *nidaioshō*, a title indicating high respect and accomplishment. But in 1989 the Shūmuchō took off the prefix *ni* (which means nun), 尼 for they were concerned that this prefix was a remnant of discrimination.[9] Indeed, the nuns have blossomed during this century. They established the first Zen nunneries to train nuns exclusively, they gained equal rank with monks, and they continue to live in accordance with traditional Zen values.

Through surveys and interviews I have gained a fuller picture of the present conditions of the nuns in contemporary Japan. I sent surveys to 150 Sōtō nuns all over the country. I also conducted extensive interviews of all the nuns I was in training with in 1989. They have helped me understand the motivations of women who chose to commit their lives to Zen training in the modern age. Through them I gained some insight into their self-perception and the way in which they are perceived by Buddhist laity. Many seem to perceive their monastic experience to be fundamentally different from that of their male counterparts in terms of motivation, incentive, obstacles, and attitude towards the monastic regulations in daily life. The profile of the nuns that emerged through this data elucidated the practical and cultural functions of Sōtō nuns in Japanese society. These nuns both continue the traditions of Zen culture that began to blossom in the Muromachi period (1338–1573) and cultivate methods and expressions that are unique to women committed to the tonsure in modern Japan.

The profile of the nuns first entering the nunnery has undergone a radical change. Just 40 years ago the average entering age of a nun was 16, but the present average entering age has risen to 43. This fact alone suggests the various other differences in the composition of the novice nuns now, versus that in the 1950s. Nuns now frequently enter the nunnery from a lay family, rather than having been raised in a temple environment. The majority of women entering now have had their own families or careers before taking their robes, whereas in the past the tender age at which most women shaved their heads precluded other life experiences. Thus, the women now make a conscious and mature decision to commit their lives to the Dharma, a difficult decision for a young girl to make who has donned a *kesa* upon the request of her parents.

Nonetheless, the survey results show that the vast majority of nuns make a serious attempt to abide by the precepts in their daily lives. It therefore seems natural that the nuns express a high level of consciousness towards social responsibility. Almost all the nuns suggested that one of their primary social responsibilities is to listen attentively to the needs of others, and to help them find peace in their daily lives. A significant number of nuns are also active in volunteer work, primarily focussing on the needs of orphans and the elderly. Nuns attempt to fill a vital niche in modern Japanese society. Their presence is critical. Although the number of nuns has diminished,[10] the quality of each nun seems to be increasing. In part this is due to the increase in quality of life and education in Japanese society as a whole, but it is precisely this increase in the quality of life in general that has bred women who seriously consider their options and deliberately choose to commit their lives to the Dharma. Herein lies the hope for the future of Buddhist nuns.

CONCLUSION

The history of Zen nuns in this century illuminates a vital stream in Japanese society and culture. Nuns can serve as a model for all women who seek liberation. In two generations they have gone from a position of little opportunity and recognition to a position of official equality, complete with independent institutions for nuns. They have taken unprecedented strides in educational possibilities by founding independent schools and nunneries for training nuns. This century saw the first nuns educated and graduated from the Sōtō-shū's prestigious Komazawa University. Sōtō nuns also formed their own organization in 1944, *Sōtō-shū Nisōdan*, which has since published its own journal entitled *Otayori*. They have gone from only being permitted ranks lower than the lowest monk's to being granted the title *Daioshō*. Yet in the midst of these significant advancements, they maintain the genuine quality of the Buddhist tradition.

The story of Zen nuns gives a more accurate account of Japanese Buddhism. Their motivations differ from most monks who take the tonsure as a result of a hereditary system. Nuns make an independent and personal commitment to the Dharma. Nuns, therefore, maintain a relatively traditional lifestyle in the midst of a technologically superior society. They also help preserve the traditional arts of Japan by teaching them in their original spirit: training for the body, mind, and heart. Contemporary Japanese society leaves little room for traditional arts and Buddhist values, yet the small number of quality nuns keep these alive. Nuns are living treasures of Japanese Buddhism.

NOTES

* This article first appeared in the *Bulletin of the Nanzan Institute for Religion & Culture* 14 (1990): 38–51. Reprinted by permission. Paula K. R. Arai received her Ph.D. in Japanese Buddhism from Harvard University and is currently Lecturer in Humanities at Hong Kong University of Science and Technology.

[1] Tajima Hakudō *Sōtōshū nisō-shi*, Tokyo: Sōtōshū Nisōdan Honbu, 1955, pp. 112–13. This work is the most comprehensive text written on Japanese Buddhist nuns. Other texts include Aichi Senmon Nisōdō's *Rokujūnen no ayumi*, written in celebration of their 60th anniversary. Various other texts help fill in the picture of the nuns, including the magazine published by the Sōtōshū Nisōdan, *Otayori*. Aichi Senmon Nisōdō also publishes a magazine, *Jōrin*.

[2] Tajima, *Sōtōshū nisō-shi*, p. 14.

[3] This is a temple headed by a nun. *Ama* means nun and *tera* or *dera* means temple. There is no equivalent in English, since there is no situation calling for one. I therefore prefer to use the transliteration.

[4] Tajima, *Sōtōshū nisō-shi*, p. 14.

[5] *Shūkyō nenkan* [Religion yearbook], Tokyo: Gyōsei. It is extremely difficult to get an accurate count of the number of nuns in each sect, for the definition of female teacher *(kyōshi)* has broadened considerably in recent years. Before World War II this term referred primarily to nuns, but now it also includes lay women teachers. I have tried to calculate the number of nuns in a traditional definition of nun: women who shave their heads, have taken the bodhisattva precepts, trained at a nunnery, live in a temple, and wear a *kesa* all the time. Tendai and Shingon nuns also exist, but I have only been able to determine that their numbers are less than those of the Rinzai sect.

[6] Nuns generally retain this rhythm of life even after leaving the nunnery. They continue to rise early, clean their own temple daily, chant sūtras, arrange the flowers, and cook. I have yet to meet a lazy Zen nun.

[7] See Holmes Welch's *The Practice of Chinese Buddhism 1900–1950* (Cambridge: Harvard University Press, 1967), chapter 1, for a more complete description of the traditional division of labor in a monastery.

[8] The Sōtō-shū Shūmuchō is the official administrative office of the Sōtō sect. It determines the regulations, keeps the records, and functions as the guiding force behind Sōtō affairs. The major Buddhist sects in Japan have their own *shūmuchō*. The Sōtō Shūmuchō is located in the Tokyo Grand Hotel near the Tokyo Tower.

[9] I am concerned, however, that without the distinction of monk or nun *Daioshō*, it is easier to hide the fact that few nuns are granted this status. I would rather see them keep the prefix *ni* and add the prefix *nan* to monks who gain this title.

[10] The present numbers are also on the brink of a drastic reduction, for 52% of present Sōtō nuns were born before 1928.

PART 4

New Religious Movements

Introduction to Part 4

New Religious Movements

SHIMAZONO Susumu

*J*APANESE SOCIETY entered a period of rapid modernization from the mid-nineteenth century. As in other areas
of social activity, religious communities also underwent drastic change. On the one hand, traditional religions
and religious institutions rooted in village communities faced
decline, and on the other hand, religions with their social
base in urban areas increased significantly. Over the past century, a variety of new religious movements have attracted
many followers and created many new religious groups.

CHRISTIANITY AND NEW RELIGIONS

Christianity also found its place in the context of these new
religious groups. By the 1870s Protestant and Catholic missionaries from various Western countries had arrived in
Japan and established strong bases for evangelism in places
such as Nagasaki, Yokohama, Tokyo, and Sapporo. Since
then and in spite of intense efforts, however, the Christian
churches have not been able to attract a large number of
members. Even today only about 1% of the population claim
membership in a Christian church. There are a number of factors related to Christianity's lack of success in Japan. Until
the end of World War II, educational policies based on State
Shinto and nationalistic sentiments inhibited the development of Christian churches. Furthermore, because Christianity was initially accepted by the old samurai (*bushi*) upper
class, it was not able to gain a widespread following among
the common people.

In contrast to the situation in Korea, where Christianity
has become deeply rooted in the religious life of the common
people, both Protestant and Catholic forms of Christianity
remain alien to the religious life of most Japanese. In addition

to these transplanted forms of Christianity, there are also some indigenous Christian organizations or communities founded by so-called "minor founders" (see the article by **Mark Mullins**). These indigenous movements, along with Christian-related new religions such as the Mormons, Jehovah's Witnesses, and the Unification Church, are movements that deserve serious consideration in this context.

The role that Christianity is playing in Korea has been filled in Japan by the so-called New Religions. Already by the end of the Edo Period (early to mid-19th century), Kurozumi-kyō and Misogi-kyō had gained a considerable number of followers. At the turn of the century (early Meiji Era) Tenri-kyō, Konkō-kyō, and Honmon Butsuryū-shū achieved rapid growth. This is considered the first period of new religious movements. Ōmoto is representative of the second period, from late Meiji through the Taishō eras (early 20th century). The third period (Shōwa era, around 1926 to the mid-1970s) includes the period of rapid growth for groups such as Hito-no-Michi (later Perfect Liberty Kyōdan), Reiyū-kai, Seichō-no-Ie, Sekai Kyūsei-kyō, Risshō Kōsei-kai, and Sōka Gakkai. Increasing numbers of organizations were founded, particularly in the postwar period, with more and more people joining these groups.

Sōka Gakkai, the largest of these new religious movements, claims a membership of over seventeen million. However, the actual active membership is probably nearer to three to four million. Statistics are not available on the true number of new religious groups, but some scholars have estimated that they number over three thousand. It is also estimated that between ten to twenty percent of the total Japanese population is involved in one or more of the new religions.

The founders of these new religious movements in many cases have been men or women without a high social standing, who have experienced many personal hardships and created their own religious faith after involvement in a variety of religious practices and traditions. Since their faith is often syncretistic and eclectic, it is often difficult—not to say misleading—to identify one religious tradition as the only source of their religious inspiration. Another prominent feature of these new religious movements is the great diversity of their teachings, practices, and rituals. The tendency in the Japanese religious world to combine and mix elements from

Buddhism, Shinto, folk religion, and various other sources, is reflected in the pluralism of the New Religions. In spite of this diversity, it can be said that there are two main sources for most new religious movements. One is the Nichiren tradition based on the *Lotus Sūtra*, represented by such groups as Sōka Gakkai and Risshō Kōsei-kai. The other is the syncretistic folk tradition characterized by the quest for magical healing and salvation. In this collection we have included an article on each of these types: **Anson Shupe**'s study of Sōka Gakkai and **Richard Young**'s study of Mahikari.

CHARACTERISTICS OF THE NEW RELIGIONS

A this-worldly orientation is one of the defining characteristics of the New Religions. Rather than rejecting this world and seeking salvation in the world after death, New Religions tend to place great value on this current life, and offer the hope of relief from suffering in this world. The strong appeal of New Religions lies in the promise of this-worldly benefits, such as deliverance through faith in the gods (kami) and/or buddhas from problems that arise due to illness and poverty. Many people have been attracted to them by their promise to cure illness through magical rituals.

It goes without saying that physical "healing" (*byōki* 病気なおし *naoshi*) is not the only goal of the New Religions. Many have also been concerned with solving the fundamental problems of Japanese society and creating an ideal society through faith in the power to transform the world (*yonaoshi*). Rooted in 世直し this *yonaoshi* faith, Ōmoto and Sōka Gakkai are two New Religions that became active in movements for political reform. However, the aspiration to realize religious ideals in this world through political means met with strong opposition from society at large. In time, the ambition to transform the world did not translate into concrete results, and these movements were forced either to find hope in an ideal society in the future or compromise and take a more realistic position with regard to social reform. As Shupe's study shows, Sōka Gakkai has taken the latter path.

Many of the New Religions also have the goal of personal transformation, often referred to as "healing the heart" (*kokoro* 心なおし *naoshi*). There are a variety of causes leading to human unhappiness. There are groups, like Mahikari, that place a great emphasis on spirits of the dead (human or animal), while other movements prefer to explain misfortune in connection with the ancestors or previous lives. Even more widespread is the explanation of problems in terms of evil or impure "hearts." In this case, the causes of unhappiness are the conditions of the heart, including malice, jealousy, ill-will, or self-centered desires and feelings, rather than human behavior or action. Consequently, in order to be delivered from unhappiness, one's heart must be transformed into a "good" or "pure" heart. In concrete terms, *kokoro naoshi* means developing a "good" heart that avoids conflict and is kind and accepting of others—in short, strives for harmonious human relationships.

The moral norms implied in such ideals are closely related to the group-oriented values of Japanese society. By teaching and encouraging the practice of these moral norms, New Religions contribute to the stability and cohesion of the family and other social groupings. At times New Relgions function in a conservative way to maintain the established social order, but in many cases they serve to provide stability in the face of new social environments and new human relationships. The new religious organizations provide the basis for new and intimate human relationships apart from previously existing social groups. This is one of the roles of Japanese New Religions overseas (see the article by **Shimazono**).

A conspicuous feature of the religious activities and social organization of the New Religions is large-scale popular participation. The activities of local groups are characterized by close relationships and gatherings of fellow members. Problems of everyday life are understood in religious terms that all the members share and discuss together. Any and all members are expected to actively participate in group activities and the propagation of their faith. No distinction is made between clergy and laity, and one's religious advancement depends on effort and ability rather than on one's social class or background. In fact, the most powerful social group supporting local activities and giving birth to numerous leaders has been middle-aged housewives, who suffer from a relatively low social standing.

THE POST-1970 SITUATION

Since the 1970s the established New Religions entered a difficult period of development. Japanese New Religions outside of Japan began to flourish from about this time, but within Japan many established New Religions, such as Sōka Gakkai, faced the problem of stagnation. Accompanying the decline of the established New Religions has been the development of the so-called "new New Religions" (the fourth period of the New Religions).

A variety of groups fall under this category of "new New Religions," and many are not so different from previous New Religions. However, it is possible to identify some new distinguishing features. First of all, it could be said that the strong concern with this-worldly healing has weakened to a certain extent. In its place there is a greater concern with the problem of meaninglessness and the loss of fulfillment in life. Changes in the type of problems faced by the Japanese have brought with them changes in the goals and aspirations offered by the New Religions. The concern for a happy family and working life has declined, and in its stead there is an increasing concern with life after death and personal inner fulfillment. Although miracles and mystical techniques and practices are still regarded as important, the emphasis has shifted from their practical application in group life to that of personal experience and individual fulfillment.

Changes in religious group life have accompanied this shift in emphasis. Previously, local religious groups were characterized by members helping each other with the problems of everyday life. Today, however, when these close-knit groups are created there is a tendency to separate from the larger society and create a monastic or separate religious community, as seen in the Unification Church or Aum Shinri-kyō. In other cases new New Religions use the mass media and sponsor large gatherings and events, and do not rely so much on local groups to maintain religious activities. These types of activities are certainly more appealing to contemporary youth in Japan, and in fact many more members of the younger generation have joined in a new New Religion than was the case with the earlier movements.

It could be, however, that the new New Religions are not the most representative religious movements of the period since the 1970s. In urban areas in modernized societies around the world, there are growing religious movements that do not create religious organizations nor emphasize participation in group activities. These movements are shaping each other as they develop simultaneously. In the West this is often referred to as the "New Age" movement, while in Japan it is often referred to in terms of the "spiritual world." These movements can be seen as local manifestations of a single global phenomenon, which I call "new spirituality movements."

From the point of view of these new spirituality movements, earlier religions with their hardened doctrines and institutional forms have restricted individuals and prevented them from realizing their full spiritual potential. What is important is that each individual search and discover their own inner being, develop their own spirituality, and bring about their own spiritual transformation. For such personal purposes, techniques such as meditation, ascetic training, bodywork, and psychotherapy are offered as forms of practice and combined with the study of ancient mysticism, archaic religions and myths and shamanistic rituals, and psychological theories. Followers of these new spirituality movements maintain that the age of doctrinal-type religions is over, and that humanity is entering a new stage in the evolution of consciousness, of which they are the new representatives.

It is not that there were no such individualistic religious movements before the 1970s, but since that time their development has been particularly prominent. One long-term trend over the past century has been the continual decline of traditional religious groups and communities, and the corresponding development of New Religions. Since the 1970s, however, the situation has changed significantly. It appears that we have entered a period in which movements that sought to create New Religions have declined, while the number of people pursuing an individualistic spiritual quest have increased. It appears that this trend will continue well into the 1990s.

➤   ➤   ➤

The following tables give a list of the major New Religions, the names of their founders, and membership figures for representative years. Table 2 provides information on representative new New Religions.

TABLE 1

STATISTICS FOR MAJOR NEW RELIGIONS

	Organization	Founder	Founded	Number of Members		
				1954	1974	1990
1st Period	Nyorai-kyō	Isson-nyorai Kino (1756–1826)	1802	75,480	407,558	295,225
	Tenri-kyō	Nakayama Miki (1798–1887)	1838	1,912,208	2,298,420	1,839,009
	Kurozumi-kyō	Kurozumi Munetada (1780–1850)	1814	715,650	407,558	295,225
	Konkō-kyō	Konkō Daijin (1814–1883)	1859	646,206	500,868	442,584
	Honmon-Butsuryū-shū	Nagamatsu Nissen (1817–1890)	1857	339,800	515,991	526,337
	Maruyama-kyō	Itō Rokurōbei (1829–1894)	1870	92,011	3,200	10,725
2nd Period	Ōmoto	Deguchi Nao (1837–1918) Deguchi Onisaburō (1871–1948)	1899	73,604	153,397	172,460
	Nakayama-Shingoshō-shū	Kihara Matsutarō (1870–1942)	1912	282,650	467,910	382,040
	Honmichi	Ōnishi Aijirō (1881–1958)	1913	225,386	288,700	316,825
3rd Period	En'nō-kyō	Fukada Chiyoko (1887–1925)	1919	71,654	266,782	419,452
	Nenpō-shinkyō	Ogura Reigen (1886–1982)	1925	153,846	751,214	807,486
	Reiyū-kai	Kubo Kakutarō (1892–1944)	1924	2,284,172	2,477,907	3,202,172
	Perfect Liberty Kyōdan	Miki Tokuharu (1871–1938)	(1925)*	500,950	2,520,430	1,259,064
		Miki Tokuchika (1900–1983)	1946			
	Seichō-no-le	Taniguchi Masaharu (1893–1985)	1930	1,461,604	2,375,705	838,496
	Sōka Gakkai	Makiguchi Tsunesaburō (1871–1944) Toda Jōsei (1900–1956)	1930	341,146	16,111,375	†17,736,757
	Sekai Kyūsei-kyō	Okada Mokichi (1882–1955)	1935	373,173	661,263	835,756
	Shin'nyoen	Itō Shinjō (1906–1989)	1936	155,500	296,514	679,414
	Kōdō Kyōdan	Okano Shōdō (1900–1978)	1936	172,671	417,638	400,720
	Risshō Kōsei-kai	Naganuma Myōkō (1889–1957) Niwano Nikkyō (1906–)	1938	1,041,124	4,562,304	6,348,120
	Bussho Gonenkai Kyōdan	Sekiguchi Kaichi (1897–1961) Sekiguchi Tomino (1905–)	1950	352,170	1,210,227	2,196,813
	Tenshō Kōtai Jingū-kyō	Kitamura Sayo (1900–1967)	1945	89,374	386,062	439,011
	Zenrin-kyō	Rikihisa Tatsusai (1906–1977)	1947	404,157	483,239	513,321
	Myōchikai Kyōdan	Miyamoto Mitsu (1900–1984)	1950	515,122	673,913	962,611

TABLE 2

STATISTICS FOR THE NEW NEW RELIGIONS (4TH PERIOD)

Organization	Founder	Founded	Number of Members 1974	1990
Ōyama Nezunomikoto Shinji Kyōkai	Inaii Sadao (1906–1988)	1948	59,493	826,022
Byakkō Shinkō-kai	Goi Masahisa (1916–1980)	1951		(1989) 500,000
Agon-shū	Kiriyama Seiyū (1921–)	1954	500	206,606
Reiha-no-Hikari Kyōkai	Hase Yoshio (1915–1984)	1954		761,175
Jōdoshinshū Shinran-kai	Takamori Kentetsu (1934–)	1958		(1984) ‡100,000
Unification Church	Moon Sun Myung (1920–)	1959		—
Sekai Mahikari Bunmei Kyōdan	Okada Kōtama (1901–1974)	1959		97,838
Sūkyō Mahikari		1978		501,328
Honbushin	Ōnishi Tama (1916–1969)	1961		‡900,000
G.L.A. Sōgō Honbu	Takahashi Shinji (1927–1976)	1969		12,981
Shinji Shūmei-kai	Koyama Mihoko (1910–)	1970		(1988) ‡440,000
Nihon Seidō Kyōdan	Iwasaki Shōkō (1934–)	1974		69,450
ESP Kagaku Kenkyūjo	Ishii Katao (1918–1993)	1975		‡16,000
Hō-no-Hana Sanpōgyō	Fukunaga Hōgen (1945–)	1980		‡70,000
Japanese Raelian Movement	Claude B. Rael (1946–)	1980		‡3,000
Yamato-no-Miya	Ajiki Tenkei (1952–)	1981		‡5,000
Aum Shinri-kyo	Asahara Shōkō (1955–)	1984		
Cosmomate	Fukami Seizan (1951–)	1986		‡30,000
Kōfuku-no-Kagaku	Ōkawa Ryūhō (1956–)	1986		(1989) ‡13,300 (1991) ‡1,527,278

* The (1925) date refers to the Hito-no-Michi Kyōdan, the mother organization of Perfect Liberty Kyōdan.

† Sōka Gakkai has not released figures for 1989 and 1990, so this figure is the membership numbers for 1988.

‡ Most of the statistics in these charts are from the 1991 edition of the *Shūkyō Nenkan* (Religion Yearbook, Tokyo: Gyōsei). Numbers marked with ‡ are from other sources reporting the organizations' own membership statistics around 1990.

§ For religions introduced from abroad, the year of its establishment in Japan is given as the "founding" date.

Note: These are membership statistics for Japan only, and do not include members outside Japan.

FURTHER SUGGESTED READINGS

DAVIS, Winston. *Dojo: Magic and Exorcism in Contemporary Japan*. Stanford: Stanford University Press, 1980.

EARHART, H. Byron. *The New Religions of Japan: A Bibliography of Western-Language Materials*. Second Edition. Ann Arbor: Center for Japanese Studies, The University of Michigan, 1983.

———. *Gedatsu-Kai and Religion in Contemporary Japan: Returning to the Center*. Bloomington and Indianapolis: Indiana University Press, 1989.

GUTHRIE, Stewart. *A Japanese New Religion: Risshō Kōsei-kai in a Mountain Hamlet*. Ann Arbor: The University of Michigan, 1988.

HARDACRE, Helen. *Lay Buddhism in Contemporary Japan: Reiyūkai Kyōdan*. Princeton: Princeton University Press, 1984.

———. *Kurozumikyō and the New Religions of Japan*. Princeton: Princeton University Press, 1986.

———. "Gender and the Millenium in Ōmotokyō." In *Religious Innovation*, M. Williams and C. Cox, eds. Leiden: E. J. Brill, 1992.

INOUE Nobutaka, ed. *New Religions*. Contemporary Papers in Japanese Religion, vol. 2. Translated by Norman Havens. Tokyo: Institute for Japanese Culture and Classics, Kokugakuin University, 1991.

MCFARLAND, H. Neill. *The Rush Hour of the Gods. A Study of New Religious Movements in Japan*. New York: The Macmillan Company, 1967.

MULLINS, Mark R. "Japan's New Age and Neo-New Religions: Sociological Interpretations." In *Perspectives on the New Age*, James R. Lewis and J. Gordon Melton, eds. Albany, NY: State University of New York Press, 1992.

MULLINS, Mark R., and Richard F. YOUNG, eds. *Japanese New Religions Abroad*. Special double issue of *Japanese Journal of Religious Studies* 18/2–3, 1991.

READER, Ian. "The rise of a Japanese 'new New Religion'—Themes in the development of Agonshū." *Japanese Journal of Religious Studies* 15/4: 235–62, 1988.

SHIMAZONO Susumu. "Charisma and the evolution of religious consciousness: The rise of the early New Religions of Japan." *The Annual Review of the Social Sciences of Religion* 6, 1982.

———. "Spirit-belief in new religious movements and popular culture: The case of Japan's New Religions." *The Journal of Oriental Philosophy* 26/1: 90–100, 1987.

———. The development of millennialistic thought in Japan's New Religions: From Tenrikyō to Honmichi." In *New*

Religious Movements and Rapid Social Change, James A. Beckford, ed. Newbury Park, CA: Sage, 1987

Tsushima Michihito, et al. "The vitalistic conception of salvation in Japanese New Religions: An aspect of modern religious consciousness." *Japanese Journal of Religious Studies* 6/1–2: 139–61, 1979.

Wilson, Byran R. "The New Religions: Some preliminary considerations." *Japanese Journal of Religious Studies* 6/1–2: 193–216, 1979.

Sōka Gakkai and the Slippery Slope from Militancy to Accommodation

Anson SHUPE

ELIGION, AS GERMAN sociologist Max WEBER (1964) observed, has both *prophetic* and *priestly* forms. Prophetic religion is challenging, unsettling, and even revolutionary. Priestly religion, on the other hand, settles in, makes peace with the status quo, and casts off the faith's raw, unconventional "edges." Priests and prophets, even within the same religious tradition, make poor bedfellows because they are fundamentally antithetical types.

The transformation from prophetic to priestly religion is of interest to sociologists because it involves the organizational transition from a deviant social movement to an establishment institution. Part of this transition concerns the religion's relation to the state. Young prophetic religions often reject the larger society (of which politics is a part) as corrupt and unholy, and thus they may discourage members from active political involvement. But a more mature group must come to terms with the state and, indeed, may even seek to influence it. What then are the implications of political activism for the prophetic mission of such a religion? Can a prophetic form of religion survive encounters with the political establishment without coming out compromised, dirtied, and co-opted? This essay examines the process of religio-political accommodation in post–World War II Japan, using the Sōka Gakkai movement as a case in point.

NICHIREN SHŌSHŪ AND SŌKA GAKKAI

Nichiren Shōshū [the "True" Nichiren school] was founded in thirteenth-century Japan by Nichiren (1222–1292), a charismatic figure in whom were mixed the roles of ultra-nationalistic patriot, saint, and prophet. After studying various forms of traditional Mahāyāna Buddhism, Nichiren became convinced that the *Lotus Sūtra* contained the most succinct and essential form of the historical Buddha's message. Nichiren went so far as to teach that all other scriptures and Buddhist schools were either heretical or at best redundant with the truth in the *Lotus Sūtra*. He preached that merely chanting the name of the *Lotus Sūtra* (*namu myōhō renge kyō*—"Hail to the Wonderful Truth of the *Lotus Sūtra*") could invoke divine benefits and gain salvation for the believer in the next existence while also bestowing such temporal benefits as good health and prosperity in this life.

南無妙法蓮華経

According to Nichiren Buddhism, Nichiren Daishōnin (the "Great Holy Sage") surpassed the accomplishments of even Śākyamuni, the historical Buddha. Such a claim is not unusual in Japanese religious history. Members of various "new religions" (*shinkō shūkyō*) have often elevated their prophets and sect founders to the status of demigods or divine beings, creating numerous "founder cults" (see HOSHINO 1987). An article in *The Soka Gakkai News* (1978), for example, explains that:

新興宗教

> He [Nichiren] revealed the ultimate Buddhist teaching, to which his two predecessors Śākyamuni, or Gautama, and the Tendai sect in which Nichiren studied had aspired yet never realized in practice. Nichiren Daishōnin took as his starting point the secret, ultimate wisdom that all outstanding Buddhists since the time of Śākyamuni had acquired as part of final enlightenment, yet never had been able to expound because the time was not ripe.

Thus, Nichiren himself came to be regarded as a Buddha. And not merely a Buddha, but instead the Buddha for our doomed age of *mappō* (the "last days" of the Buddhist Law), when all other religions have become misguided or downright malevolent. It is clear that Nichiren the man believed that true faith was to vanish from the earth until the coming of the future (messianic) Maitreya Buddha (ELLWOOD 1974: 84). The world had become so hopelessly corrupt, he preached, that the path to nirvāṇa as originally taught by Śākyamuni was no longer possible for most persons. The assistance of Bodhisattvas—advanced beings who sought out enlightenment not only for themselves but for others—was necessary. The key to success in the spiritual life, Nichiren claimed, lay solely in the *Lotus Sūtra*, a claim that later Nichiren followers used to justify an exclusivist, intolerant approach toward other sects and religions.

末法

Sōka Gakkai (Society for the Creation of Value) is a lay Buddhist movement, officially established in 1951 and until recently affiliated with the Nichiren Shōshū sect.[1] An earlier, more secular version was founded in 1937 as Sōka Kyōiku Gakkai (Society for Education in the Creation of Values) by Makiguchi Tsunesaburō, a Tokyo elementary-school principal with a philosophical bent towards what we now call existentialism. He was later joined by another public-school official, Toda Jōsei, who added managerial talent to Makiguchi's intellectual interests. Together they formed a social movement of personal regeneration and affiliated it with Nichiren Shōshū shortly before World War II.

In 1941 Nichiren Shōshū resisted a government decree to consolidate with eight other Nichiren groups and participate in obligatory State Shinto worship. Both Makiguchi and Toda were imprisoned in 1943, and Makiguchi died a martyr in prison. The allied Occupation in 1945 brought release for Toda Jōsei, however, and he took charge of the surviving Sōka Kyōiku Gakkai. He shortened its official name to Sōka Gakkai, substituting more emphasis on evangelistic, practical Buddhism for Makiguchi's educational thrust. In doing so he transformed the movement into its postwar form: a proselytizing/mobilizing arm of Nichiren Shōshū, some ten to fifteen million members strong (BRETT 1979: 366; ELLWOOD 1974: 91).

As with most successful modern religious movements, the evolution of Sōka Gakkai has been rapid. The movement has "mellowed" many of its more belligerent (some say outrageous) proselytizing tactics and shifted beyond concerns of mere personal salvation to global humanitarian outreach. However, its political entrepreneurship is the best indicator of the extent of Sōka Gakkai's accommodation to mainstream Japanese society.

THE SŌKA GAKKAI FORAY INTO POLITICS

Sōka Gakkai entered Japanese politics within a decade after World War II and only four years after its inception. In 1955 a member of the group's board of directors was elected to Tokyo's prefectural assembly, and thirty-three other Sōka Gakkai candidates were elected to their ward (neighborhood) assemblies. In 1962 the Gakkai-affiliated Kōmekai, or Clean Government Association, first registered with the national government, and in 1964 this became the Kōmeitō (Clean 公明党

Government Party), a full-fledged political party.

The Kōmeitō was much publicized as a distinct "alternative" to the corrupt status-quo politics of the dominant Liberal Democratic Party. Both Kōmeitō and Sōka Gakkai leaders boldly proclaimed reformist intentions for the party. They denounced the amorality of Japan's entire electoral system and proclaimed to the nation that their candidates and elected officials would—because of their high Buddhist moral principles—be immune to the bribery and corruption so rife in Japanese electoral politics. Their Buddhist commitment to world peace would presumably lead them to resist all military entanglements (such as permitting United States military bases in Japan), and their steadfast religious faith would help stem the danger of atheistic communist influence in Japan. More broadly, it was hinted that their grounding in the nationalist zeal of Nichiren would restore Japanese pride and return the nation to its preeminent place in the community of nations.

Since 1955 Kōmeitō (or Sōka Gakkai–related) candidates have vigorously taken part in local, prefectural, and national races. In 1956, for example, three of four Sōka Gakkai candidates won seats in the House of Councilors (the National Diet's Upper House). Six Sōka Gakkai candidates won Upper House seats in 1959, each obtaining nearly three million votes. By the late 1960s the Kōmeitō had grown to become the third-largest political power in the National Diet (taking into account both the Upper and Lower Houses), behind the conservative Liberal Democrats and the Japan Socialist Party, but ahead of the older Democrat Socialist Party and the Japan Communist Party. As the Liberal Democrats have gradually lost seats, the Kōmeitō has been able to achieve a considerable amount of leverage in Japan's parliamentary system. Although the party formally separated from Sōka Gakkai in 1970, almost all of Kōmeitō's candidates and supporters are Sōka Gakkai members (BRETT 1979: 370; JOHNSON 1976: 39).

The Kōmeitō is not the only example of a Japanese "New Religion" becoming involved in the political system. Various scholars concur that it is a common practice for these groups to endorse and openly support particular political candidates.[2] However, most of these groups do not possess either local constituencies that can successfully field local candidates or sufficiently large national memberships to elect their own members. Sōka Gakkai has both. In large cities (particularly Tokyo) its "dense" interpersonal networks have successfully recruited uncommitted "floating votes," i.e., persons not integrated into tightly structured bailiwicks whose votes were once "delivered" to politicians by landlords, village headmen, office managers, union officials, or local politicos. Floating votes tend to be those of migrants, young semiskilled laborers, and apprentices not tied to big corporations or to labor unions (and therefore missed by both the Japan Communist Party and the Japan Socialist Party; see IKADO 1968: 106–108). They fit the profile of the typical Sōka Gakkai member: lower-class socioeconomically and of low formal education (DATOR 1969: 59–105).

SŌKA GAKKAI AND POLITICAL COMPROMISE

Although prophetic religion shuns compromise, pragmatism constitutes the essence of politics. Dogmatic or idealistic intransigence never provides access to the corridors of power or leads to change in a parliamentary democracy. The Kōmeitō has had to deal with this fact.

For example, numerous candidates may register in a particular district. In this sense, Japanese political races resemble American party primaries. Ten candidates of party X may hypothetically run for three seats, but few will receive enough votes to win, and most will simply be siphoning off votes from the others. Thus the number of same-party candidates in any race is delicately negotiated by potential candidates and party officials. In the same way, if candidates from separate parties are sufficiently similar so that they will be appealing to the same type of voters, it may be decided through discussion (however tacitly or informally) how to avoid pitting "redundant" candidates against each other, splitting a finite number of votes and possibly allowing some mutually disliked third-party candidate to win.

During the past decade and a half the Kōmeitō has cooperated in various elections with the moderate Democratic Socialist Party so as to maximize the chances of the former's candidates winning office. The Kōmeitō has likewise done parallel maneuvering with the majority conservative Liberal Democratic Party (LDP), which has seen its own support base eroding in recent years.[3] This cooperation is ironic, since the LDP was once the prime target of the Kōmeitō's denunciations about corruption and big money. Now, however, the LDP is more often in need of allies than it once was, and with the Kōmeitō the third largest party in the Japanese National Diet, the LDP is in more of a position to grant concessions in exchange for participation in coalitions. At present the two parties' overlapping stances on such conservative issues as pro-nationalism are more often stressed than the rhetoric of corruption and reform. Such cooperation between the LDP and the politicians of the Kōmeitō also contributes to the latter's appearance of respectability (SAMUELS 1982: 633).

Also aiding the Kōmeitō's political efforts is what many observers see as a "centrist" trend in postwar Japanese elections. Voters seem weary of the unkept promises and radical rhetoric of the left (i.e., Japan Socialist Party and Japanese Communist Party) as well as the "business-as-usual," ethically gray politics of the reigning LDP (e.g., the bribery scandals of the 1970s and 1980s; see UCHIDA and BAERWALD 1978; SAMUELS 1982). BLAKER (1978) sees an "emerging consensus" along moderate lines on which the Kōmeitō (with its claims to be following a nonaligned "middle way" in politics) has been able to capitalize. This suggests that the Kōmeitō has surrendered its pretensions to be a genuine alternative to the murky partisan world of Japanese political life in exchange for political legitimacy. In the process it has transformed itself into a valuable bargaining ally of the status-quo party, the LDP.

On the other hand, both the Kōmeitō and Sōka Gakkai can be accused of opportunism and violation of their own principles. In October 1977 the Kōmeitō and Democratic Socialist Party leaders announced their mutual intention never to enter into any local coalition in which communists were participating. (Kōmeitō leaders stressed their party's standard objection to Marxism's atheistic doctrines.) Yet, despite this agreement there was actually an increase in the number of coalitions across the nation in which the three parties participated (SAMUELS 1982: 634). Even more indicative of Kōmeitō and Sōka Gakkai willingness to accommodate to political temptation was their *sub-rosa* dealings with the "atheistic" communists. It is now well known that the secretary general of the Japanese Communist Party sought an alliance with the Kōmeitō through Sōka Gakkai during the mid-1970s. Meetings were held between various leaders of the JCP and Sōka

Gakkai, including the latter's president, Ikeda Daisaku. By December 1974, a "secret" ten-year accord of rapprochement was reached and signed without other Kōmeitō leaders being informed (JOHNSON 1976: 39). The Kōmeitō immediately renounced the agreement. Sōka Gakkai leaders quickly tried to back-peddle, claiming that they only had meant "coexistence" with the JCP, but the JCP insisted that the understanding of the agreement was "joint struggle" and cooperation. The issue was never resolved and proved an embarrassment for Sōka Gakkai. Needless to say, a number of persons in both camps felt betrayed.

THE LESSONS OF SŌKA GAKKAI AND THE KŌMEITŌ

The pressures on any unconventional religion to modify its doctrines and activities toward less radical forms are obvious. Respectability and legitimacy ease persecution and rejection, and are beneficial for recruitment and membership retention. Fewer resources need be expended to repel attacks by opponents and competitors, freeing time and energy for more productive pursuits.

The pressures within such a group to achieve *proximate* as well as *ultimate* goals are strong. Achieving proximate goals lends a sense of successive approximation toward ultimate goals. The former serve as immediate rewards, or reinforcers, that help morale and promote a sense of validity about the latter. Each rung on the ladder achieved, believers reason, confirms the validity and practicality of seeking larger ultimate ends.

But a common fate awaits prophetic religions that wish to achieve political structural change and decide to use nonviolent or conventional means to do so. Proximate goals such as increased public respectability, influence in legislative bodies, better relations with the mass media, and cooperation of other power groups—which are what the Sōka Gakkai/ Kōmeitō have achieved in Japan—become consuming. They involve moderation and compromise that divert the movement from its ultimate goals.

Prophetic religion deals with ultimate goals, as do prophetic/ revolutionary politics. Together they can upset regimes and create new large-scale possibilities. Neither set of values and goals have much stake in the status quo. However, prophetic religion and proximate politics (e.g., "the politics of moderation") are a poor mix from the religion's standpoint. Prophetic religion is inevitably the loser in such instances, for it ends up compromising its principles. For all its rhetoric about meaningful reform, Sōka Gakkai's Clean Government Party has had to wade into the swamp of Japanese electoral politics and has come away muddied. Those politics, on the other hand, have remained relatively unchanged from their contact with the Kōmeitō. It is Sōka Gakkai and the Kōmeitō that have had to adapt to a new set of rules. With the loss of their affiliation to the strident Nichiren Shōshū sect, it is conceivable that both Sōka Gakkai and the Kōmeitō may move even closer to embracing the politics of compromise and jettison their more exclusivist religious values.

NOTES

* Anson Shupe is Professor in the Department of Sociology and Anthropology at Indiana University–Purdue University, Fort Wayne, Indiana.

[1] The recent parting of the lay group and the sect seems to have been over matters of financial and administrative control and may prove irrevocable. Certainly neither side seems willing to make the first move toward reconciliation. See ASTLEY 1992 and MÉTRAUX 1992.

[2] See, for example, DAVIS 1980: 257, and CURTIS 1971: 198.

[3] For example, the Kōmeitō supported the same candidate as the Liberal Democrats in eight prefectures in 1979 and opposed no Liberal Democrats (see SAMUELS 1982: 633).

Magic and Morality in Modern Japanese Exorcistic Technologies

A Study of Mahikari

Richard Fox YOUNG

O BSERVERS OF JAPANESE New Religions are much perplexed by the unanticipated resurgence, especially among the new New Religions (*shinshinshūkyō*) such as Mahikari and Agon-shū, of belief in spirits, the decline of which had long been predicted as an unavoidable sacrifice to modernization. Contrary to some social-science theorists who maintain that rationality—the sine qua non of all processes by which societies transcend primitive or feudal institutions—is antithetical to spiritism, what we see in Japan today suggests the very opposite. Rather than an archaic cognitive anomaly, contemporary spirit-belief might better be understood as an expanded rationality with its own modality of logic. Spiritism is not simply compatible with modernity but is also capable of enhancing the meaning of life in Japan's highly urbanized and industrialized society, where often a sense of disconnectedness prevails that no dose of pure, scientific, or empirical reason appears able to cure.

新新宗教

Not only disinterested specialists but also those who actively preserve Japan's elite or established religions, which, at least in principle if not in practice, have traditionally been antagonistic to spirit-belief, are puzzled by its revival. Their consternation is articulated by Sasaki Shōten, a Jōdo Shinshū theologian, who laments,

> We, who had been looking down on the New Religions as premodern, even primitive, and have made great efforts to show that our Buddhism can coexist with science, now are confronted with the idea that the true match for a scientific-technical world is spirit-belief, the magical, pseudo-scientific, manipulative type of religion (SASAKI 1988: 32).

Elite religion, as Sasaki notes, has in the modern era aligned itself with elite culture by reasserting the intrinsic rationality of Buddhist theories of causality, without, it should be added, discarding the necessity of faith in the absolute efficacy of savior deities such as Amida whose compassion resolves the apparent contradictions of life. Nonetheless, traditional salvation religions, just as modern rationalism, appear to be ineffective in counteracting the trend in popular culture and religion toward belief in spirits, precisely because of their simplicity. Such spirits are increasingly regarded as a wrongly neglected link in the chain of cause and effect, and to recognize their existence seems to more satisfactorily interpret the complex world of today that the creative forces originally released by rationalism generated but no longer fully explain.

What follows below is not concerned with establishing whether or not spirits exist as scientific fact, but rather to explore the logic of, and the meaning derived from, the beliefs of individuals who have joined New Religions that regard their reality as indisputable. First, I will briefly draw attention to what current research has to say in connection with the revitalization of spirit-belief. To sort this complex data out, I will differentiate, as H. Byron EARHART has done in his most recent study of a Japanese New Religion (1989), between enabling and precipitating factors. However, as I am convinced that socio-historical forces alone cannot account for the reemergence of spirit-belief, I will introduce the exorcistic ritual of Mahikari as an instance of innovation in Japanese spiritism that can, as such, be considered paradigmatic of a whole cluster of contemporary New Religions. Finally, in view of the fact that modern forms of spirit-belief are an explicit challenge not only to modernity itself and to traditional Japanese salvation religions but also to Christianity, I offer some reflections on how the spiritism exemplified by Mahikari has universalistic aspects embedded in its Japanese particularity that have elicited a vigorous if not yet massive response from abroad.

MEAN STREETS, MALEVOLENT SPIRITS

What enables spirit-belief to emerge in present-day Japan in the first place? For, as far as the wider society is concerned, spiritism is unorthodox, an offense against reason, and a return to premodern thought.

The at-hand answer is that its antecedents are the worship of household divinities, the ancestors, and the pacification of wandering and angry spirits that has characterized the totality of Japanese religion (with the possible exception of Christianity) in varying degrees at all levels of popular and elite religion from the earliest times until the beginning of modernization. Although transformed in a manner that shall be noted later, current spirit-belief arises out of this vast reservoir.

This matrix of spiritism was a necessary precondition for the reappearance of similar beliefs in modern society, but what precipitated their reawakening from a period of relative dormancy, considering the primacy of rationalism in Japan's furious pace of modern nation-building dating from the second half of the nineteenth century?

With the onset of modernization, the social cohesion of village communities broke down when the solidarity of individual households was weakened by the departure of second and third sons as emigrés to cities where the infrastructure of the newly industrialized, market-based economy of Japan was being developed. In rebellion against the anonymity of urbanized life and to counteract the arbitrary groupings of unrelated peoples whose interaction was mainly governed by competitive commercial instincts, utilitarian and communitarian religious movements emerged that promised to restore the communal support and solidarity of the old rural social order, albeit in the changed context of the city.

Chronologically, however, the first New Religions arose in the first half of the nineteenth century, before modernization, in village environments where one would assume that spirit-belief was most deeply rooted. In point of fact, rural-based movements such as Tenri-kyō and Konkō-kyō, which have never enjoyed a substantial urban following, were centered on parent-deities (*oyagami*), which, though they did not deny the existence of ancestral and other spirits, relegated them to a position of relative unimportance.　親神

Beginning with the Meiji era, however, and with heightened intensity in the Taishō and early Shōwa eras, by which time the most dramatic aspects of demographic change in Japan were largely complete, such urban New Religions as Ōmoto-kyō, Seichō-no-Ie, and Reiyū-kai had outpaced older village-based rivals. Symptomatic of these newer urban movements was a renewed conviction that spirits exist, not merely benign ancestral spirits but also spirits so malevolent that even the benevolent parent-gods of rural Japan seemed weak in comparison.

Why, then, did this trend toward spiritism occur in tandem with the process of modernization? In his analysis of spirit belief in modern Japanese urban society, SHIMAZONO Susumu (1987) has traced this phenomenon to a number of factors, among which only a few can be mentioned here.

According to Shimazono, if spirits are factored into the environment as but one among many causal elements that can be organized, dominated, and manipulated, they can then complement, without competing with, the technological-manipulative frame of mind that scientific reasoning and rationalistic education foster. Belief in savior- or parent-deities, on the contrary, cannot key into this modern attitude, because of its tendency toward unicausality, or the conviction that the will of God determines all the seemingly contradictory phenomena of life. The implication here is that the individual ego is not negated in spiritism, as it tends to be in traditional salvation religions and village-based New Religions. On the contrary, the I-Thou relationship with God, although present in spirit-belief, is less restrictive. There the ego is free to give full play to its powers of experiential and inductive logic to construct meaning in apparently happenstance situations without the necessity of introducing a compassionate God as *deus ex machina* (SHIMAZONO 1987: 96–97).

Shimazono further argues that urban life, unlike rural life—at least as it used to be before modernization—is never static; it demands a constant input of new configurations of knowledge to keep abreast of change. But without the psychological backup of the traditional household religion, the pressure-cooker atmosphere of cities becomes nerve-wracking. There has consequently been an increased vulnerability among relocated branch-families in urban settings to fear of disturbances caused by spirits. Such spirits are meaner and more malicious relative to the perceived threat in the surrounding environment.

But to live with a sense of resigned arbitrariness, that all is determined by chance or necessity, is alien to the contemporary belief in spirits, just as it is to modern rationalism.

Spiritism today functions in an urban environment more complex and uncertain than was envisioned by traditional salvation religions or pre-modernization New Religions. Yet it does empower individuals to live with more certitude, precisely because its expanded vision of rationality, which includes hidden factors of causality (spirits), does not deny the basic validity of natural or empirical chains of cause and effect.

The perceived inadequacy of rationalism is not that it fails to explain how events occur but rather that it abstains from saying why. Medical science, for instance, teaches that germs or bacteria cause illness, but according to the etiology of illness as understood by spiritism, people become sick because they ingest illness-causing agents at the behest of spirits. Spirit-belief thus draws a tighter net of causality around the experience of what the world-at-large calls misfortune or plain bad luck.

There can be no question, however, but that involvement with malevolent spirits, especially those that inhabit this world, is regarded by the public-at-large as deviant behavior, even by many who continue to believe in the presence of ancestors who are near at hand. This bias, too, derives from modernization; it is not just a feeling, as I have often heard Japanese put it, that talk of spirits is "creepy." As SHIMAZONO notes,

> When rationalism seeps down to the masses, it carries with it the ascetical ideal of hard work and frugality. In order to survive within the mercantile economy of capitalism, one needs to succumb to the ascetical ethos, systematizing the things of life and investing energy in highly efficient economic activities. The ascetical ethos...rejects the expenditure of energies on sentimental behavior and emotional satisfaction. Things like belief in spirits are dispensed with as literally worthless. By the 1970s, however, the booming Japanese economy reached a critical transition point, marked by a decline in the "ascetical ethos," that is, a tendency toward less preoccupation with production and more willingness to attribute value to introspective, emotional, or non-rational activities. (1987: 98)

THE DIVINE MAGICIAN-PHYSICIAN

The above observations have outlined how spirit-belief has not only been preserved in modern Japan but also transformed so that nowadays it dovetails neatly with the demands of urban life and even reinforces the values of industrial society. What has not yet been pinpointed precisely is the innovation in *tekhnē*, skill, that sets as its objective the manipulation of means to exert control over the hidden spirits believed to be external to the self, for only a development in this connection could continue to fuel the resurgence of spiritism. As an instance of a significantly new spiritual technology, the exorcistic ritual of Mahikari called *mahikari no waza* (the Mahikari technique), or, more simply, *okiyome* (purification), will be discussed below.[1]

真光の業
お浄め

Mahikari's institutional history spans no more than three decades, but its prototype, "world-renewal" religion (*yonaoshi-shūkyō*), appeared first in the late nineteenth century with the advent of Ōmoto (The Great Foundation). Originally, Ōmoto pivoted around a parent-like divinity, Ushitora no Konjin. He was believed to have returned to this world after aeons of enforced exile, having been overthrown by the collective power of lesser deities, under whose slack administration the world had declined into chaos.

世直し

Deguchi Nao (1837–1918), the foundress of Ōmoto, saw evidence of the world's need of renewal mainly in the socio-political upheavals brought on by Japan's rapid industrialization. This radical emphasis was muted when her successor, Deguchi Onisaburō (1871–1948), affirmed modernization and instead found proof of impending world catastrophe in an alleged upsurge of cases of spirit possession. Onisaburō revived the ancient mediumistic practice of *chinkon kishin* (pacification of spirits–return to divinity), a ritual whereby individuals were exorcised of evil spirits, which were then transformed into guardian spirits (*shugorei*).

鎮魂帰神

守護霊

In one form or another, the world-renewal motif of the eclipse and return of the good god, combined with an exorcistic technique to dispel evil influences, characterizes the entire cluster of New Religions descended from Ōmoto (e.g., Sekai Kyūsei-kyō [World Messianity] and Byakkō [White Light], including its most recent offshoot, Mahikari).[2]

The origin of Mahikari dates to 1959 when its founder, Okada Kōtama (1901–1974), according to his own account, was awakened from his sleep at five in the morning and inspired with a revelation from the Revered-Parent Origin-Lord True-Light Great God, who, like other world-renewal deities, had returned to this world after a time of withdrawal. Su-God, as his elegant name is abbreviated, who is a deity of yang-like attributes: austere, righteous, strict, and whose essence is fire announced to Okada that he would no longer tolerate a world maladministered by inferior deities of yin-like attributes: sensual, apathetic, and lenient, whose essence is water. The priority of Su-God, as a deity of fire and light and preeminently of the sun, is to cleanse the world of the evil spirits that lesser deities could not constrain, and to purge the human body of defilement, especially the toxins and wastes produced by modernization that result in illness and unnatural death.

Having chosen Okada to be the savior, Su-God, the True God of Light (whence the organizational name, Mahikari [True Light], is derived), declared his intention of bathing the world in a Baptism of Fire, a healing light for the people who respond to it, but a burning and destructive light to those who hide themselves from it. If the imbalance between good and evil in the world cannot be corrected, Su-God will incinerate the world. The deadline is said to be A.D. 2000.

Aside from Su-God himself as the original source, True Light is emitted from his throne on earth, the shrine called Suza,[3] and from the scroll inscribed with the characters "True Light" that hangs over the altar in every Mahikari practice hall (*dōjō*), and from an amulet (*omitama*) worn by members 御み霊 (the efficacy, or thickness of the rays of this light is in descending order of listing). The world is said to be constantly flooded in True Light, but the practice hall is where its power is primarily put into effect as the purification ritual is enacted, during which an intricately standardized procedure is carried out. Members sign an attendance register on arrival at the practice hall, write a wish (generally accompanied by a donation), offer a prayer to Su-God, bow and clap in several sequences, greet other believers, pair off, and intone another prayer, the Prayer of Heaven, in classical Japanese with Shintoesque diction. Only then do they commence to purify one another with True Light, one person at a time in alternating active-passive roles. Considered to be the focal point of True Light, the palm of the hand is directed at the partner's forehead, behind which the primary soul is said to be located. Possessing spirits are thought to reside here, and the purification ritual invariably begins with a ten-minute exorcistic phase, followed by thirty minutes or more of irradiating the body at various vital points to heal a variety of ills, from stiff shoulders to malignant tumors.

Of principal interest here is the exorcistic phase of purification. Insofar as recruitment is concerned, Mahikari promises quick and miraculous healing, and recovery of health is a primary motivation of most first-time visitors to the practice hall. But health is a commonplace this-worldly benefit (*genze riyaku*) of many New Religions, and to follow this further would be to digress. The Savior was quite explicit that evil spirits can be held accountable for about eighty percent of humanity's misfortunes, and it is therefore to the question of how spirits are purified that attention will be directed.

現世利益

"I am the Divine Magician," Su-God declared to the Savior in one revelation (15/8/1961), and, in another, "human beings can become magicians," too (15/10/1960; OKADA 1982: 129, 105). The source of this empowerment is the amulet. How the amulet is thought to function is a matter of considerable dispute, but to *kamikumite* (lit., "they who walk hand in hand with each other and God"), as Mahikarians are called, it encircles the wearer in protective light. Its energy has no half-life; unlike a battery, it never dies out. Even if the amulet lies disused on a shelf, it has a residual power, although senior members claim that frequent usage by a devout believer will enhance its effectiveness (i.e., the thickness of its rays). Unless it is defiled (e.g., dropped in dirt or water or stepped on), the *omitama* will accompany a *kamikumite* into the afterlife, for it is now customary for the amulet to be cremated with a deceased member. The magic of Mahikari, in short, is that the amulet requires neither belief nor faith to be activated. The "try it and see" advice of *kamikumite* to newcomers is not just pragmatic but symptomatic of the manipulative art or technique of the magician.

神組手

The amulet is thus a shield against harmful influences from the outside, but spirits already residing in one's body can only be dislodged by undergoing the exorcism ritual called *okiyome*, or purification, the invariable format of which runs as follows: The preliminaries described earlier having been completed, the active performer raises a palm over the forehead of the partner in the passive role, discharging True Light. When the primary soul is being cleansed, the

Healing light. Two young women perform *mahikari no waza* at Sekai Mahikari Bunmei Kyōdan headquarters in Izu.

passive participant may begin to sway from side to side. A defensive response to True Light called spirit-movement is considered proof of possession.

Insofar as Mahikari is concerned, possession is an induced or learned behavior. That is to say, it occurs only inside the practice hall during the exorcism ritual. The experience of possession is lucid; members are conscious throughout and remember afterwards what happened. Although *kamikumite* often speak of "hair-raising" first-visit spirit-movements, in most cases these begin to surface only after an individual has been in the practice hall three months or more—ample time to observe and master the required routine.

Spirits that become manifest during purification are liminal. They are malevolent and therefore dangerous, but they are not absolutely evil either. They belong neither to this world nor to the afterworld. Their proper place is the astral world where they await a rebirth to be determined according to their merits by the tutelary deities of Su-God. It is characteristic of Japanese spirit-lore in general and of Mahikari as well, that aggrieved spirits who hold grudges against the living, or who are hungry and cold without the warmth of human flesh, are believed to roam the world of the living in search of appropriate victims. The difference is that Mahikari links the alleged increase in the number of such spirits to the disruption of natural lifestyles due to modernization.

Possession is not, however, an arbitrary misfortune; there is always an explanation based on cause-and-effect logic—no matter how forced, eccentric, and irrational it may seem to nonbelievers. The original casus belli is reconstructed as follows: When the spirit movements of a *kamikumite* become pronounced, a staff member trained to perform spirit investigation (*reisa*) interrogates the manifesting spirit (who speaks or gestures with the mouth or body of the passive participant) and from its responses pieces together a diagnosis, a process that may take months or even longer. Admonition (*osatoshi*) is an essential element of the ritual, for the spirit must be told to return to the astral world because to torment the living will only make its destiny worse. Each session is concluded with the command "*Oshizumari!*" (Peace! Be still!).

霊査

お諭し

The originality of Mahikari is mainly its radical re-identification of who the real victims and assailants in an instance of possession are, as they are unmasked during the purification ritual. Possession is indeed a crisis, but the word "possession," which is suggestive of intent to harm, is problematic in the context of Mahikari. Following the analysis of MIYANAGA Kuniko (1983), a pattern that can be found almost invariably in accounts of spirit-investigations is that the victim of possession in this life was the assailant of the aggrieved spirit in a previous life. To redress this wrong, the victim in the past becomes the assailant in the present. The exchange of roles can be diagrammed thus:

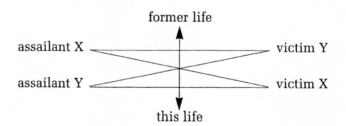

"The assailant," as Miyanaga puts it, "has to experience the misery of the victim by himself being victimized by his original victim" (1983: 222). In this light, possession is to be understood less as punishment than as a plea for the redress of a wrong. What appears, then, to be a crisis is actually the initiation of reconciliation.

Possessing spirits are generally resentful spirits, less often ancestors, and only rarely animal-spirits. To illustrate this process, the third-person testimonial (*taiken*) of a *kami-kumite* will be narrated below, even though it concerns the spirit of an animal. Entitled "Miss Doggie's Story," it runs as follows:

> A middle-aged woman, the mother of two children, visited a [Mahikari] center for consultation because her husband began to have an affair with another woman three months earlier. Immediately she was given a purification ritual. Her possessing spirit was identified as a female dog she had kept in her family for seven years.
>
> Under spirit investigation, [the spirit of the dog said:] "When I was kept in her house, she threw water over my men [male dogs] and blocked me from fulfilling my natural desire to preserve my bloodline. She even locked me up inside the house, so I barked and bit around in vain to let her know I wanted intercourse, which I understood was my right given by the divinity. But she was totally oblivious to my communication. After all I had to leave this present world for the astral world [i.e., died], because of too much frustration. As my resentment remained as strong as before, I possessed her body for revenge. I also drove her good husband to go to another woman to let her know the importance of compassion and harmony. However, she did not reflect on her own misdeed but wished to get her husband back. She is too selfish. Please, make her know that even a dog has this much [sense]." This was an opinion that Miss Doggie stated with a sad and annoyed expression.
>
> [In giving admonition, the teacher says:]
> Your agony is the result of your own defilement. Do understand it and try to be engaged in spiritual discipline and ask for a divine pardon. Furthermore, do not forget about the kindness given by your mistress for seven years. Go back to the astral world.
>
> [The problem was resolved, the woman's husband returned, and the story ends with a moral:]
> This story tells us that we must have compassion and sincerity for all the living beings and spirits. (MIYANAGA 1983: 216ff.)

Possession in the Mahikari context is usually homeopathic and frequently concerned with sexual karma. As the above testimonial indicates, Miss Doggie, resentful of being constrained while in heat, reciprocates by denying her master the normal sexual relations she had enjoyed with her husband, who begins to chase other women. The sequence of role-exchange is exactly as diagrammed above: The victim (Miss Doggie) resents the assailant (her master), and after death possesses the assailant, who in turn becomes the victim. Reconciliation is achieved through spirit-investigation, and knowing what originally went wrong—no matter how outrageous it may seem—results in mutual compassion. Their bondage to one another is thereby terminated, the dog-spirit returns to the astral world, and husband to wife. "The real magic of the [exorcism ritual]", as Winston DAVIS observes, "lies in the fact that some people emerge from the experience in greater control of their lives, and with their health restored" (1980: 153).

It has already been observed above that evil is not understood in Mahikari to be absolute. Possessing spirits are not intrinsically demonic; their salvation is also the salvation of the *kamikumite*. In the overall monistic structure of world-renewal religion, there is no room for a rigid dichotomy between good and evil, even where Su-God himself is concerned, for he is the totality of yang (strict) and yin (lenient) tutelary deities and human spirits, who in the process of creation were refracted from his originally unitary essence. World-renewal deities, beginning with Ōmoto's Ushitora no Konjin, have all undergone a process of self-discipline to refine themselves or, as it is often said, polish their souls, so that they become even better at being gods. They are not less than divine for having had to do so, for the critical quality is their capacity for readjustment. Cosmic imbalances can and do occur—the present age is one such instance. Likewise, the emphasis in Mahikari is on renewal through harmonization, not punitive retribution.

If divine beings occasionally stand in need of some self-correction, so much more so do the children of God, as their human offspring are called in the idiom of world-renewal religion. The process of moral reformation usually commences before an individual becomes a *kamikumite*, when the onset of crisis (prolonged illness, cold human relations, business difficulties, etc.) is sensed. Most first-time visitors to the practice hall arrive in a state of anxiety, having experienced an impasse in life and hoping for a breakthrough. Once the individual has been recruited, trained, and given *okiyome*, the experience of spirit-seizure almost comes as a relief, for it signifies that the crisis is beginning to be resolved.

Symptomatic of crisis-resolution by spirit-investigation is that neither party, the possessing spirit or its victim-in-this-life, demands repentance (*zange*) of the other. Despite the 懺悔 often terrifying stories that circulate in Mahikari, what spirits require is that their victims own up to their mistakes. Genuine malicious intent is rare, if not unknown. Exorcism reveals wrongs that have been committed almost invariably out of ignorance, as in the case of the woman who did what any sensible pet-owner should do—restrain her dog from breeding indiscriminately. Saving knowledge is thus a new awareness of mistakes that could have been avoided, if one had only known better (MIYANAGA 1983: 251). What *kamikumite* learn from their experience of exorcism becomes the basis of their operational, day-to-day morality, and to hear them speak of a newfound concern with altruistic love (*rita-* 利他愛 *ai*) as a result of their purification is not uncommon.

Once *kamikumite* have become sensitized to the reality of the spirit-world, they remain wary of further signs of disturbance. It is imperative, however, that seizures decrease in frequency and intensity after the loose ends of an investigation have been tied together, otherwise the power of Su-God could be called into question. Repeated possessions are therefore rare. But precisely why the ritual is therapeutic is problematic in the extreme, and the symbolic projection of repressed guilt has been one line of interpretation provocatively discussed by Winston DAVIS (1980: 115–60).

Externalization of nearly all life's problems is indeed distinctive of Mahikari (and of much of world-renewal religion in general) and differentiates it from heart-renewal religions (*kokoro-naoshi shūkyō*) such as Risshō Kōsei-kai that inter- 心なおし nalize difficulties encountered in the outside world. Whether despite or because of the exorcism, numerous *kamikumite* among the many I have known claim to have been subjectively renewed, if not always absolutely healed in an objective, empirical, or scientific sense. Nonetheless, the dropout rate among *kamikumite* is high, estimated at eighty percent, and remains high at all ranks, especially if a dilemma arises between trusting Su-God or modern medicine.

THE LAST OPENING OF THE CELESTIAL ROCK DOOR

Religion in Japan has long been geared to the satisfaction of specific human needs and the fulfillment of personal wishes. In modern urban society, this expectation has, if anything, been heightened. Deprived of the solidarity of the household system mentioned earlier, and often engaged in occupations that do not guarantee lifetime employment, the clientele of New Religions seeks an instantaneous payoff to its investment in religion in terms of this-worldly benefits . Mahikari's self-understanding vis-à-vis other established religions arises out of this general orientation: religions that do not deliver the required goods and services (better health, financial rewards, personal happiness, etc.) have outlived their usefulness.

It was noted above that modernity has induced in Mahikari a sense of imminent cataclysm, the Baptism of Fire, toward which the world is accelerating. To slow this headlong rush toward self-destruction so that humanity might develop the spirituality to avert catastrophe, Su-God established the great historical religions of the world, which Mahikari calls brake-religions (*bureiki-shūkyō*). The vitality these religions once had, however, is no longer available, for they have declined into mere "teachings" disinterested in salvific action against possessing spirits. Considering the danger to which these worn-out religions are exposing the world, Su-God elected Okada to be the savior by revealing to him the supra-religion (*sūkyō*) of True Light, a religion of action and not only talk, in comparison to which the established religions (in a wordplay on the character "religion" [*shūkyō*]) are ugly teachings and group-insanity.

崇教

宗教　醜教
衆狂

Critical as it is of the established religions, Mahikari sees itself as the agent of their renewal and not at all discontinuous with them. As such, the Mahikari attitude toward other religions is symptomatic of world-renewal religion as a whole and its myth of Su-God is but a variant of the withdrawal and return of the good god found in Ōmoto. All such world-renewal myths pivot around a motif originally derived from *Kojiki*, an early Japanese chronicle which includes the story of Amaterasu, who hid within a cave in the High Plain of

　　　RELIGION AND SOCIETY IN MODERN JAPAN

Heaven to protect herself from the impertinence of her brother Susano-ō and other kami. As she is the solar-deity, her withdrawal is naturally catastrophic, and her subsequent return is world-renewing.

In the modern revision of the *Kojiki* myth, the present age is the final opportunity for humanity to open the Rock Door of Heaven. This act of emerging from hiding is expressed in a spatial metaphor as the coming of God from the rear to the fore of salvation history. God has, however, spoken fragmentarily during his absence through messengers, the founders of the world's great religions. Paralleling the polarity between "front" and "rear" is therefore another pair of opposites: "revealed truth" and "concealed truth." What has thus far been revealed in the existing religions has proved insufficient to brake the downward spiral of humanity, and now is the critical moment to "put on the throttle" in renewal of the world.

In the idiom specific to Mahikari, this is the era of unification of the five religions (Buddhism, Taoism, Confucianism, Islam, and Christianity), which can be reinvigorated by the practice of exorcism and healing: "[*Mahikari no waza*] is the wondrous method to revive the Five Major Religions and all other teachings" (OKADA 1986: 12). Orthodoxy in the overall structure of the Savior's teachings was, however, a priority almost as high as orthopraxy, and Okada invested immense energy in unveiling what he considered to be the esoteric parts of other religions, Christianity in particular. Okada saw himself as the agent of its renewal in part because he believed he had had an intimate association with Jesus Christ in a former life—a not at all unprecedented claim in world-renewal religions—and that he was the "Spirit of truth" whose coming Jesus had prophesied. With this license, a nationalistic view of world history centered on Japan, and utilizing a discredited pseudo-scientific etymological art called *kotodama* (lit., "word-spirit"), the arcane catalog of 言霊 Okada's "concealed truths" fills several Mahikari volumes. A prominent theme is that Moses and Jesus were Japanese-Jews and that both died in Japan.

Insofar as public relations are concerned, Mahikari refers to the process of religious revitalization as a return to the origin, Su-God, whereby the religions again become what they were intended to be when they began. The esoteric knowledge described above is largely kept by Mahikari to itself, and *kamikumite* are initiated into such matters mainly at the intermediate and advanced levels of training. If the public position is that Mahikari is helping religions recover their original efficacy, in private it teaches that the religions, as presently constituted, are beyond repair and that Christians and others ought to "jump ship" while they still can.

THE TRUE JINGLE BELLS OF GOD ARE RINGING FAR AND WIDE

神
来 鈴

The Savior was fond of the Christmas tune, "Jingle Bells," and—with a play on its phonetic characters in Japanese: *jin* (God), *guru* (or *kuru*; coming), *beru* (bell)—it has become a metaphor of Mahikari's overseas missionary expansion. Evangelism in foreign parts is ardently encouraged, and in North and South America, the traditional fields of missionary endeavor by Japanese New Religions, Mahikari has made more rapid progress than, for instance, Nichiren Shōshū, in enlisting recruits from outside of Japanese immigrant communities.

As is often the case with new religious movements worldwide, Mahikari in the West has been especially effective in recruiting disillusioned or disaffected Christians. But the Francophone nations of black Africa and the Caribbean, where a colonial syndrome is still prevalent, are the spheres of Mahikari's most spectacular progress. French, Swiss, and Belgian missionaries first introduced Mahikari to the Ivory Coast, the Congo, and Zaire, from which it spread to French Caribbean islands such as Martinique and Guadalupe where African slave-culture and spiritism continue to flourish (see HURBON 1991).

Even in the post-colonial context, the equilibrium of traditional culture is precarious, threatened both by modernity and the Christian monotheism of established, Western-educated elites. In these areas, Mahikari and its corollary, Japanization, is to a certain extent displacing Christianity and Westernization as a role-model. Those who see themselves as victims of colonial ideologies, who in private adhere to the beliefs and practices of African primal religions but in public profess abhorrence of them in order to secure educational and occupational privileges, are now enabled to find in Mahikari an alternative legitimation of indigenous ways. Associated abroad with the immense prestige of Japanese economic power, Mahikari reinforces the values of techno-logical society toward which developing nations aspire at the same time that it preserves and transforms premodern spiritism. In short, as Laënnec HURBON (1986: 158) says:

> Mahikari is a way of renewing links with the traditional her-itage; but at the same time it is an instrument for criticizing modernity, and it can rid the individual of his inferiority com-plexes.

Over the past several years, I have collected a number of testimonies and life-histories from African *kamikumite* in Tokyo, from which the following has been selected in order to exemplify the pattern of meaning such individuals find in Mahikari:

Jean, a Congolese in his mid-30s, studied at the Sorbonne and recently graduated from Tokyo's Keiō University with a doctorate in economics that he hopes will qualify him for a position with the finance ministry in Brazzaville. As an intel-lectual, it would seem he has radically assimilated Western values (and a degree of Marxist ideology) through his educa-tion abroad, but this process actually began at home, where he was raised a Jehovah's Witness. From the Witnesses Jean acquired a church-and-culture-in-conflict attitude, the "asceti-cal ethos" of the discipline of hard work, and a conviction that those who believe in the Bible will be immune to spirit possession.

This faith in the Witnesses' teaching was shattered when two of Jean's brothers died in circumstances he felt so strange he could comprehend them only as an act of traditional sor-cery—the curse of a neighbor with whom his family had been feuding over several generations. Convinced that the Witnesses were helpless to prevent him from becoming the next victim, Jean took initiation into the mysteries of the Rosicrucians, who are active in the Congo, but was likewise disappointed. While consulting practitioners of traditional magic, Jean's latent, indigenous world-view underwent reconstruction, and he became resentful of having to disguise his belief in spiritism in order to excel in the mission-school system.

Jean described to me his first experience of the Mahikari purification ritual, performed by *kamikumite* he met after coming to Japan for advanced studies, as an "electric shock" from head to toe. Indeed, his reaction was so virulent that *kamikumite* advised him to receive purification for shorter periods and at longer intervals than is usual, so malevolent was his possessing spirit thought to be. His spirit-seizures are nowadays less violent than they were when he was recruited several years ago, and Jean feels that spirit-investigation will eventually reveal the breach between his family and its assailants. While he awaits the final exorcism, Jean is confident that the power of True Light is superior to both the good and evil forces of African primal religion, but—most significantly—that Mahikari, unlike Christianity, fulfills rather than destroys what he proudly calls his *négritude*.

While the penetration of Mahikari into black Africa requires far more systematic research than has been possible here, we who have been assuming—as the Jōdo Shinshū theologian, Sasaki Shōten, quoted at the outset of this study—that Japanese New Religions such as Mahikari are premodern and outdated, are now confronted with the possibility that spirit-belief is not only a match for modern*ized* Japan but also for modern*izing* Africa.

NOTES

* This article appeared originally in a slightly expanded form in the *Japanese Journal of Religious Studies* 17/1: 29–49 (March 1990). Richard Fox Young is Professor in the Faculty of International Studies at Meiji Gakuin University in Yokohama.

1 For a detailed study of Mahikari ritualistic behavior in relation to secular technological processes, see MIYANAGA 1983.

2 Although there are two Mahikari, Sekai Mahikari Bunmei Kyōdan (Church of the World True-Light Civilization) and Sūkyō Mahikari (True-Light Supra-Religious Organization), I do not differentiate between them, as the division mainly results from a successional dispute.

3 There are two rival claimants, administered by the two Mahikari respectively: one in Takayama, Gifu Prefecture, and the other in the Izu Peninsula, Shizuoka Prefecture.

4 On the Celestial Rock Gate symbol in world-renewal religions, see YOUNG 1989b, and on the origin of the unity teaching in the same tradition see YOUNG 1988.

Christianity as a New Religion

Charisma, Minor Founders, and Indigenous Movements

Mark R. MULLINS

*J*APANESE HISTORY provides rich data for the study of the transplantation and indigenization of religions. This process can be documented and analyzed with reference to several religious traditions in vastly different socio-historical circumstances. The Buddhist tradition was introduced to Japan via China and Korea from the late sixth century, Roman Catholic Christianity was transplanted in the sixteenth century, and various Protestant denominations began missionary efforts from the latter half of the nineteenth century after Japan reopened its doors to the West.

Considerable attention has been given to the study of early Protestant missionary efforts and the subsequent transplantation of churches from Europe and North America. By contrast, comparatively little is known regarding the many indigenous and independent movements that broke away from the mission churches. The reference to Christianity as a New Religion in the title of this paper is not because it is a foreign-born religion and a relatively recent arrival to Japan. Rather, "newness" is related primarily to the fact that indigenous Christian movements broke away from the mission churches and resemble New Religions in so many respects. These movements have charismatic founders and involve significant innovations in beliefs, rituals, and social organization. In this sense, therefore, these Christian-related movements may be viewed as "New Religions" in the Japanese context.

CHURCH-SECT THEORY AND THE STUDY OF INDIGENIZATION

Over the course of a century scores of Protestant mission organizations from Europe and North America established churches in Japan. During this same period nativistic reactions to these imported expressions of Christianity eventually led

---

to the creation of a number of movements or sects organizationally independent of the mission churches. Japanese scholars refer to many of these movements as Christian-related New Religions, and several such groups were included in the massive reference work on New Religions published in 1990.[1] These groups, however, do not fit easily into typologies of Japanese New Religions because of their indebtedness to the established Christian traditions. For this reason, in fact, SHIMAZONO (1992: 72) recently suggested that a separate typology was needed to adequately deal with Christian-related New Religions in Japan.

Adapting church-sect theory, figure 1 provides a comparative typological framework for understanding Christian religious organizations in Japan according to three criteria: basic orientation, self-definition, and degree of indigenization. This typology is hardly intended to provide a definitive statement, but it should clarify in a new way the complex relationship between imported and indigenous religions. Readers will note that some groups included in this figure are often regarded as heretical by established or dominant churches. They are included here because this typology is based on an interpretative sociology of religion, rather than theological criteria, and priority is given to the actors' definition of the situation. As BERGER and KELLNER (1981: 40) explain, sociological concepts "must relate to the typifications that are already operative in the situation being studied." Therefore, groups that define themselves in Christian terms or in continuity with the Christian tradition are also included in this typology.

First of all, it is necessary to distinguish indigenous movements from the imported denominations and independent evangelical churches in terms of their basic orientation or dominant reference group. The basic orientation of a Christian religious body in Japan tends to be either "foreign-oriented" or "native-oriented." Transplanted religious organizations, including the Anglican Church, Roman Catholic Church, Lutheran denominations, and the United Church of Christ (the largest Protestant religious body in Japan that incorporates Methodist, Reformed, Presbyterian, and Congregational churches) are still "foreign-oriented" in many respects and therefore located at the non-indigenous end of the continuum. These denominations still receive foreign missionaries and their understanding of theological ortho-

FIGURE 1		
TYPOLOGY OF INDIGENIZATION		

Self-Definition (Claims to Legitimacy)	Degree of Change	
	Indigenous ←————————————→ Non-Indigenous	
	Self-support, self-control, self-propagation	

	Native-Oriented	Foreign-Oriented
Monopolistic (Sectarian)	Spirit of Jesus Church Original Gospel	Mormons Jehovah's Witnesses Baptist International Mission
Pluralistic (Denominational)	Non-Church (Mukyōkai) Christ Heart Church The Way	United Church of Christ Roman Catholic Church Anglican Church Lutheran Church* Baptist Church* Reformed Church

* There are a number of Lutheran and Baptist churches in Japan that represent various European (German, Norwegian, Finnish) and North American traditions.

doxy and models for church polity and organization are taken primarily from Western churches.[2] Similarly, there are scores of independent evangelical groups in Japan whose dominant reference group tends to be American evangelicalism. While these independent groups are indigenous in terms of the standard criteria of self-government, self-support, and self-propagation, their "foreign-orientation" is still apparent in their literature, tracts, and theology, which is largely "translated" materials from North America.

Indigenous movements, on the other hand, are "native-oriented" and do not measure their perception of religious truth by the standards of orthodoxy defined by Western theology or ancient church councils. According to most indigenous movements, God's self-revelation did not end with the canon of the Christian Scriptures. God continues to reveal deeper truths to those who are open to the ongoing work of the Holy Spirit. While some of these movements operate with the closed canon (the Non-Church movement, for example), many share a common belief that God continues to reveal

new truths hidden from or as yet ungrasped by Weste
churches. Most of these groups produce their own literatur
including monthly or quarterly magazines, editions of tl
Bible (sometimes specially edited versions), and collectio:
of the founder's writings and lectures. If not revealing rac
cally new truths, indigenous movements at least share
common the conviction that God is calling them to devel(
Japanese cultural expressions of the Christian faith that are
least as legitimate as the national churches and denomin
tional forms that have emerged over centuries in Europe ar
North America.

Although indigenous movements share many comm(
features, they can be distinguished in terms of their sel
understanding and claims to legitimacy. Religious organiz
tions can be distinguished by whether they claim to l
"uniquely legitimate," thus denying the legitimacy claims
other groups, or "collegially legitimate," thus accepting tl
claims of other groups. Several movements, for example, a
placed in the denominational category (for want of a bett
term) because they make only modest claims for themselves

無教会 道会 The Non-Church movement (Mukyōkai), the Way (Dōkai
基督心宗教団 and Christ Heart Church (Kirisuto Shinshū Kyōdan), f(
example, only claim to be Japanese expressions of Christianit
not the exclusive path to salvation.

Two groups are placed in the category of indigenous se
because of their tendency to emphasize exclusive trut
claims. The Spirit of Jesus Church (Iesu no Mitama Kyōka
イエス之御霊教会 and the Original Gospel (Genshi Fukuin, sometimes referre
原始福音 to as Makuya or the Tabernacle movement), for example, bo
幕屋 regard Western churches and Christian traditions as inad(
quate and distortions of New Testament Christianity. Whi
some of the publications produced by Makuya (including tl
writings of the founder, Teshima Ikurō) seem rather collegi(
and inclusive, both groups claim to have recovered authent
Christianity before it was corrupted by Hellenistic cultur(
This movement has cultivated "ecumenical relations" wit
many Jewish organizations in an effort to recover the Hebre
roots of Christianity. It continues to sponsor annual pilgrin
ages to Israel and sends leaders to study Hebrew on a kibbut
but it has maintained a sectarian stance toward oth(
Christian churches.

It has been noted in many different contexts that foreign missionaries often fail to distinguish their national culture from the religious faith they seek to transplant. Protestant missionaries to Japan have been no exception. Transplanting the faith has usually included denominational distinctives and loyalties, church polity, forms of leadership, and church architecture, all born in very different socio-cultural situations. Summarizing this tendency in the early period of Protestant mission to Japan, KITAGAWA (1961: 40–41) explains that:

> More often than not, European and American missionaries attempted to Westernize as well as Christianize the Japanese people and culture. Japanese converts were made to feel, consciously or unconsciously, that to decide for Christ also implied the total surrender of their souls to the missionaries. The task of evangelism was interpreted by most missionaries as transplanting *in toto* the church in the West on Japanese soil, including the ugly features of denominationalism—an unhappy assumption, indeed.

After Japanese converts were introduced to the Scriptures and went on to pursue serious theological study, many realized that it was possible to distinguish the Christian faith and biblical tradition from the theology, church polity, and cultural values of American and European missionaries.

As native leaders gained a more critical understanding of the Christian tradition and became aware of the significant differences in doctrine and practice among the mission churches, they began to assert more confidently their own ideas as equals of their missionary teachers. The fact that numerous denominations were competing for converts on Japanese soil (each with their own doctrinal peculiarities and forms of government) indicated to many native leaders that there might be room for Japanese interpretations and cultural expressions of Christianity. Missionaries, however, found it difficult to receive instruction from their Japanese disciples. UCHIMURA Kanzō (1916: 233), the founder of Mukyōkai (Non-Church) and one of the most articulate critics of the mission churches, expressed the sentiments of many Japanese Christians in the following passage:

Missionaries come to us to patronize us, to exercise lordship over us, in a word, to "convert" us; *not* to become our equals and friends, certainly not to become our servants and wash our feet.... We believe that the Gospel of Christ is the power of God unto salvation to every one that believeth; but unless through God's grace we save ourselves, we shall not be saved—certainly not by foreign churches and missionaries.[4] [Emphasis in the original]

It is important to recognize that indigenous Christian movements were not merely the result of personality conflicts and power struggles with foreign missionaries. By the late Meiji period the social climate had become decidedly anti-Western and nationalistic, after an earlier phase of worshipping everything Western (*seiyō sūhai*). In his study of attitudes toward modernization in Japan, Marius JANSEN (1965: 5) notes that "the responses of representative and leading Japanese were necessarily conditioned by the climate of opinion within which they moved." This statement is equally valid with respect to Japanese Christian leaders active during this period. The establishment of State Shinto and revival of Confucianism, on the one hand, were accompanied by parallel developments among Japanese Christians. Many Christians exchanged the displacement theology of the missionaries for a fulfillment theology in an effort to recover and legitimate the cultural riches of native traditions. The approach of missionaries came to be regarded by many indigenous leaders as "smelling of butter" (*batākusai*) or "smelling of the West" (*seiyōkusai*) This identification of Christianity with the West had become a stumbling block to propagation and many leaders became convinced that "Japanization" or "de-Westernization" was the only way forward. Independent indigenous movements became the most extreme examples of this process. While nationalism and conflict with missionaries were important "precipitating factors" that clarify the "timing" of these movements, we must consider other factors to explain their "content."

西洋崇拝

THE ENABLING FACTOR: IMPORTED AND NATIVE RELIGIOUS ELEMENTS

In referring to indigenous Christian movements as New Religions I do not intend to suggest that they are created ex-nihilo. New Religions do not appear out of thin air: they draw

FIGURE 2
SELECTED MINOR FOUNDERS AND INDIGENOUS MOVEMENTS

MINOR FOUNDER	MOVEMENT	DOMINANT WESTERN INflUENCES	DOMINANT NATIVE INflUENCES
Uchimura Kanzō (1861–1930)	Non-Church (1901)	William S. Clark, Professor and lay Christian, Sapporo Agricultural College, Amherst	Confucianism, Bushidō
Matsumura Kaiseki (1859–1939)	Church of Japan (1907), The Way (1912)	James Ballagh, Dutch Reformed Church, Yokohama Band, New Theology, Darwinism	Neo-Confucianism (Yōmeigaku), Shinto
Kawai Shinsui (1867–1962)	Christ Heart Church (1927)	Tōhoku Gakuin College (German Reformed Church)	Confucianism, Buddhism, mountain asceticism, Kyōkenjutsu
Murai Jun (1897–1970)	Spirit of Jesus Church (1941)	Aoyama Gakuin College (Methodism), True Jesus Church, Taiwan, Unitarian Pentecostalism	Folk religious traditions and the ancestor cult
Teshima Ikuro (1910–1970)	Original Gospel or Tabernacle of Christ (1948)	Zionism, Jewish Traditions	Uchimura Kanzō and Non-Church principles, folk religious traditions, mountain asceticism
Nakahara Masao (1948–)	Okinawa Christian Evangelical Center (1977)	Plymouth Brethren Missionary influence, Dispensationalism	Okinawan shamanism

on "vital elements of the religious heritage" (EARHART 1989: 236). Consequently, we must give attention to this "enabling factor" in the development of New Religions. In the Japanese context, New Religions draw from a vast reservoir of beliefs and practices related to ancestors, the spirit world, Buddhist, Shinto, and Confucian traditions. Similarly, the charismatic founders of Christian movements may have unusual insights and be creative individuals, but they do not start from scratch when organizing a new church or movement. They draw on the imported teachings, rituals, and organizational forms of the mission churches, as well as on various indigenous religious traditions. Native and exogenous elements are creatively adapted by minor founders and form the basis for new organizations. The religious experiences of these leaders and their unique combination of foreign and indigenous elements give rise to new formulations of belief-systems, new rituals and forms of religious practice, sometimes an enlarged canon, and even new forms of social organization.

Notwithstanding the popular myth of the homogeneous Japanese, it is necessary for us to recognize the cultural diversity of this receiving society in order to understand these new indigenous forms of Christianity. Religious diversity (folk religion, Shinto, Buddhist sects, Confucianism) and competing group loyalties (rival clans, social classes, and regions) provided the complex matrix for Japan's encounter with Christianity. The various reinterpretations of Christianity result from this complex interaction between imported foreign elements and diverse native traditions. Figure 2 highlights the dominant foreign and native influences on selected minor founders and movements.[5] Only through in-depth case studies will we be able to unravel and assess the actual impact of various religious traditions on founders and adherents. Here we have only briefly indicated that many different streams of foreign influence (reformed theology, pentecostalism, dispensationalism, unitarianism) have been mixed in unique ways with indigenous elements to produce new expressions of Christianity.

MINOR FOUNDERS, INNOVATION, AND CHARISMATIC AUTHORITY

The anti-Western social climate, growing nationalism, and dissatisfaction of Japanese Christians with Western missionaries are important precipitating factors that illuminate the development of indigenous Christian movements. These factors alone, however, do not provide an adequate explanation for the birth of these movements. Like other Japanese New Religions, indigenous Christian movements represent much more than social crisis and "reaction" to imported Christianity. The break with Western mission churches and the creation of viable alternative forms required strong charismatic leaders. "The innovative decision of the founder," EARHART (1989: 236) points out, "cannot be completely subsumed by either social factors or the influence of prior religious factors." How are we to understand the charismatic leaders who play such a key role in the development of indigenous movements? WEBER (1964: 46) made no distinction between charismatic individuals who renewed an old religion and those who founded new religions, but subsumed both under the category of prophet. Werner STARK (1970: 84), however, drew attention to the need for another concept to deal with innovations within a religious tradition:

> In order to describe Paul of Tarsus correctly, we need some such concept as that of a minor founder. In Paul, we behold an archetype which was to be re-incarnated many times in the history of the Church. Behind him, there appear such figures as Benedict, Francis, Dominic, Bernard, Ignatius, Alphonso, and many others. They were all minor founders, revolutionaries and reformers and even reactionaries (goers back to the original) rolled into one, and certainly not routinizers in the sense of Kipling and Weber.

Although Stark's comments are limited to the role of minor founders in the history of European or Western Christianity, this category seems equally relevant to understanding the development of Christianity in non-Western contexts.

More recently, Anthony BLASI has drawn attention to the category of "minor founder" again in his study of early Christianity, *Making Charisma: The Social Construction of Paul's Public Image* (1991). Arguing that Paul was much more than a "routinizer" of the charisma of Jesus, BLASI (14–15) explains that he "....was a 'minor founder,' a founder who resembles major founders in so far as he was an agent of change but who was more conservative than they insofar as he maintained a basic continuity with what had come before him. Paul did something new, but he did it within an already recognizable Christian subculture." Similarly, the charismatic leaders of indigenous Christian movements also create something new, but in recognizable continuity with an existing religious tradition. Minor founders in Japan departed from the religious traditions imported by foreign missionaries in significant ways, but at the same time passed the Christian heritage on to people in this new cultural context. Perhaps we could summarize by saying that a "minor founder" is a charismatic individual who gives birth to a new religious movement in an effort to address the needs of a new type of member, while at the same time conceptualizing the movement as an extension, elaboration, or fulfillment of an existing religious tradition.

From a sociological perspective, "charisma" and "charismatic authority" can only be understood in terms of the social relationship between a "leader" and "followers." Individuals can claim to have direct contact with God and to have received new revelations, but a movement will not be born if the new message does not meet the needs and aspirations of a significant audience. The message must have some appeal and followers must be convinced that these particular individuals have a special connection with the sacred. The break with an existing tradition, in this case with imported mission churches, requires a powerful figure whose personhood authenticates the claims. While founders and movements vary in the degree to which they reject existing traditions and introduce new elements, at the very least they claim to have direct access to the sacred and to have an independent basis of religious authority. UCHIMURA Kanzō (1920: 592), for example, one of the strongest advocates for an indigenous Christianity and founder of Mukyōkai, claimed:

> Japanese Christianity is not a Christianity peculiar to Japanese. **It is Christianity received by Japanese directly from God without any foreign intermediary; no more, no less.** In this sense, there is German Christianity, English Christianity, Scotch Christianity, American Christianity, etc; and in this sense, there will be, and already is, Japanese Christianity. "There is a spirit in man: and the inspiration of the Almighty giveth him understanding." The spirit of Japan inspired by the Almighty is Japanese Christianity. It is free, independent, original and productive, as true Christianity always is.
>
> No man was ever saved by other men's faith, and no nation will ever be saved by other nations' religion. Neither American Christianity nor Anglican faith, be it the best of the kind, will ever save Japan. Only Japanese Christianity will save Japan and the Japanese. (Emphasis mine)

The charismatic authority of minor founders is based on their convincing claims to direct contact with the sacred, sometimes additional revelations, and their persuasive personalities. It is also not uncommon to find claims of miraculous healings in the early stages of these movements. Matsumura, Kawai, Murai, Teshima, and Nakahara, for example, five of the six founders included in figure 2, each claimed to have either experienced personal healing or been used by God to heal others. During subsequent phases of the institutionalization process, the charismatic authority of these minor founders is reconfirmed and routinized. In some cases, the teachings and writings of the founder came to be viewed with equal or similar authority to the Bible. Even if religious groups distinguish in principle between the canon (Bible) and the founder's writings, in practice they tend to function with similar authority in the community. Religious services normally include readings from the Bible as well as numerous references to the founder's teachings, example, or quotations from his or her writings. Just as Christians normally view the Hebrew Bible and Jesus' interpretations of these ancient texts as "sacred," members of indigenous Christian movements tend to merge the Scriptures and their founder's interpretation.

These minor founders sometimes even become the object of veneration and special ritual respect. Kawai Shinsui, for example, the founder of Kirisuto Shinshū Kyōdan (Christ Heart Church) is paid ritual respect with bows to his photograph at the beginning and end of each service. His writings are also quoted as frequently as the Judeo-Christian scriptures. On a number of occasions I have even heard the deceased founder addressed in prayer ("Chichinaru Kami-sama, Iesu Kirisuto, Kawai Shinsui Sensei" ["Father God, Jesus Christ, Kawai Shinsui ..."]), as though he has become a part of the Holy Trinity in the minds of some followers. This tendency to venerate minor founders has a long history, as NAKAMURA Hajime (1964: 454) explains with reference to Japanese Buddhism:

> One result of this absolute devotion to a specific person is that the faithful of the various Japanese sects are extreme in the veneration with which they acknowledge the founder of the sect and perform religious ceremonies around him as the nucleus. **One has absolute faith in the master as well as in the Buddha, without feeling that there is the slightest contradiction.** It is not that one pays less attention to the Buddha, but the idea is perhaps that a profound faith in the master and devotion to the Buddha have the same significance. [Emphasis mine]

In much the same way, members of Christ Heart Church appear to experience no cognitive conflict in "believing in Jesus Christ" and venerating the founder, Kawai Shinsui, who made the salvific significance of Christ real to them through his teaching and example.

What distinguishes indigenous Christian movements from other New Religions is the fact that minor founders link their new insights to the existing religious tradition. This can take the form of "fulfillment" or "restorationist" explanations. In fulfillment explanations, the teaching of these founders is understood as the additional truth Jesus promised his disciples ("when the Spirit comes he will guide you into all truth"). The new insight fulfills or even supersedes the understanding of Christianity found in the Western churches. In restorationist explanations, Western churches are viewed as degenerate, and indigenous movements assert that they are only recovering or restoring important truths once held by the early church. No matter how severely these movements are assessed or criticized by mission churches or the dominant orthodoxy, in one form or another each regards itself in continuity with the Christian religion or, at the very least, more fully expressing the teachings and intention of Jesus.

FUTURE DIRECTIONS

The foregoing discussion can be regarded as no more than the preliminary spade work needed for constructing a more adequate understanding of indigenous Christianity. In concluding this essay, I would like to suggest areas for future study and comparative research.

First of all, we still need a basic inventory and documentation of indigenous Christian movements. There are at least six other movements I am aware of about which almost nothing is known. Case studies of these movements are needed before we can move on to more reliable generalizations regarding these types of movements in Japan. While each movement developed out of a particular set of circumstances (specific foreign influences, personality conflicts, and indigenous proclivities), comparative analysis of these groups will likely reveal a number of common features. Religious authority in major Buddhist sects in Japan, for example, is transmitted through father-son blood lineage.[6] To what extent have Christian movements adopted or adapted this traditional pattern of leadership succession? So far I have discovered a similar pattern in at least three movements. While not always passed from father to son, religious authority tends to stay in the family of the founder. In the Spirit of Jesus Church, authority was transferred to the founder's wife and, according to my informants, his daughter is in line to be the next bishop. Christ Heart Church is now in its third generation of leadership. The founder's authority was first transferred to his son and recently to his grandson. Matsumura Kaiseki and his wife were childless, but adopted a son to take over as head of The Way. The adopted son's wife, and then daughter, succeeded him as head (*kaichō*) of this religious body. It seems, therefore, that the imported organizational forms and authority structures (representative forms of government) are not readily adopted by Japanese if they have a choice. This is just one area that deserves additional consideration in future comparative studies.

The relationship between charismatic leadership, indigenization, and numerical growth also needs to be addressed. According to Robert Lee's *Stranger in the Land: A Study of the Church in Japan* (1967), the Westernness of Christianity is a major obstacle to numerical growth. Without indigenization, he argues, significant growth cannot be expected. All of the movements in figure 2 experienced significant growth at one time in their history, but today most are barely holding their own or are in a state of rapid decline. The current membership of these groups varies widely, but ranges from several hundred to twenty or thirty thousand.

Mukyōkai, for example, was estimated to have between fifty and one hundred thousand members in the late 1950s,[7] but two decades later Caldarola's study (1979) placed the membership at about 35,000. A follow-up study is needed, but my guess is that Mukyōkai has continued to experience decline since then. In the late 1970s, the Original Gospel consisted of close to 60,000 members, organized into some 500 home Bible-study groups around the country. In 1990, however, I was informed by a leader in the Tokyo office that there were only 150 groups meeting nationwide and approximately 25,000 subscribers to their magazine *Seimei no hikari* (Light of Life). The headquarters of the Spirit of Jesus Church reports that it has over 300 ministers, close to 200 churches, and a total membership of 420,000. The membership figure is clearly inflated and cannot be accepted at face value. This church practices baptism for the dead, more specifically baptism for the ancestors of living members. Some observers have been overheard suggesting rather cynically that this is guaranteed to be one of the fastest methods of church growth! Although still a generous figure, the active membership of 23,283 reported by church headquarters provides us with a more accurate picture of the actual strength of this movement. Christ Heart Church has declined to a membership of approximately 1,300 and adherents to The Way number less than 300 nationwide. Nakahara's Okinawa Christian Evangelical Center, the most recently organized group included in figure 2, is currently in a phase of rapid growth and has baptized over one thousand adherents in just over a decade.

A study of growth and decline patterns in these movements raises the question of whether groups can dig their own graves through "over-indigenization." Comparative studies of religious movements indicates that those maintaining a "medium level of tension" with the larger society are the ones that are growing. STARK (1987: 16) explains that a "movement must maintain a substantial sense of difference and considerable tension with the environment if it is to prosper. Without significant differences from the conventional faith(s) a movement lacks a basis for successful conversion." In the case of some indigenous Christian movements in Japan, they have become so indigenous that there is minimal tension and ineffective mobilization of members for recruitment activities. This is clearly the case with Christ Heart Church and The Way. While these two movements experienced significant growth under charismatic founders, the routinized indigenous forms have not provided an adequate foundation for long-term growth. It is also undeniable that the conservative Confucian character of movements organized decades ago appear rather austere to contemporary Japanese. "What will give one generation a sense of unifying tradition," YINGER (1970: 112) correctly notes, "may alienate parts of another generation who have been subjected to different social and cultural influences."

Finally, we need to consider the role and significance of indigenous Christian movements for the larger Japanese society. To what extent, in other words, do these movements represent significant social change? In his study of the New Religion Gedatsu-Kai, for example, EARHART (1989) discovered that in spite of the new elements introduced by the founder it was in many respects a revitalization movement of traditional Japanese religiosity, or a "return to the center." In fact, involvement in Gedatsu-kai leads to increased participation in traditional religious practices, such as worship before

a *kamidana* (Shinto god shelf) and *butsudan* (Buddhist altar), 　神棚　仏壇
and visits to the local Shinto shrine and to the family
Buddhist parish temple. Similarly, HARDACRE's (1984) study
of Reiyūkai Kyōdan revealed that it attempted to revitalize
the traditional extended family (*ie*) and ancestor veneration,
and that the role of women was largely confined to domestic
and religious duties. Only a serious study of the teachings of
indigenous Christian movements, an analysis of social relations, gender roles and status, and a survey of the actual practices of members will reveal whether they represent
alternative cultural values and social roles, or in fact reinforce traditional Confucian ideals. We may also discover
that many indigenous Christian movements represent primarily "a return to the center" rather than significant social
change.

NOTES

* A longer version of this article appears in *Syzygy: Journal of
Alternative Religion and Culture* 2/1 (Winter), 1993. Mark R. Mullins
is Associate Professor at Meiji Gakuin University in Tokyo and
Yokohama.

[1] See INOUE Nobutaka, et al., eds., *Shinshūkyō jiten* [Encyclopedia
of the New Religions], Tokyo: Kōbundō, 1990. This indispensable
volume contains over a thousand pages of information on New
Religions in Japan.

[2] Readers should keep in mind that this framework is based on a
continuum. I am not arguing that indigenization has not occurred in
these foreign-oriented religious bodies, only that the process has proceeded more slowly than in indigenous movements with minor
founders. See REID (1991) for studies of indigenization within the
United Church of Christ in Japan, NISHIYAMA (1985) on the Anglican
Church, and DOERNER (1977) on the Roman Catholic Church.

[3] I have used the denominational category in order to emphasize
the self-understanding of these groups, even though they lack the
characteristics normally associated with a denomination in the West
(i.e., central bureaucracy, complex organizational structure, and a formal system for ministerial training and ordination).

[4] UCHIMURA's (1886: 159) pessimism regarding the prospects of
Western Christianity was expressed as early as 1886, when he wrote:
"Which of the nineteen different Christian denominations which are
now engaged in evangelizing Japan is to gain the strongest foot-hold
there? In our view, —and let us express this view with the most hearty
sympathy toward the earnest endeavors of the missionaries of all the
denominations—none of them. One reason is that mere transplanting

of anything exotic is never known on Japanese soil. Be it a political, scientific, or social matter, before it can be acclimatized in Japan, it must pass through great modifications in the hands of the Japanese."

[5] Several of the founders and movements in figure 2 have already been the focus of serious field research. CALDAROLA (1979) provided a helpful study of Uchimura and the Non-Church movement, considering in particular the role of Confucianism and the samurai code (Bushidō) in this reinterpretation of Christianity. It is not coincidental that Uchimura, whose Non-Church movement became the inspiration for many other groups, was introduced to the Christian faith by a lay Christian, Dr. Clark, who was not preoccupied with the ecclesiastical concerns of most missionaries. Caldarola also analyzed the influence of folk religion and shamanism on Teshima's application of non-church principles in the formation of the Original Gospel or Makuya. In an earlier paper (MULLINS 1990) I sketched the development of the Spirit of Jesus Church (Iesu no Mitama Kyōkai) and considered the dual influence of imported Pentecostalism and dispensationalism, as well as the indigenous ancestor cult on Murai's reformulation of Christianity. Most recently, IKEGAMI (1991) has provided a major study of Nakahara Masao and the Okinawa Christian Evangelical Center established in 1977; this is now a rapidly growing movement combining Plymouth Brethren Christianity and Okinawan shamanism.

Christ Heart Church and the Way are the focus of my current research. The founders, Kawai Shinsui and Matsumura Kaiseki, were both educated in mission schools dominated by the Reformed tradition. After disagreements with missionaries on a variety of matters, they began independent churches and drew on various Asian religious traditions in their interpretations of Christianity. The creed of Christ Heart Church, for example, includes the following confession: "We believe the ways of the ancient saints are not destroyed but rather fulfilled by the coming of Christ." For Kawai Shinsui, the "ancient saints" included Buddha, Confucius, Mencius, and others. Zen meditation and Kyōkenjutsu (another influential form of bodily training and discipline) also greatly influenced the religious practice of both Kawai and his followers. Matsumura Kaiseki initially organized the Nihon Kyōkai (Church of Japan) in order to create a Japanese Christianity independent of Western control. He became widely known as an advocate of Confucian Christianity, but eventually claimed to be establishing a "New Religion" of the eternal way. While Neo-Confucianism provided the primary categories of Matsumura's perspective, the Christian teaching of a personal God and Jesus' teaching of neighborly love were key elements of "the way."

[6] See FUJII (1986: 164) for a discussion of transmission of leadership and authority in Japanese Buddhist sects.

[7] This is the estimate provided by HOWES (1957: 125) and is based on attendance at Bible study meetings and lectures as well as subscriptions to Mukyōkai magazines.

The Expansion of Japan's
New Religions into Foreign Cultures

SHIMAZONO Susumu

THE BEGINNINGS OF THE expansion of Japan's New Religions overseas go back as far as the Meiji period.[1] At first it spread to nearby colonies and among emigrants to new continents. Then war brought an end to propagation in migrant communities, and defeat in the war checked propagation in colonial territories. Most of the New Religions at first restricted their postwar propagation activities to Japan. But it was not long before they were renewing their efforts in emigrant communities. Eventually propagation to people of non-Japanese descent "took off," using prewar propagation bases in colonial territories and emigrant communities as springboards. Following the economic boom of the 1960s, propagation within Japan eventually approached an upper limit, and there was renewed enthusiasm for overseas expansion. This enthusiasm came just at a time when second and third generations of migrants were assimilating in local societies. The overseas expansion of the New Religions entered a new phase from the 1960s on: that of expansion into foreign cultures. As a result of defeat in the war, Japan suffered an almost complete loss of the foundations upon which its imperialistic, authoritarian control overseas rested. Until the 1960s, it also lacked economic reserves for overseas expansion. As a result, the New Religions relied on Japanese ethnic communities in North and Latin America. With the exception of the old colonial territories of Taiwan and Korea, until the beginning of the 1960s the spread of Japanese New Religions overseas was almost exclusively in Japanese ethnic communities, where Japan's cultural traditions were strongly preserved.[2]

After the 1960s, however, Japan's New Religions were slowly accepted by non-Japanese. In North and Latin America, where there were migrant ethnic communities, non-

Japanese believers in New Religions would increase steadily. This was a period when new migrants were few in number and assimilation of Japanese communities into local societies proceeded apace. The situation in Taiwan and Korea was slightly different. The results of propagation in colonial times were not completely negated by defeat in the war. Churches run by local people carried on religious activities independently of organizations within Japan. Expansion of membership, begun even in the 1950s, became conspicuous in the 1960s and afterwards. And in the 1970s relations with the organizations in Japan tended to be restored, so that, with increased exchanges of personnel and the propping up of operations by organizations in Japan, the amount of energy put into propagation also increased greatly.

The aim of this study is to consider the significance of this spread of New Religions to non-Japanese, so conspicuous from the 1960s on. At present Sōka Gakkai and other groups have reached out to virtually every corner of the world through their missionary activity. The teachings and thought of Japan's New Religions have been translated into many languages and have been accepted by people of widely different cultural backgrounds. What has made this situation possible is, first and foremost, the rapid improvement in Japan's economic strength; another factor has been the rapid growth in world communication and information distribution. The expansion of Japan's New Religions overseas is primarily the result of changes in economic life. This question of the influence of economic change on Japan's New Religions is itself a deeply interesting subject for study. The aim of this present study is a little wider. The entrance of New Religions into foreign cultures may even provide hints for thinking about what changes are at present occurring in religions around the world, and also about what special position Japan's New Religions occupy in the history of world religions.

PRESENT STATUS OF EXPANSION

To what extent have Japan's New Religions spread among non-Japanese?[3] As of 1990, non-Japanese believers in New Religions are decidedly most numerous in Latin America and East and Southeast Asia; next comes North America (including Hawaii). Brazil and Korea far exceed all other countries in membership, with the United States and Asian countries distant seconds. While there are some believers in Europe, Oceania, South Asia, West Asia, and Africa, their numbers are insignificant in comparison with those in the Americas and East and Southeast Asia.

BRAZIL

Seichō-no-Ie boasts the largest membership, followed by Sekai Kyūsei-kyō, Perfect Liberty Kyōdan (PL), and Sōka Gakkai.[4] Brazil's news weekly, *Veja*, carried an article in its 28 March 1990 issue entitled "The Gods of the Sun: The Progress of Eastern Religions Promising Heaven on Earth and Prosperity in the Present World." According to this article, Seichō-no-Ie had 2,500,000 members, Sekai Kyūsei-kyō and PL 250,000 each, and Sōka Gakkai 150,000. Not mentioned in the article but growing remarkably in recent years are Sūkyō Mahikari, with several tens of thousands of followers, and Reiyūkai, with 44,000 (as of March 1989; see INOUE et al. 1990: 650). Other groups as well, such as Sekai Mahikari Bunmei Kyōdan, include many non-Japanese believers, as do such groups as Burajiru Kannon Jiin and the Inarikai begun in Brazil by Japanese. There are said to be 800,000 people of Japanese descent in Brazil, and another 300,000 of mixed descent; thus the influence of Japanese New Religions goes far beyond Japanese circles. If one accepts the figures given in *Veja*, more than 2% of Brazil's population of 150 million people are members of Japanese New Religions.

Those figures are, however, considerably exaggerated. NAKAMAKI Hirochika has said of PL that, as of 1984, "active believers are estimated to have peaked in the neighborhood of 30,000 people" (1989: 417); if this is true, then actual membership is about one-eighth that of the figure given in *Veja*. Of course, it is difficult to say exactly what "active believers" means. In the case of Seichō-no-Ie, the official overseas membership is 1,257,907 (as of the end of 1989), of whom roughly 1,200,000 are in Latin America. One of the most important religious practices in Seichō-no-Ie is subscription to their official publications; as of December 1989, 608,000 copies of the two Portuguese-language publications, *Acendedo* and *Pomba Branca*, were printed. No data is available for exact numbers of copies of the Japanese-language publications printed in Brazil, but it is estimated that about 10% of Brazil's Japanese belong to Seichō-no-Ie (MATSUDA 1989). Of the members of Shirohatokai [White dove society], the women's group, approximately three belong to the Portuguese section for every one who belongs to the Japanese section. Again, there were about 362,000 (as of December 1989) who were paying monthly dues to the Seishimeikai [Holy vocation society], while the same year there were 821,998 Seishimeikai members in Japan. When looking at these comparisons, however, one must take into account that Brazilians tend to feel it odd to pay membership fees to the religious group one believes in, so that canvassing among members of the Seishimeikai is not done as aggressively as it is in Japan.

UNITED STATES OF AMERICA

In the United States the NSA (Nichiren Shōshū Sōka Gakkai of America) far surpasses all others in its spread among non-Japanese. According to Sōka Gakkai's own statistics, it had 333,000 adherents in North America as of 1985, very few of whom were Canadians. George WILLIAMS (1989) states that the racial makeup of NSA membership in that year was 25.6% Asian, 47.9% white, 20.4% black, and 6.1% others. Since most of the Asians are of Japanese descent, roughly three-fourths can be regarded as of non-Japanese descent.

Aside from NSA, it seems no other New Religion has succeeded in going from Japan and gaining several tens of thousands of adherents. There are some Japanese New Religions, however, that spread in the United States without initiatives from groups in Japan, such as the Reiki of Mikao Usui and Macrobiotic, founded by Sakurazawa Yukikazu and propagated in the United States by Michio Kushi (see ALBANESE 1990). *East West Journal*, which Macrobiotic started publishing in 1970, was printing close to 80,000 copies in 1985. Another New Religion, the Unification Church (Holy Spirit Association for the Unification of World Christianity) founded in Korea, spread its forces to Japan and then to the United States, where at the end of the 1970s it claimed a membership of approximately 30,000 (BROMLEY and SHUPE 1981).

ASIA

In Korea the Sōka Gakkai and Tenri-kyō have made the greatest impact. The former group maintains that it has 709,000 adherents in the Asia/Oceania area (as of 1985); we can safely assume that two-thirds of these are Koreans. Tenri-kyō puts the number of its adherents at about 370,000. Similar figures are given in Korean government reports. Still, officials of the religious groups themselves consider actual figures to be far lower. One mark of deepening faith in Tenri-kyō is participation in a three-month "character-building course" at the group's headquarters in Japan. Because people could not travel freely from Korea to Japan, from 1973 several sites were set up in the country where these long training sessions could be carried out. As of April 1990, there were fifty-one churches scattered throughout Korea, with prospects for that number to increase. By February 1990 the total number of people who completed these courses came to 37,000.

In the rest of Asia, there has been a considerable growth among communities of ethnic Chinese in Taiwan, Hong Kong, Singapore, and other countries. Sōka Gakkai has enjoyed far and away the greatest success overall, but in Hong Kong Shinji Shūmei-kai has been quite strong, and in Thailand Sekai Kyūsei-kyō claims over 60,000 adherents.

This summarizes the countries and groups with the largest numbers of adherents, but I would like to conclude this section with a quick look at the range over which some of the groups have extended their propagation activities overseas. Sōka Gakkai and Seichō-no-Ie are the two groups with the largest number of overseas adherents, with the former's membership scattered all over the world and the latter's heavily concentrated in Brazil. In 1985 Sōka Gakkai was estimated to have 1,262,000 members in 115 countries outside Japan. Another wide-ranging group is Sūkyō Mahikari, with approximately 100,000 adherents spread over 75 countries outside Japan.

PERIODS OF EXPANSION INTO FOREIGN CULTURES

BRAZIL

Expansion into Brazil practically began with the first migrations of Japanese in 1908. Groups of Honmon-Butsuryū-shū and Tenri-kyō adherents were already formed by 1930. Seichō-no-Ie had also gained a considerable number of followers by the end of the war. But all of these members were restricted to Japanese ethnic communities. The one exception was Ōmoto, which from about 1930 had begun propagation;

right from the start it reached out to non-Japanese (MAEYAMA and SMITH 1983). But because of stiff local opposition, the dissolution of Japanese headquarters due to government suppression, and the death of missionaries, Ōmoto was unable to form a large group of adherents. At the end of the 1960s solid members numbered only a few hundred.

From the early 1960s large-scale penetration into non-Japanese society began. The two groups that took the lead in this regard, PL and Sekai Kyūsei-kyō, had no bases in the migrant communities prior to this period. Tables 1 and 2 present the number of adherents by group and the proportion of Japanese to non-Japanese in 1967 as reported by MAEYAMA Takashi (1983, pp. 192–93). At this stage Japanese were still in the majority in the New Religions as a whole, though signs of the expansion to non-Japanese were already evident in Sekai Kyūsei-kyō in particular as well as in PL. From the end of the 1960s Seichō-no-Ie began an explosive penetration into non-Japanese society. And according to NAKAMAKI, by 1984 non-Japanese amounted to more than 90% of total PL overseas membership (1989: 417). Therefore, the rapid develop-

TABLE 1

THE ADHERENTS OF NEW RELIGIONS IN BRAZIL (1967)

Sect	Initiation of Propagation	Estimated Number of Adherents
Ōmoto	1926	600
Tenri-kyō	1929	4,000
Seichō-no-Ie	1932	15,000
Sekai Kyūsei-kyō	1955	5,000–7,000
PL	1957	8,000–10,000
Sōka Gakkai	1960	15,000–20,000
Total		47,600–56,600

TABLE 2

ETHNICITY OF ADHERENTS OF NEW RELIGIONS IN BRAZIL IN 1967 (EST.)

Sect	Japanese (%)	Non-Japanese (%)
Ōmoto	50	50
Tenri-kyō	100	0
Seichō-no-Ie	99–100	0–1
Sekai Kyūsei-kyō	40	60
PL	80–90	10–20
Sōka Gakkai	100	0

ment of Japanese New Religions from the late 1960s was clearly a result of the spread of activities to non-Japanese.

In the 1980s Sekai Kyūsei-kyō and PL membership tended to remain stagnant, but Seichō-no-Ie continued to grow, and other groups, such as Mahikari, have recently shown conspicuous growth. Overall one can say that diversification and expansion of Japanese New Religions has continued.

UNITED STATES OF AMERICA

Missionary activity in the United States had an early start through the activities of such groups as Kurozumi-kyō in Hawaii, which has a history of immigration from Japan going back to 1868. From the late 1920s groups such as Tenri-kyō and Konkō-kyō carried on organized propagation in Hawaii and California. They were followed later by Seichō-no-Ie, Tenshō Kōtai Jingū-kyō, and several others. Propagation, however, was mainly confined to people of Japanese descent (INOUE et al. 1990, YANAGAWA and MORIOKA 1979 and 1981, and INOUE 1985).

It was Sekai Kyūsei-kyō and PL that, as in Brazil, were the first to stress propagation to non-Japanese; they were unable, however, to achieve the same conspicuous penetration of non-Japanese society that they achieved in Brazil. The breakthrough in the United States was made by NSA. The first group of Sōka Gakkai members was formed in 1960.[5] At first the mainstays were women who had married American men and gone to live in America, and other people of Japanese descent. As early as 1964 there were discussion meetings in English, the journal *World Tribune* was being published, and other early efforts were being taken to penetrate non-Japanese society. In the latter half of the 1960s a remarkable number of non-Japanese, especially white youths, joined the New Religions, even exceeding the number of Japanese who joined. NSA's most surprising growth took place in the latter half of the 1960s, and the impetus continued on into the first half of the 1970s. Official adherent numbers are given as 200,000 in 1970, rising to 245,000 by 1975.

After that, however, NSA membership fell rapidly. The number of copies of *World Tribune* printed in 1975 was 60,000; this dropped to 33,000 in 1975, and down to 19,000 in 1980. The drop in membership was not to prove a long-term phenomenon, however, for in the early 1980s there was a resurgence in strength, and by 1985 the number of copies of *World Tribune* printed rose to 94,000. Still, the figure of 333,000 given for North American membership in 1985 does not reflect actual numbers. Also, penetration into non-Japanese society to such an extent that non-Japanese made up three-fourths of the membership had already been realized in the late 1960s. According to NSA's own survey of 1970, members who identified their racial background as Asian were already no more than 30% of the total.

ASIA

Propagation in this part of the world was begun by Tenri-kyō missionaries working in Korea in the 1920s. Along with colonial expansion after the Sino-Japanese and Russo-Japanese wars, many religious groups made inroads into colonial territories; groups such as Tenri-kyō, Konkō-kyō, the Kokuchū-kai, Ōmoto, and Nihonzan-myōhōji had bases established before 1925, while groups such as Hito-no-Michi and Seichō-no-Ie achieved rapid growth after 1925. Of all the groups, the inroads made by Tenri-kyō were something spectacular: by 1944 they had 211 churches in Korea, 39 in Taiwan, 124 in Manchuria, and 46 in China (INOUE et al. 1990: 644). This expansion of New Religions along with imperialistic expansion naturally aimed not only at Japanese but also at local inhabitants. And these New Religions were also accepted by non-Japanese (mainly Koreans) within Japan, people who either moved to Japan or were sent as conscript labor. Prior to 1945, therefore, penetration of New Religions into non-Japanese society was evident in many regions of East Asia.

Nearly all of the fruits of imperialistic expansion were lost by defeat in World War II. Still, some remained, and Tenri-kyō used some of its prewar propagation achievements to renew missionary activity in East Asia after the war. In fact, of all the New Religions that were active before the war, it was only Tenri-kyō that had some of its churches maintained by local inhabitants. Of the 51 churches it had in Korea as of April 1990, eight were churches that had been founded in the thirty-one years between 1912 and 1943. In Taiwan only one of its churches remained. Up to a certain point in time after the war, these churches all barely managed to survive despite violent anti-Japanese feelings, and it is easy to surmise that open propagation was not easy.[6]

Nevertheless, some brave souls proceeded to former colonial territories after the war in order to carry out missionary activity. The most representative of these is Choi Jae-Whan, who established the Won Nam Seong church in Pusan (YAMAMOTO 1982). Choi had come to Japan in 1927 at the age of sixteen and joined Tenri-kyō in 1947 after suffering from Hansen's disease. Following some time in missionary activity among Koreans living in northern Kyūshū and Hiroshima, he smuggled himself into Korea in 1955 and thereafter achieved spectacular results. By the time of his death in 1988, the Won Nam Seong church had given birth to seventeen other churches. Propagation continued after his death through the efforts of other Koreans living in Japan who returned to Korea. It is estimated that there are now more Tenri-kyō adherents belonging to churches established by such repatriates than members belonging to churches from prewar days. We can safely conclude that Tenri-kyō's membership expansion in postwar Korea went hand in hand with the development of Choi's Won Nam Seong church, and hence took place in the 1960s and 1970s. It would seem that Tenri-kyō's growth in Taiwan followed a similar timetable, with remarkable growth occurring in the 1980s.

In contrast, the situation has been very different for Sekai Kyūsei-kyō in Thailand. Prior to 1970 there was almost no penetration by Japanese New Religions into Thailand. Sekai Kyūsei-kyō missionaries had taken up residence in Bangkok in 1968 and begun propagation, but up to the beginning of the 1980s there had been no great progress made. In early 1982, however, rapid growth finally began. By 1990 membership exceeded 60,000, and a yearly increase of over 10,000 members is expected. Tenri-kyō also reports remarkable growth recently in Thailand.

At present I do not have available to me data on Sōka Gakkai, which has had the biggest expansion in membership in Asia, so I am unable to say where and when its growth has been most notable. Judging from the above data on Tenri-kyō and Seichō-no-Ie, however, we could conclude that the expansion of Japanese New Religions into Asian cultures began with notable progress in Korea, then spread among ethnic Chinese communities, and more recently reached out into Thailand and other countries.

Why is it that Japanese New Religions succeeded in penetrating foreign cultures at this time? It is a belief of most of the New Religion groups that each member of the human race has dignity as a human being, but existence involves suffering, and for this very reason human beings are in need of salvation. Hence they have a strong desire to extend, if possible, their teaching to people of other cultures as well. Besides, New Religions are in general extremely keen to expand membership, and not only out of a desire to save people. In a capitalistic competitive society, one's legitimacy is graphically brought home on the basis of success in expanding numbers. What is more, when the following of one's teaching by people of other cultures is felt to be proof of your religion's universal adequacy, missionary activity to people of other cultures overseas can stir up stronger impulses than propagation among one's compatriots.

Still, sometimes propagation does not produce great results, regardless of how strong the desires or how much energy is poured into it. For propagation to succeed, suitable conditions must exist in the receiving society. Also, the religion doing the propagation must have, along with strong desires, certain features making it easily acceptable by people of foreign cultures. In other words, by considering the special features of both the receiving society and the religion being propagated, we shall be better prepared to understand why, in a certain place at a certain time, particular religions succeeded in expanding. In this section, we shall first consider the special features of the receiving societies.

The first condition for expansion is the cultural and political condition, i.e., how generally tolerant the local government and inhabitants are toward a religion derived from another culture, and how favorable and friendly they are toward that culture, especially a Japanese, Oriental culture. In the period of imperialistic expansion, the fact that the religion belonged to the culture of the side exerting authoritative control was in itself a major cause for expansion. Colonial authority is keen to surround local inhabitants with influences of that authority's own culture. This is especially true when assimilation is deliberately pursued. Under such a political, legal, and military aegis, propagation has an extremely high chance of success.

Yet the postwar expansion of the New Religions did not take place under this kind of powerful political aegis. On the contrary, by being different from the existing, dominant religions, in many cases they had to expand by overcoming governmental regulation and the opposition of local inhabitants. Also, success would be difficult if the religion were too exotic for the dominant culture, thus becoming an object of antipathy. This is the condition I am referring to when I talk about a degree of political and cultural freedom and tolerance. When the Japanese community has excellent relations with the outside world, as in Brazil, Japanese culture in general naturally enjoys a good reputation. Economic expansion through the export of goods and capital and personnel exchanges, even if they invite antipathy at first, eventually serve to make people feel attracted to the new culture, and they soften people's antipathies.

But it is even more important that cultural freedom be expanded widely in that society and that the authority of the traditional cultural system be seen as relative. In a society where the traditional religion has monopolistic authority—where freedom of religion is not recognized—one cannot expect success in propagation. Progress in industrialization and urbanization, along with progress in a worldwide interchange of personnel and information, are eroding these cultural and political barriers.

In both Brazil and Korea in the 1960s and 1970s, when there was so much expansion of the Japanese New Religions, the countries were in the midst of development through rapid industrialization under authoritarian military-rule systems; it was not a coincidence that both military rules were as a result in a process of breaking down. Thailand in the 1980s, too, was in a state of rapid industrialization and cultural liberalization and relativization. In both Brazil and Thailand, prior to those changes, there was little scope for tolerance of any other religions besides Christianity or Theravāda Buddhism. Even in the case of Korea, which had religious diversity, political regulation was strict. Industrialization brought change in its wake, however. Industrialization requires free accumulation and investment of capital, the formation of a competent middle class, and the creation of a free labor force. For these ends, even though doing so carries the risk of a certain amount of social unrest, it is necessary to recognize freedom of belief and thought. Also, the liberation of people from traditional ways of life linked with the dominant religions must, if anything, be encouraged. Added to this process of liberalization that follows industrialization are the waves of worldwide information exchange and cultural relativization.

In Korea there was fierce opposition from the inhabitants towards Japanese culture. Yet the expansion of general cultural freedom and the increase in everyday contacts with things Japanese as a result of economic expansion to some extent softened the opposition to Japanese culture on the level of everyday life. In the case of the United States, despite the outward facade of freedom of thought and belief, there always existed a strong confidence in the superiority of Christian, Occidental culture, with a corresponding rejection of Oriental culture. This rejection mechanism, and people's confidence in Christian Occidental culture, began to be badly shaken in the 1960s, a tendency that has continued to the present day. One of the striking manifestations of this unrest is the counterculture movement revolving around young middle-class whites. Positive interest in Oriental religions supported the most powerful wing of this counterculture movement. Disappointment with the Christian Occidental culture manifested itself in a yearning for its antithesis, Oriental religion. The expansion of Sōka Gakkai and Sekai Kyūsei-kyō into the foreign culture of the United States of America was something that accompanied the tide of interest in Oriental religions stemming from this aspect of the counterculture movement (INOUE 1985: 170–73, 204–206).

To sum up what happened in Brazil, Korea, and the United States of America in the 1960s and in Thailand in the 1980s: greater expansion of capitalism than ever before; advances in communication, transportation, information exchange, and the concomitant relativization of culture. In Japan, driven by a desire to catch up with and surpass Western nations, political leaders were quick to try to build a strong nation by aggressive introduction of Western culture, and they were ruthless in destroying the authority of traditional religions such as Confucianism and Buddhism. Defeat in World War II and the Allied occupation added further impetus in this direction. What emerged and developed from that experience of cultural relativization were Japan's New Religions; they not only emerged under these conditions, they also offered people many cultural resources for coping with these new conditions. On the other hand, countries like Brazil and the United States had absorbed immigrants from all parts of the world, and as a result were more accustomed to cultural diversity than Europe; consequently, they had a tendency to prefer a pragmatic way of thinking that did not insist upon a single tradition.[7] There can be no doubt that in these countries the essential prerequisite of familiarity with cultural diversity encouraged openness to and acceptance of Japanese New Religions.

The second condition for expansion is the emergence of a demand for new religions as a result of socioeconomic changes. The various New Religions in Japan grew and developed by satisfying the new spiritual yearnings of people living in the midst of modern Japan's socioeconomic changes. One of the common characteristics of the New Religions is their response to strongly felt needs of individuals in their daily lives, their solutions to discord in interpersonal relations, their practical teaching that offers concrete solutions for carrying on a stable social life, and their provision, to individuals who have been cut off from traditional communities, of a place for group activities where congenial company and a spirit of mutual support can be found. As capitalistic industrialization and urbanization advance, large numbers of individuals are thrown into new living environments, thus producing conditions that require spiritual support for the individual. Many people have lost the support of their traditional communities and face a situation in which they must get by on their own resources in the midst of the pressures of competition and the dangers of isolation. Those who have overcome such problems no doubt make up the lion's share of the stable middle-class urban population (including the lower stratum of middle-class laborers). Japanese New Religions are abundantly equipped with cultural resources that answer the needs of just these people in the process of treading the path towards the urban middle class. The second condition for expansion, therefore, is the existence of socio-economic conditions that nurture a latent demand among people for a religion that gives guidance in daily life.

In Brazil and Korea from the 1960s, and in Thailand in the 1980s, such socio-economic conditions did in fact exist. Let

---

us take a brief look at Brazil. Brazil, whose principal industry was a monocultural agriculture based mostly on coffee, began to tread the path of industrialization in 1934, with the "Vargas Revolution." Amidst the trade slump that accompanied worldwide depression, and backed by the military, the new government forced through the domestic production of many industrial products that had been previously imported. This policy of industrialization imposed from above was to bear fruit in the 1960s, after a period of democratization following World War II. The military rule that began in 1964 would prove to be a period of large-scale development and high growth. The result was a rapid increase in population coupled with a rapid decrease in the rural population, which had once constituted the greater portion of the nation's population. Between 1940 and 1980 Brazil's total population grew 2.8 times larger, and the ratio of urban to rural population reversed itself from 3:7 to 7:3 (NAKAMAKI 1989: 421–22). Whereas 54% of workers were engaged in primary industries in 1960, in 1970 this figure was down to 44.3%, and in 1980 down even more, to 29.3%. The rapid economic growth that drew attention to Brazil as one of the Newly Industrialized Countries (NICS) took place from 1968 to 1973, exactly the same time that Seichō-no-Ie's expansion to foreign cultures was being energetically promoted.

During the course of such industrialization and urbanization the Japanese community occupied a singular position. Japanese immigrants very early purchased small plots of farmland (as compared to the huge plantation-type farms that were the mainstay of Brazilian agriculture) and set out to produce on self-managed farms commodity crops for sale to urban residents. While accumulating wealth through their characteristic industriousness, the majority of people of Japanese descent were extremely keen on giving their children a good education. As a result, Japanese were quick to improve their status to that of the urban middle class along with the industrialization and urbanization of Brazilian society. Japanese stood for the dream of the new industrialized society: individual success through self-reliant effort. From the 1960s on, Japanese New Religions took over this idea of individual success, and in addition presented themselves to Brazilian society as the religions of these urban middle-class Japanese, religions that were eager to form congenial communities, that were deserving of respect and affection.

In respect to socio-economic conditions the situation in the United States of America was somewhat different. There, propagation of the Japanese New Religions succeeded in a society where industrialization had already reached a certain stage and society was about to move into a postindustrial period. In the United States of the 1960s there was also a large number of inhabitants who had left rural areas for the big cities, from the South and Midwest as well as from Central and South America, Korea, and other places. Yet it was not necessarily such people that the NSA attracted in its growth period. Rather, it attracted urban residents isolated in an advanced industrial society, represented most often by young whites in California and in large eastern-seaboard cities such as New York (WILLIAMS 1989). Offering a pragmatic value system, a congenial community, and an alternative to the individualistic, rationalistic Western civilization became the role of the Japanese New Religions in this country. NSA, Sekai Kyūseikyō, and Macrobiotic were accepted because they belonged to a group of New Religions that were countercultural, in that they counteracted the existing Christian, utilitarian culture (see INOUE 1985, YAMADA 1983, and ALBANESE 1990).

Some of the Japanese New Religions responded to the fact that it was possible to retain their vigor within a postindustrial environment as well as within an industrial one. Most of Japan's New Religions developed in response to the religious needs of lower-class inhabitants who had left rural areas for urban areas with the advent of industrialization. Still, between these nuclei of the New Religions in their growth periods and upper middle-class people with a higher education there was not a great cultural gap. When in the course of time the living standards of the Japanese people improved overall, the number of well-educated people who joined the New Religions also increased. As a result, the cultural resources of the teachings and group management skills that members of the New Religions had nurtured so long were available in sufficient amounts to enable those religions to meet the needs of urban middle-class residents isolated in postindustrial society. This phenomenon can be compared with the way the Pentecostal movement, which began in the United States at the beginning of this century as a movement among the lower middle class, developed from the 1960s into a movement that involved the whole middle class, including those with a higher education.

In this way, though there are differences in the socio-economic conditions forming the background to the New Religions' expansion into the United States and other places, still, if taken as the formative process of an urban culture common to cities worldwide in the wake of international capitalism, the phenomenon can surely be seen as the product of one and the same socioeconomic condition.[8] In other words, the New Religions gained the support of urban residents by offering in the midst of worldwide urbanization the support of congenial communities and cultural resources that deal with things in a practical, realistic way and preserve stable identities in the midst of diverse human relationships.

THE FEATURES OF EXPANDING NEW RELIGIONS AND THEIR APPEAL

The preceding section outlined the way New Religions as a whole might appeal to inhabitants of a society accepting them, showing the connections with cultural and political conditions and with socioeconomic conditions. In this section I would like to consider the way those New Religions that were accepted appealed to local inhabitants. First, I will note which specific groups expanded successfully into foreign cultures and then consider their particular features.

Though there are hundreds of New Religions in Japan, only a few have garnered a sizable following in foreign fields. Representative of the successful groups are Sōka Gakkai, Seichō-no-Ie, Sekai Kyūsei-kyō, PL, and Sūkyō Mahikari. While Tenri-kyō has been successful in Korea and Taiwan, it has not produced notable results in other regions. Two groups representative of New Religions whose expansion into foreign cultures has been relatively unsuccessful despite the size of their membership within Japan would be Risshō Kōsei-kai and Shin'nyo-en. Lack of success overseas, however, is also greatly affected by accidental circumstances. For example, Seichō-no-Ie in Brazil was accepted as a religion offering the wartime and postwar Japanese community support for their identity as Japanese. When the Japanese community built up a large foothold in Brazilian society, a foundation for expansion was available to Seichō-no-Ie without any extra effort on its part.[9]

It is still possible to say that religions that succeed in expansion into other cultures have some inherent features making them deserving of that success. For example, Sōka Gakkai's spirit of aggressive, argumentative proselytization of complete strangers is easily surmised to be effective in circumstances where isolation in urban society has increased and diverse cultures coexist and clash with one another. Here I do not intend, however, to go into the self-evident factor of aggressive proselytization; what I want to do is consider what aspects in the contents of the teachings and beliefs are suited to expansion into foreign cultures.

STRAIGHTFORWARD MAGICAL PRACTICE

Sōka Gakkai, Seichō-no-Ie, Sekai Kyūsei-kyō, PL, and Sūkyō Mahikari are, all of them, groups in which straightforward magical practice forms the essence (or at least is one of the things forming the essence) of religious life. In Sōka Gakkai, performing *gongyō* and reciting the *daimoku* before the *go-honzon*; in Seichō-no-Ie, performing the simple meditation of *shinsōkan* and intonation of the sacred scriptures for the spirits of the ancestors; in Sekai Kyūsei-kyō and Sūkyō Mahikari, pouring the deity's "light" into the body through the outstretched palm; and in PL, praying to have one's problems transferred to the instructor together with a vow by means of the *oyashikiri* ("magical prayer")—these are the main, or some of the main, religious practices. The belief that such magical practices produce mysterious, miraculous effects needs no explaining, one merely observes the practice and one understands it at once. And one can try it for oneself and see that it works. When this belief is transmitted to people of another culture, it is attended by almost no difficulties in communication. That is because it is something in the physical, experiential sphere, which needs little meaningful articulation on the linguistic level.

勤行

神想観

親遂断

　　Similar types of religious groups did not just happen to form by chance. Except for Sūkyō Mahikari, which can be considered an offshoot of Sekai Kyūsei-kyō, all these groups were founded between 1910 and 1930 by intellectually gifted founders with large cities for their bases. In the context of the clashes of diverse value systems and the relativization of traditional culture, both keenly experienced in large cities, they all intended to present straightforward magic as the foundation for unswerving faith, and by this means overcome relativism. The expansion into foreign cultures of those religious groups was advanced with the intention of transcending the relativization of culture in places where such relativization was on the increase.

PRACTICAL LIFE ETHICS

NAKAMAKI (1989) has made a very interesting study of the reasons for PL's success in Brazil. One of the things about PL that is appealing is the belief in miracles based on the magical prayer referred to as the *oyashikiri*. Still, merely a miracle belief based on magical practice is not enough to take hold of large numbers of people. The reason why people make an effort to follow PL over a long period of time is, he says, the appeal of its ethical teachings and guidance. Its ethics are adapted to the concrete situations of daily life. It preaches the mutual support of equal partners in a nuclear, rather than a patriarchal, family; a work ethic that includes not only honesty and industry but also working for society and for one's neighbors, and regards work as a form of self-expression; and an ethic of "citizenship" that encourages service to the local community. Furthermore, through one-to-one counseling it provides concrete, practical guidelines. All these things were, he says, lacking in the traditional Catholic Church and were features that appealed to Brazil's rapidly growing urban population. Nakamaki also mentions actual cases of people who talked of the appeal of the teaching that responsibility for one's good or bad fortune rests with oneself, or the appeal of the teaching that labor freely and gladly rendered ultimately redounds to one's own happiness. Practical ethics that include the utilitarian idea that service ultimately brings happiness reveals particularly well the characteristic feature of ethics in the New Religions (see SHIMAZONO 1991).

Explaining the appeal of PL in terms of its miracle beliefs and practical urban ethics would also apply to most of the other groups that have succeeded in advancing into other cultures. Whether Brazil, or the United States of America, or Korea, or Thailand, cultural resources that were lacking in the traditional religious groups but abundantly available in Japan's New Religions appear here in their classic form. Only, in the case of PL, the manner of presenting the practical ethics is systematic and thoroughgoing, and herein lies the reason why it has had a greater appeal than the other groups. As Nakamaki explains, PL's ethical guidance reaches out into the practical details of living in an exhaustive and minute way. Another feature of its ethical statements, like those of Seichō-no-Ie, is that they pay careful attention to subtle shifts of mentality and present technical, mind-control-type methods for bringing about psychological stability. Like the "new thought" and "positive thinking" that has been popular in the United States since the end of the nineteenth century, or the "human potential" movement of recent years, techniques for preserving mental stability in the midst of urban living, with its isolation and stressfulness, have been linked with ethical practice.

LOGICAL STATEMENTS

What accounts for the appeal of Seichō-no-Ie and Sekai Kyūsei-kyō? They, too, stress miracle belief and preach practical ethics for living. In this respect they have something in common with PL. Yet they also have a slightly different appeal: their systematic, logical statements. The founder of Seichō-no-Ie, Taniguchi Masaharu, and the founder of Sekai Kyūsei-kyō, Okada Mokichi, both were culturally refined men blessed with a gift for writing discourse in a coherent way. In this they were both quite different from other founders. In the cases of female founders most at home in the world of oral tradition, or male founders lacking in literary knowledge, the words they left behind are not too logical, but what they want to say is conveyed through delicate nuances. This makes translation of their teachings extremely difficult. Also, such religious groups tend to be averse to logical explanations of their teachings and to learning. Typical examples of this are the groups in the Reiyūkai family tree. These groups are not suited for expansion to other cultures when one considers the importance of transmitting teachings in a readily understandable form. In contrast, Seichō-no-Ie and Sekai Kyūsei-kyō are able to draw non-Japanese to the world of their teachings through written expression that, while easy to understand, is logical and coherent, rather than a delicately nuanced mode of expression that is bound to one determinate culture.

In addition, I believe that Seichō-no-Ie's stress on the importance of members reading its literature is one of the very important points of its appeal. In present-day urban

---

society, being proficient in written expression and having a habit of reading is an important condition for social success. As was true in Japan in the 1930s, in a society where urbanization advances rapidly, religions that make positive use of easily comprehensible literature as a tool for propagation are, by that fact alone, already attractive. Also, if easy-to-read, easy-to-understand doctrinal literature is available in translation, the message can get across even without the mediation of close person-to-person contact. In propagation to people of a different language, and in an age of cultural diversity, propagation that relies on the medium of literature that is not so bound by the delicate nuances of a specific culture is especially effective.[10]

A POSITIVE APPROACH TO RELIGIOUS PLURALISM

What was said in the preceding section could almost be said about Sōka Gakkai as well.[11] But there is one important difference between Sōka Gakkai and Seichō-no-Ie, Sekai Kyūsei-kyō, and PL. This is the attitude towards other religions, especially the attitude towards the traditional religion dominant in the overseas country. Seichō-no-Ie, Sekai Kyūsei-kyō, and PL take a positive attitude to the dominant traditional religion and allow their members to continue to belong to, for example, the Catholic Church. This attitude is based on the idea that all religions are in fact rooted in the same reality and seek the same thing. They preach that their religion and Christianity are not fundamentally different, but they are merely complementing and perfecting what was lacking in the earlier Christian religion. They therefore adopt a flexible policy of leaving such things as rites of passage to the Catholic Church. This line of thinking is readily accepted by people who have taken on traditional Catholic views and rites out of custom. Also, the adoption of such a generous attitude has the additional benefit that it avoids the troubles that arise when people with many ties to a traditional religion sever those ties to join these new religious groups.

Sōka Gakkai, on the other hand, demands exclusive commitment. Its members must sever their relations with their traditional religion. This can be the cause of troubles with the traditional religious bodies, with relatives, and with neighbors. In this respect, Sōka Gakkai can be described as putting itself in a slightly unfavorable position.

Yet, seen from another perspective, these two types of groups have something in common: both assume the coexistence of diverse religions, both have prepared coherent statements for handling this situation and have prepared positive measures to cope with it.[12] People in present-day society are placed in circumstances that make them keenly aware of the coexistence of diverse religions. For a person to choose one from among the different religions and be committed to it, something is needed that will convince the person. By insisting that other religions are wrong and that it is correct, Sōka Gakkai is showing one type of a response to the pluralistic coexistence of religions. What this means is that Seichō-no-Ie, Sekai Kyūsei-kyō, and PL on the one hand, and Sōka Gakkai on the other, are adopting differing approaches to a situation they all consciously recognize, that of the coexistence of diverse religions.

I have attempted to explore the appeal of Japanese New Religions to local residents by analyzing the features of those groups that have succeeded in expansion into other cultures. It is necessary, though, to consider also the basic feature shared by all the New Religions of Japan, that of their being this-worldly oriented religions.[13]

To be this-worldly oriented first of all implies that a systematic conception of salvation provides the framework for these religions of magical, this-worldly salvation. In Japan's New Religions, the healing of sickness, harmony in the family, and success in one's work are directly linked to the highest goal of belief: salvation. Secondly, it means putting weight on self-help and effort in one's present life. This is closely connected with the PL characteristic described earlier. An extremely large number of Japanese New Religions do not preach reliance on the power of God, the power of Buddha, the power of this or that holy person, but preach that happiness cannot be attained unless one changes one's own mental attitude and manner of daily life.

This-worldly orientation in the above two meanings is linked with an immanentist view of the divine that recognizes the divinity of the human being and recognizes divinity in existence in the present world in general. These characteristics were lacking in traditional religions with their strong tendency to be affirmative with regard to the other world and negative toward this world. It is easy to understand why such

---

this-worldly orientation and an immanentist view of the divine are attractive to people living in a competitive society where industrialization and urbanization have advanced and changes are extreme.

CULTURAL DISCORD DUE TO EXPANSION OVERSEAS AND RELIGIOUS UNIFICATION

It has been reported many times that religious groups propagating their religion in other cultures have attempted to adapt themselves to the respective alien cultures. PL, for example, takes a variety of steps to make their translations of documents readily understandable to the local people. It has also been reported that they have also introduced elements that differ significantly from the way ceremonies and assemblies are conducted in Japan (NAKAMAKI 1989: 440–45). Seichō-no-Ie is said to have omitted from its translation of *Seimei no jissō* and other documents passages that might encounter resistance from Brazilians. The NSA has also made repeated efforts to Americanize; one example is its "pioneer spirit" catch phrase in connection with its active involvement in the Bicentenary of American Independence (WILLIAMS 1989).

Apart from these attempts to adapt on the part of the religious groups themselves, there can be spontaneous changes made to the contents of teachings or practice by the non-Japanese members of the groups. Consciously or unconsciously, local religious culture or local ways of group management can be introduced, leading to ways that differ from the parent body in Japan. If steps are taken to ensure control by dint of force, discontent can arise among local believers, and this in turn can even lead to a splitting off of whole groups. While adaptations made by religious groups are done for the sake of more effective propagation, at the same time they can be viewed as strategies to control local believers within the framework of the larger group. This means that New Religions accepted by people of alien cultures have to face new problems of cultural discord and religious unification as a result of their adaptations.

Even within Japan itself it is not unusual for groups of believers in a particular religious organization to deviate from the regulation of the central body, or even split off entirely. Reiyū-kai and Sekai Kyūsei-kyō, for example, have seen large numbers of groups escape control of the central body—some have branched off completely—and perhaps there are but few examples of medium-sized groups that could not be classified as branches from larger groups. In the case of groups overseas, it is probably even more difficult to maintain control, given the geographical and cultural distances separating them.

Deviation of overseas believer groups from the control of headquarters in Japan already occurred in various places around the time of World War II as a result of loss of contact. In Brazil a group of Ōmoto followers that included a large number of non-Japanese was beginning to form from around 1930, but contact with Ōmoto headquarters ceased after government oppression of the group within Japan in 1935 (MAEYAMA and SMITH 1983). The group of believers in Brazil developed rather independently and began to engage in activities similar to those of such popular Brazilian religions as spiritism and Umbanda. After the war contact with headquarters was restored, and organizational affiliation was formally renewed, but the contents of its religious activities underwent no change; headquarters has done almost nothing to intervene.

In the case of Tenri-kyō in Taiwan, contact with headquarters was cut after the war, and the Chiaitungmen church, which was run solely by local believers, adopted *poe* (divination stones) and the drawing of lots to divine the right times to pray, the offering of gilt paper to gods and ancestors, and other elements of Chinese folk religion (HUANG 1989). But with the resumption of operations of the Tenri propagation office in Taiwan in 1967, slowly but steadily the church was restored to something similar to what exists in Japan. Still, it is said that some subordinate missionary stations even now maintain deviant elements. In Korea, where anti-Japanese feelings run high, problems of this sort are even more serious, and control by headquarters is a difficult matter, including the problem of church unity within Korea itself.

A recent example of discord occurred in Sōka Gakkai's overseas organization. NSA (Sōka Gakkai in the U.S.A.), which achieved explosive growth at the end of the 1960s, attempted to hand over leadership of the local organization to non-Japanese (WILLIAMS 1989). But the new leadership stratum made up principally of non-Japanese did not like the central-administrative, organization-mobilizing nature of the group and attempted to adopt policies that set a value on the autonomous activities of regional groups and on democratic procedures for running NSA as a whole. This happened to coincide, however, with a sudden slowdown in NSA growth and even signs of decline. From the 1980s, under the guidance of headquarters, there was a return to a central-administrative, organization-mobilizing type of religious group along with a return to a leadership setup in which Japanese formed the core. In the process, a group of people, mainly whites who for a time had been in leadership positions, separated and began independent activities. While detailed information is not available, a similar large-scale secession also has occurred in Indonesia.

Judging from the experiences of groups splitting away from parent bodies within Japan, we can anticipate that the problem of regulating overseas believer groups will occur often in the future. There will no doubt be some groups in which the overseas believers will be numerically stronger. There is already a faction, the Shinsei-ha, within Sekai Kyūsei-kyō in Brazil, that is larger than its sponsoring body in Japan. Also, the sources of propagation activity have shifted in recent years with, for example, Brazilian members of Seichō-no-Ie and Sekai Kyūsei-kyō doing successful missionary work in Europe, and with a Korean member of Tenri-kyō propagating in Argentina.[14] At present, it appears that in most of the groups the authority of Japanese propagators is preserved, but it is only a matter of time before local propagators will have more say. In the future, financial aid coming from headquarters will undoubtedly decrease when Japan's status as an economic superpower begins to decline. When that happens, the question will surely arise, how will the central body in Japan be able to maintain control over religious bodies overseas? It is impossible to predict whether or not it will be able to maintain its present unity as a single multinational organization. New Religions that have expanded overseas can be compared to multinational enterprises, it has been argued, and they can be characterized as multinational religions (INOUE 1985; NAKAMAKI 1986, 1989), but when separations occur overseas and a religion ceases to be a single organization, we shall have to think again about the appropriateness of this designation.

SIGNIFICANCE FROM A HISTORY OF RELIGIONS PERSPECTIVE

The expansion of Japan's New Religions into other cultures from the 1960s on was founded on the imperialist-inspired invasions before the war as well as massive migrations from Japan, which continued even after the war. Without these two factors there probably would not have been such an extensive expansion into other cultures. It is also clear that Japan's economic prosperity is another contributing factor to recent expansion into other cultures. The success of Sekai Kyūsei-kyō and Sōka Gakkai in Thailand, for example, cannot be fully comprehended unless one takes into account the huge economic influence wielded by Japanese businesses in the country and the financial and spiritual help liberally poured into Thailand from Japan for the sake of propagation. In a certain sense, then, the expansion into alien cultures of Japan's New Religions must be seen from one viewpoint as the fruit of the growth in economic and military influence of the Japanese.

Still, the expansion into alien cultures from the 1960s on also has to be grasped in the light of the rapid expansion in cultural exchange worldwide, with movements of personnel and information on the increase. This is also linked with a spread of cultural tolerance. Societies that previously were closed to other religions have in the past twenty years become open to missionary activity. In years to come, places like the Soviet Union, Eastern Europe, and China will no doubt be thrown open as markets where propagation can be freely conducted. We can expect that places for extensive activity will open anew to those religions in the world that favor propagation and evangelism, and that they will expand.

What sorts of religions will be active in these new markets and vying for results from missionary activity? There are four categories:

1 the Catholic Church, Greek Orthodox Church, and Islam will probably extend their influence to neighboring regions by enlarging their present bases;
2 the various Protestant sects will probably show growth in Catholic areas and other regions where traditional Christian culture still has strong influence; they will also probably grow in places like Korea and ethnic Chinese societies, where the influence of Confucianism,

which shares the Protestant character of a religion of moral duties and stress on scriptures, is strong;

3 loosely organized religious philosophies that are mystical and psychotherapeutic in character, such as the "New Age" in the United States of America and the Anthroposophie movement in Germany, will probably gain wide acceptance among people in the higher education class; and

4 new religions that have been born in various parts of the globe, with the potential for huge development side by side with all of the above, especially as a force to compete with the Protestant sects.[15]

The most conspicuous cradles of these new religions have been the United States and Japan. The new religious groups originating in the United States are also often called "cults": the Mormons, Jehovah's Witnesses, Scientology, etc. The Unification Church that was born in Korea is also powerful. The Wat Dhammakāya movement begun in the 1960s in Thailand is an example of a new religious movement with a high potential for spreading to other countries. Seen in a global perspective, Japan's New Religions have much in common with these religious groups and movements.

As I suggested above, Japan's New Religions have garnered great success in societies where urban populations have increased as a result of industrialization. Again, in those societies where industrialization has already been attained and the loneliness of urban living has deepened, they are considered to have the potential for a certain degree of success in missionary activity. In such societies the New Religions try to indicate concrete, practical guidelines for overcoming the problems isolated individuals face in ordinary daily life. And they offer such people spiritual support for self-help and mutual-support communities. In doing this, they offer something people can hang on to as they acquire moral self-discipline and continue to live as urban middle-class citizens. Furthermore, they have more this-world intentionality than sects, and they try to respond to urban residents' this-worldly aspirations.

In a world community characterized by increasing industrialization and urbanization, the demand for religions that fulfill such functions will probably increase. The various New Religions in Japan have, alongside cults originating in the United States, been in the vanguard in various regions throughout the world, nurturing and storing up the cultural resources for meeting that demand.

NOTES

* This article first appeared in the special issue on "Japanese New Religions Abroad" edited by Mark R. Mullins and Richard F. Young, *Japanese Journal of Religious Studies* 18/2–3 (June–September 1991), pp. 105–32. It was translated from the Japanese by Edmund R. Skrzypczak. SHIMAZONO Susumu is Associate Professor in the Department of Religious Studies at the University of Tokyo.

1 The history of the overseas expansion of Japan's New Religions can be found in summary form in INOUE et al. 1990, pp. 608–57.

2 One exception was Ōmoto. More will be said about this group in the sections below.

3 Most of what follows is based on information I received and materials presented to me when I visited, in summer and autumn 1990, the headquarters of Sōka Gakkai, Seichō-no-Ie, Sekai Kyūsei-kyō (Shinsei-ha), PL, Tenri-kyō, and Sūkyō Mahikari.

4 Sōka Gakkai's overseas organizations are known by a variety of names. In this study I shall refer to them all simply as "Sōka Gakkai," except for the organization in the United States, which is widely known as NSA.

5 The following description is dependent on WILLIAMS 1989.

6 One can obtain some idea of conditions during this period from YAMAMOTO 1982 and HUANG 1989.

7 For a consideration of these features of Brazilian culture and their relationship to features of the religious situation, with a comparison with the United States and Japan, see NAKAMAKI 1986, pp. 204–28.

8 For a work that presents this point of view, see Shōji Kōkichi, ed., *Sekai shakai no kōzō to dōtai*, Tokyo: Hōsei Daigaku Shuppan-kai, 1986.

9 See SEICHŌ NO IE HONBU 1980, MAEYAMA 1983, and MATSUDA 1988, 1989. STARK and ROBERTS (1982, pp. 53–68) point out that sometimes a new religious movement that began in a large-scale society is forced to remain a minor movement there, and so early hopes wither and die, but when it shifts to a small-scale society it reaps unexpected success—that is, supported by many influential members at first, it develops into a powerful, prestigious religion in that small society. The assumption that another religion might have reaped the greatest success in Brazil if it had become the most influential in the Japanese community, cannot be completely groundless.

10 The leader of Seichō-no-Ie's Brazilian propagation program,

Matsuda Miyoshi, has written that "another unique and absolute deciding factor in Seichō-no-Ie's enlightening not only of Brazil but also of the whole world, is the new campaign method of propagation through the written word. There can be no denying that Seichō-no-Ie's spread to the most distant land from Japan, Brazil, in the very same year Seichō-no-Ie began in Japan (1930), its spread to the remotest corners of Brazil, and the fact that the Brazilian translation of *Seimei no jissō* was widely diffused and became a pillar of strength, are all due to the power of propagation through the written word" (MATSUDA 1989, 331–32).

[11] This also has a bearing on what I said earlier: Seichō-no-Ie, Sekai Kyūsei-kyō, and Sōka Gakkai have in common the fact that they were founded by men of intellectual ability familiar with history, religious doctrine, modern thought, and scientific statement. This sort of religious group forms a large type within the New Religions, standing alongside the "indigenous-emergent type" that a fairly unlettered founder began from a folk-religion background, and the "moral-cultivation type" in which popular ideas of character building and virtue come to be linked to a salvation belief—a type that can be called the "intellectual-thought type." Further, the groups in the Reiyū-kai tradition and most of the groups derived from Shin'nyo-en fall midway between the "indigenous-emergent type" and the "intellectual-thought type," so they belong to a fourth type we might refer to as an intermediate type. According to my tentative classification of the New Religions, most of the religious groups that have succeeded in expanding into alien cultures belong to the "intellectual-thought type." In contrast, the lack of success overseas of the quite numerically large "intermediate-type" groups is particularly striking (SHIMA-ZONO 1990, 216–23).

[12] For the philosophy of Ōmoto, which was the source of Seichō-no-Ie's and Sekai Kyūsei-kyō's idea that all religions are the same, see YOUNG 1988.

[13] The brief discussion that follows can be fleshed out by consulting TSUSHIMA et al., 1979.

[14] NAKAMAKI (1989, pp. 445–47) draws attention to this aspect of PL.

[15] STARK and BAINBRIDGE (1985) divide religious groups in contemporary North America and Europe into three categories and attempt to depict the ways in which they have taken turns being influential. The categories are: "church," "sect," and "cult." "Cult" is subdivided into "cult movement," "client cult," and "audience cult." I have made four categories, but they are not that far apart from Stark and Bainbridge's. I have singled out their "cult movement" and taken it to be "new religions." Again, what I have placed in my third category to a great extent overlaps with their "audience cult" and "client cult," though not completely.

CUMULATIVE BIBLIOGRAPHY

This list includes only works cited in this book and is not intended to serve as a comprehensive bibliography on the subject of Japanese religions.

ABEGGLEN, James C. *Management and Worker: The Japanese Solution.* Tokyo: Sophia University, in co-operation with Kodansha International Ltd. (An expanded and updated edition of *The Japanese Factory*, 1973), 1975.

AKAMATSU Toshihide and Philip YAMPOLSKY. "Muromachi Zen and the Gozan system." In *Japan in the Muromachi Age*, J. W. Hall and T. Toyoda, eds., 313–29. Berkeley: University of California Press, 1977.

ALBANESE, Catherine L. *Nature Religion in America.* Chicago: University of Chicago Press, 1990.

ANESAKI Masaharu. *History of Japanese Religion.* London: Kegan Paul, 1930 (reprint 1963, Tokyo: Tuttle).

ARIYOSHI Sawako. *Kōkotsu no hito* [A man in ecstasy]. Tokyo: Shinchōsha, 1972.

ASHIZU Yoshihiko. "The Shinto directive and the constitution." *Contemporary Religions in Japan* 1/2: 16–34, 1960.

ASTLEY, Trevor. "A matter of principles: A note on the recent conflict between Nichiren Shōshū and Sōka Gakkai." *Japanese Religions* 17/2: 167–75, 1992.

ASTON, W. G. *Shinto (The Way of the Gods).* London: Longmans Green and Co., 1905.

BELLAH, Robert. "Civil religion in America." *Daedalus* 96: 1–20, 1967.

———. "Religious evolution." *American Sociological Review* 29: 358–74, 1964.

———. *Tokugawa Religion: The Values of Pre-Industrial Japan.* Boston: Beacon Press, 1970.

BELLAH, Robert, and P. HAMMOND. *Varieties of Civil Religion.* San Francisco: Harper & Row, 1980.

BENEDICT, Ruth. *The Chrysanthemum and the Sword.* Boston: Houghton Mifflin, 1946 (1954 ed., Tokyo: Tuttle).

BERGER, Peter and Hansfried KELLNER. *Sociology Reinterpreted: An Essay on Method and Vocation.* Garden City, New York: Anchor Books, 1981.

BLACKER, Carmen. *The Catalpa Bow: A Study of Shamanistic Practices in Japan.* London: George Allen and Unwin, 1975.

BLAKER, Michael. "Japan in 1977: An emerging consensus." *Asian Survey* 18 (January): 91–102, 1978.

BLASI, Anthony J. *Making Charisma: The Social Construction of Paul's Public Image.* New Brunswick, New Jersey: Transaction Publishers, 1991.

BOCK, Felicia Gressit, trans. *Engi-Shiki. Procedures of the Engi Era, Books I–V.* Monumenta Nipponica monograph. Tokyo: Sophia University, 1970.

BODIFORD, William M. *Sōtō Zen in Medieval Japan*. Studies in East Asian Buddhism 8. Honolulu: University of Hawaii Press, 1993.

BRETT, Cecil C. "The Komeito and local Japanese politics." *Asian Survey* 19: 366–78, 1979.

BROMLEY, David G. and Anson D. SHUPE, Jr. *Strange Gods*. Beacon Hill & Boston: Beacon Press, 1981.

BROOKS, Anne P. "*Mizuko kuyō* and Japanese Buddhism." *Japanese Journal of Religious Studies* 8/3–4: 119–47, 1981.

BROWN, Delmer M. and ISHIDA Ichirō. *The Future and the Past—A Translation and Study of the Gukanshō, An Interpretive History of Japan Written in 1219*. Berkeley: University of California Press, 1979.

CALDAROLA, Carlo. *Christianity the Japanese Way*. Leiden: E. J. Brill, 1979.

CAMPBELL, John Creighton. *How Policies Change: The Japanese Government and the Aging Society*. Princeton: Princeton University Press, 1992.

CHAMBERLAIN, Basil Hall. *Things Japanese*. London: Kegan Paul, Trench, Trubner & Co, 1939 (6th ed. revised [reprinted, Tokyo: Meicho Fukyūkai, 1985]).

———. *The Kojiki: Records of Ancient Matters*. Reprint, Rutland/Tokyo: Tuttle, 1982.

CHIBA Tokuji and ŌTSU Tadao. *Mabiki to mizuko* [Infanticide and *mizuko*]. Tokyo: Nōsan Gyoson Bunka Kyōkai, 1983.

COLEMAN, John. "Civil religion." *Sociological Analysis* 31: 67–77, 1970.

COLLCUTT, Martin. *Five Mountains: The Rinzai Zen Monastic Institution in Medieval Japan*. Cambridge: Harvard University Press, 1981.

CURTIS, Gerald L. *Election Campaigning, Japanese Style*. New York: Columbia University Press, 1971.

DATOR, James A. *Sōka Gakkai: Builders of the Third Civilization*. Seattle: University of Washington Press, 1969.

DAVIS, Winston. *Toward Modernity: A Developmental Typology of Popular Religious Affiliations in Japan*. East Asia Papers Series. Ithaca, NY: Cornell University Press, 1977.

———. *Dojo: Magic and Exorcism in Modern Japan*. Stanford: Stanford University Press, 1980.

———. "Fundamentalism in Japan: Religious and political." In *Fundamentalisms Observed*, Martin E. Marty and R. Scott Appleby, eds., 782–813. Chicago: University of Chicago Press, 1991.

———. *Japanese Religion and Society: Paradigms of Structure and Change*. Albany, NY: State University of New York Press, 1992.

DOBBELAERE, Karel. "Civil religion and the integration of society: A theoretical reflection and an application." *Japanese Journal of Religious Studies* 13/3: 127–46, 1986.

DOERNER, David L. "Comparative analysis of life after death in folk Shinto and Christianity." *Japanese Journal of Religious Studies* 4/2–3: 151–82, 1977.

DORE, Ronald P. *British Factory, Japanese Factory*. Berkeley: University of California Press, 1973.

EARHART, H. Byron. *Japanese Religions: Unity and Diversity*. 2nd ed. Encino, CA: Dickenson Publishing, 1974. [3rd ed., Belmont, CA: Wadsworth, 1982].

———. *The New Religions of Japan: A Bibliography of Western-Language Materials*. Second Edition. Ann Arbor: Center for Japanese Studies, University of Michigan, 1983.

———. *Gedatsu-kai and Religion in Contemporary Japan: Returning to the Center*. Bloomington and Indianapolis: Indiana University Press, 1989.

———. ELLWOOD, Robert S., Jr. *The Eagle and the Rising Sun*. Philadelphia: The Westminster Press, 1974.

FAURE, Bernard. "The Daruma-shū, Dōgen, and Sōtō Zen." *Monumenta Nipponica* 42/1: 25–55, 1987.

FOARD, James. "The boundaries of compassion: Buddhism and national tradition in Japanese pilgrimage." *Journal of Asian Studies* 41/2: 231–51, 1981.

FRIDELL, Wilbur M. "Government ethics textbooks in late Meiji Japan." *Journal of Asian Studies* 29/4: 823–33, 1970.

FUJII Masao. "Founder worship in Kamakura Buddhism." In *Religion and the Family in East Asia*, George A. DeVos and Takao Sofue, eds., 155–67. Berkeley: University of California Press, 1986.

GARON, Sheldon M. "State and religion in Imperial Japan, 1912–1945." *Journal of Japanese Studies* 12/2: 273–302, 1986.

GAUNTLETT, John Owen, and Robert K. HALL. *"Kokutai no hongi"—Cardinal Principles of the National Entity of Japan*. Cambridge: Harvard University Press, 1949.

GLUCK, Carol. *Japan's Modern Myths: Ideology in the Late Meiji Period*. Princeton: Princeton University Press, 1985.

GUTHRIE, Stewart. *A Japanese New Religion: Risshō Kōsei-kai in a Mountain Hamlet*. Ann Arbor: University of Michigan, 1988.

HARDACRE, Helen. *Lay Buddhism in Contemporary Japan: Reiyūkai Kyōdan*. Princeton, New Jersey: Princeton University Press, 1984.

———. *Kurozumikyō and the New Religions of Japan*. Princeton: Princeton University Press, 1986.

———. *Shintō and the State, 1868–1988*. Princeton: Princeton University Press, 1989.

———. "Gender and the Millenium in Ōmotokyō." In *Religious Innovation*, M. Williams and C. Cox, eds. Leiden: E. J. Brill, 1992.

HOLTOM, Daniel C. *Modern Japan and Shinto Nationalism*. Revised ed. New York: Paragon Books, 1963 (reprint of 1947 edition).

———. *The National Faith of Japan: A Study in Modern Shinto*. 1938 reprint. New York: Paragon Reprint Corp., 1963.

HORI Ichirō. *Folk Religion in Japan: Continuity and Change*. Edited by Joseph M. Kitagawa and Alan L. Miller. Chicago: University of Chicago Press, 1968.

HOSHINO Eiki. "A pillar of Japanese Buddhism: Founder belief." *Journal of Oriental Studies* 26: 78–89, 1987.

HOSHINO Eiki and TAKEDA Dōshō. "Indebtedness and comfort—The undercurrents of *mizuko kuyō* in contemporary Japan." *Japanese Journal of Religious Studies* 14/4: 305–20, 1987.

HOWES, John F. "The Non-Church Christian movement in Japan." *Transactions of the Asiatic Society of Japan* 5, 1957.

HUANG Chih-huei. "Tenrikyō no Taiwan ni okeru dendō to juyō" [Evangelism and acceptance of Tenri-kyō in Taiwan]. *Minzokugaku kenkyū* 54/3: 292–306, 1989.

HURBON, Laënnec. "Mahikari in the Caribbean." *Japanese Journal of Religious Studies* 18/2–3: 243–64, 1991.

―――. "New religious movements in the Caribbean." In *New Religious Movements and Rapid Social Change*, J. A. Beckford, ed., 146–76. London: Sage Publications Ltd., 1986.

IKADO Fujio. "Trend and problems of new religions: Religion in urban society." In *The Sociology of Japanese Religion*, Morioka Kiyomi and William H. Newell, eds., 101–17. Leiden: E. J. Brill,, 1968.

IKEGAMI Yoshimasa. *Akurei to seirei no butai: Okinawa no minshū kirisutokyō ni miru kyūsai sekai* [The stage of demons and the Holy Spirit: Soteriological structure of Okinawan Charismatic Christianity]. Tokyo: Dōbutsusha, 1991.

INOUE Nobutaka. *Umi o watatta Nihon shūkyō* [Japanese religions that have crossed the seas]. Tokyo: Kōbundō, 1985.

INOUE Nobutaka, ed. *Matsuri: Festival and Rite in Japanese Life.* Contemporary Papers on Japanese Religion, vol. 1. Translated by Norman Havens. Tokyo: Institute for Japanese Culture and Classics, Kokugakuin University, 1988.

―――. *New Religions.* Contemporary Papers in Japanese Religion, vol. 2. Translated by Norman Havens. Tokyo: Institute for Japanese Culture and Classics, Kokugakuin University, 1991.

INOUE Nobutaka et al., eds. *Shinshūkyō jiten* [Encyclopedia of the New Religions]. Tokyo: Kōbundō, 1990.

ISHII Kenji. "The secularization of religion in the city." *Japanese Journal of Religious Studies* 13/2–3: 193–209, 1986.

JANSEN, Marius, ed. *Changing Japanese Attitudes toward Modernization.* Princeton: Princeton University Press, 1965.

JENSEN, Adolf E. *Mythos und Kult bei Naturvölkern* [Myth and cult among primitive peoples]. Wiesbaden: Steiner, 1960.

JOHNSON, Chalmers. "Japan 1975: Mr. Clean muddles through." *Asian Survey* 16 (January): 31–41, 1976.

KAMATA, Satoshi. *Japan in the Passing Lane.* New York: Pantheon Books, 1982.

KANEKO Satoru. "Dimensions of religiosity among believers in Japanese folk religion." *Journal for the Scientific Study of Religion* 29/1: 1–18, 1990.

KATSUDA Kichitarō. *Heiwa kenpō o utagau* [Doubts about the peace constitution]. Tokyo: Kōdansha, 1981.

KAWADA Haruo. *Jinja-shintō no jōshiki* [Basics of Shrine Shinto]. Kyoto: Seimeisha, 1982.

KETELAAR, James. *Of Heretics and Martyrs in Meiji Japan: Buddhism and Its Persecution.* Princeton: Princeton University Press, 1990.

KITAGAWA, Joseph M. "The contemporary religious situation in Japan." *Japanese Religions* 2/2–3: 24–42, 1961.
———. *Religion in Japanese History*. New York: Columbia University Press, 1966.
———. *On Understanding Japanese Religion*. Princeton: Princeton University Press, 1987.
KOMIYA Ryūtarō. "Ureubeki migi senkai—Gendai Nihon no seiji keizaiteki jōkyō" [The regretful trend to the right]. In *Kikan Gendai Keizai* 34: 4–21, 1979.
LAFLEUR, William. *Liquid Life: Abortion and Buddhism in Japan*. Princeton: Princeton University Press, 1992.
LEBRA, Takie Sugiyama. *Japanese Patterns of Behavior*. Honolulu: University of Hawaii Press, 1976.
LEBRA, Wm. P. *Okinawan Religion*. Honolulu: University of Hawaii Press, 1966.
LEE, Robert. *Stranger in the Land: A Study of the Church in Japan*. London: Lutterworth Press, 1967.
LOKOWANDT, Ernst. *Die rechtliche Entwicklung des Staats-Shintō in der ersten Hälfte der Meiji-Zeit (1868—1890)* [The juridical development of State Shinto in the first half of the Meiji period]. Wiesbaden: Harrassowitz, 1978.
———. *Zum Verhältnis von Staat und Shintō im heutigen Japan—Eine Materialsammlung* [On the relationship of State and Shinto in present Japan: A collection of materials]. Studies in Oriental Religions, vol. 6. Wiesbaden: Harrassowitz, 1981.
MAEYAMA, Takashi. "Japanese religions in southern Brazil: Change and syncretism." *Latin American Studies* (University of Tsukuba) 6: 181–238, 1983.
MAEYAMA, Takashi and Robert J. SMITH. "Ōmoto: A Japanese 'New Religion' in Brazil." *Latin American Studies* (University of Tsukuba) 5: 83–102, 1983.
MARCURE, K. "The Danka system," *Monumenta Nipponica* 40/1: 39–67, 1985.
MATSUDA Miyoshi. *Burajiru dendō no hanseiki* [An incomplete record of evangelism in Brazil]. Tokyo: Nihon Kyōbunsha, 1988.
———. *Hikari wa kokkyō o koete* [The light crosses national boundaries]. Tokyo: Nihon Kyōbunsha, 1989.
MATSUNAGA, Alicia and Daigan. *Foundation of Japanese Buddhism*. 2 vols. Los Angeles/Tokyo: Buddhist Books International, 1974–1976.
McFARLAND, H. Neill. *The Rush Hour of the Gods: A Study of New Religious Movements in Japan*. New York: Macmillan Co., 1967.
McGUIRE, Meredith. *Religion: The Social Context*. Belmont, CA: Wadsworth, 1981.
McMULLIN, Neil. *Buddhism and the State in Sixteenth-Century Japan*, Princeton: Princeton University Press, 1984.
MÉTRAUX, Daniel. "The dispute between the Sōka Gakkai and the Nichiren Shōshū priesthood: A lay revolution against a conservative clergy." *Japanese Journal of Religious Studies* 19/4: 325–36, 1992.
MIYAKE Hitoshi. "Folk religion." In *Japanese Religion*, Hori Ichirō, et al., eds., 121–43. Tokyo: Kodansha, 1972.
———. *Shugendō girei no kenkyū: Zōhoban* [Studies in Shugendō ritual; expanded edition]. Tokyo: Shunjūsha, 1985a.

———. *Shugendō shisō no kenkyū* [Studies in Shugendō thought]. Tokyo: Shunjūsha, 1985b.

———. *Shugendō jiten* [A Shugendō dictionary]. Tokyo: Tōkyōdō Shuppan, 1986.

MIYANAGA, Kuniko. "Social reproduction and transcendence: An analysis of the Sekai Mahikari Bunmei Kyodan, a heterodox religious movement in conteporary Japan." Ph.D. dissertation, University of British Columbia, 1983.

MONBUSHŌ, ed. *Kokutai no hongi* [Cardinal principles of the national entity]. Tokyo: Monbushō, 1937.

MORIOKA Kiyomi. "Gairai shūkyō no dochakuka o meguru gainenteki seiri" [A conceptual examination of the indigenization of foreign-born religions]. *Shichō* 1099: 52–57, 1972.

———. *Nihon no kindai shakai to kirisutokyō* [Japan's modern society and Christianity]. Tokyo: Hyōronsha, 1976.

———. *Religion in Changing Japanese Society*. Tokyo: University of Tokyo Press, 1975.

———. "Gendai shakai no ningen to shūkyō" [Religion and man in contemporary society]. In *Jurisuto zōkan sōgō tokushū 21—Gendaijin to shūkyō* [Jurist (extra number–special issue) 21: Religion and contemporary man], 91–96. Tokyo: Yūhikaku, 1980.

———. "Ancestor worship in contemporary Japan: Continuity and change." In *Religion and the Family in East Asia*, George A. DeVos and Takao Sofue, eds., 201–13. Los Angeles: University of California Press, 1984.

MULLINS, Mark R. "Japanese Pentecostalism and the world of the dead: A study of cultural adaptation in Iesu no Mitama Kyōkai." *Japanese Journal of Religious Studies* 17/4: 353–74, 1990.

———. "Japan's New Age and Neo-New Religions: Sociological Interpretations." In *Perspectives on the New Age*, James R. Lewis and J. Gordon Melton, eds., 232–46. Albany, NY: State University of New York Press, 1992.

MULLINS, Mark R., and Richard F. YOUNG, eds. *Japanese New Religions Abroad*. Special issue of *Japanese Journal of Religious Studies* 18/2–3, 1991.

MURAKAMI Shigeyoshi. *Irei to shōkon—Yasukuni no shisō* [Comforting and inviting the souls: The idea of Yasukuni]. Tokyo: Iwanami Shoten, 1974.

———. *Japanese Religion in the Modern Century*. Translated by H. Byron Earhart. Tokyo: University of Tokyo Press, 1980.

MURAMATSU Minoru. "Jinkō ninshin chūzetsu no tōkeiteki kansatsu" [A statistical study of abortions]. *Shūkyō to gendai* 4/5 (May): 14–18, 1983.

NAKAMAKI Hirochika. *Shinsekai no Nihon shūkyō* [Japanese religions in the new world]. Tokyo: Heibonsha, 1986.

———. *Nihon shūkyō to nikkei shūkyō no kenkyū* [Studies of Japanese religions and Japanese-derived religions]. Tokyo: Tōsui Shobō, 1989.

———. *Mukashi daimyō, ima kaisha—Kigyō to shūkyō* [In the olden days feudal lords, nowadays companies: Business enterprises and religion]. Kyoto: Tankōsha, 1992.

NAKAMURA Hajime. *Nihonjin no shii hōhō* [The ways of thinking of Japanese people]. Tokyo: Shunjūsha, 1961.

──. *Ways of Thinking of Eastern Peoples: India, China, Tibet, Japan*, ed. by Philip P. Wiener. Honolulu, Hawaii: East-West Center Press, 1964.

──. "Basic features of the legal, political, and economic thought in Japan." In *The Japanese Mind: Essentials of Japanese Philosophy and Culture*, Charles A. Moore, ed., 143–63. Honolulu: University Press of Hawaii, 1967.

NEWELL, William H., ed. *Ancestors*. Hawthorne, NY: Mouton de Gruyter, 1976.

NISHIKAWA Shigenori. "The Daijōsai, the constitution, and Christian faith," *The Japan Christian Quarterly* 56/3: 132–46, 1990.

NISHIYAMA Shigeru. "Indigenization and transformation of Christianity in a Japanese rural community." *Japanese Journal of Religious Studies* 12/1: 17–61, 1985.

NORBECK, Edward. *Religion and Society in Modern Japan: Continuity and Change*. Houston: Tourmaline Press, 1970.

NOSCO, Peter, ed. *The Emperor System and Religion in Japan*. Special issue of *Japanese Journal of Religious Studies* 17/2–3, 1990.

ŌE Shinobu. *Yasukuni Jinja* [Yasukuni Shrine]. Tokyo: Iwanami Shinsho, 1984.

OKADA Kōtama. *The Holy Words (Goseigen)*. Tujunga, CA: Mahikari of America, 1982.

──. *Yōkōshi norigoto-shū* [Yōkōshi Prayer Book]. 7th edition. Tujunga, CA: Mahikari of America, 1986.

ONO Taihaku. " Nagare kanjō kara mizuko kuyō e" [From the memorial service for women who die during childbirth to *mizuko kuyō*]. In *Dentō to gendai* [Tradition and the present day] 75. Tokyo: Dentōtogendaisha, 1982.

ONSHIZAIDAN AIIKUKAI, ed. *Nihon san'iku shūzoku shiryō shūsei* [Collection of documents on customs related to childrearing in Japan]. Vol. 9. *Hinin, datai, mabiki* [Contraception, abortion, and infanticide]. Tokyo: Dai'ichi Hōki, 1975.

PLUTSCHOW, Herbert. "The fear of evil spirits in Japanese culture." *Transactions of the Asiatic Society of Japan*, 3rd ser., 18: 133–51, 1983.

READER, Ian. "Transformations and changes in the teachings of the Sōtō Zen Buddhist sect." *Japanese Religions* 14/1: 28–48, 1985.

──. "Zazenless Zen? The position of Zazen in institutional Zen Buddhism." *Japanese Religions* 14/3: 7–27, 1986.

──. "Back to the future: Images of nostalgia and renewal in a Japanese religious context." *Japanese Journal of Religious Studies* 14/4: 287–303, 1987.

──. "The rise of a Japanese 'new New Religion': Themes in the development of Agonshū." *Japanese Journal of Religious Studies* 15/4: 235–61, 1988.

──. "Letters to the gods: The form and meaning of *ema*." *Japanese Journal of Religious Studies* 18/1: 23–50, 1991.

──. *Religion in Contemporary Japan*. London: Macmillan, 1991.

REID, David. *New Wine: The Cultural Shaping of Japanese Christianity*. Berkeley: Asian Humanities Press, 1991.

ROBERTSON, Roland. *The Sociological Interpretation of Religion*. New York: Schocken, 1970.

ROHLEN, Thomas P. *For Harmony and Strength*. Berkeley, Los Angeles, London: University of California Press, 1974.

SAMUELS, Richard J. "Local politics in Japan: The changing of the guard." *Asian Survey* 22 (July) : 630–37, 1982.

SANSOM, George B. *Japan: A Short Cultural History*. New York: Appleton-Century Company, 1943 (reprint 1981, Tokyo: Tuttle).

SASAKI Shōten. "Shinshū and folk religion: Toward a post-modern 'Shinshū theology'." *Bulletin of the Nanzan Institute for Religion & Culture* 12: 13–35, 1988.

SECKEL, Dietrich. *Buddhistische Tempelnamen in Japan* [Buddhist temple names in Japan]. Münchener Ostasiatische Studien, vol. 37, Stuttgart: Franz Steiner, 1985.

SEICHŌ NO IE HONBU. *Seichō no Ie gojūnenshi* [Fifty years of Seichō-no-Ie history]. Tokyo: Nihon Kyōbunsha, 1980.

SELL, Hans Joachim. *Der schlimme Tod bei den Völkern Indonesiens* ["Bad death" among Indonesian peoples]. The Hague: Mouton, 1955.

SHIMAGAWA Masaji. "Yasukuni—Shinkō to gakumon" [Yasukuni: Faith and scholarship]. *Sekai* 9: 19–22, 1985.

SHIMAZONO Susumu. "Charisma and the evolution of religious consciousness: The rise of the early New Religions of Japan." *The Annual Review of the Social Sciences of Religion* 6, 1982.

———. "Spirit-belief in new religious movements and popular culture: The case of Japan's New Religions." *The Journal of Oriental Studies* 26/1: 90–100, 1987.

———. The development of millennialistic thought in Japan's New Religions: From Tenrikyō to Honmichi." In *New Religious Movements and Rapid Social Change*, James A. Beckford, ed. Newbury Park, CA: Sage, 1987.

———. "Oshie no ruikei" [Types of teachings]. In *Shinshūkyō jiten*, ed. Inoue Nobutaka et al., 216–23, 1990.

———. *Sukui to toku—Shūyōdan-hōseikai no shinkō kōzō* [Salvation and virtue: Credal structure of Shūyōdan-hōseikai]. Tokyo: Kōbundō, 1991.

———. *Gendai kyūsai shūkyōron* [Salvation religions in contemporary society]. Tokyo: Seikyūsha, 1992.

SHIMIZU Ikutarō. *Sengo o utagau* [Doubts about the postwar period]. Tokyo: Kōdansha, 1980a.

———. *Nippon yo, kokka tare* [Japan, become a State!]. Tokyo: Bungei Shunjū, 1980b.

SHIMODE Sekiyo. *Nihon kodai no jingi to dōkyō* [Taoism and the Shinto deities in ancient Japan]. Tokyo: Yoshikawa Kōbunkan, 1972.

SHIVELY, Donald H. ed. *Tradition and Modernization in Japanese Culture*. Princeton: Princeton University Press, 1971.

SHŌJI Kokichi, ed. *Sekai shakai no kōzō to dōtai* [Structure and movement of the world society]. Tokyo: Hōsei Daigaku Shuppankai, 1986.

SHUPE, Anson. "Globalization versus religious nativism: Japan's Soka Gakkai in the world arena." In *Religion and Global Order,* Roland Robertson and William R. Garrett, eds., 183–99. New York: Paragon House, 1991.

SMITH, Bardwell. "Buddhism and abortion in contemporary Japan: *Mizuko kuyō* and the confrontation with death." *Japanese Journal of Religious Studies* 15/1: 3–24, 1988.

SMITH, Robert J. *Ancestor Worship in Contemporary Japan.* Stanford: Stanford University Press, 1974.

SONODA Minoru. "The traditional festival in urban society." *Japanese Journal of Religious Studies* 2/2–3: 103–36, 1975.

STARK, Rodney. "How new religions succeed: A theoretical model." In *The Future of New Religious Movements,* David G. Bromley and Phillip E. Hammond, eds. Macon, Georgia: Mercer University Press, 1987.

STARK, Rodney and Lynne ROBERTS. "The arithmetic of social movements: Theoretical implications." *Sociological Analysis* 43: 53–67, 1982.

STARK, Rodney and William Sims BAINBRIDGE. *The Future of Religion.* Berkeley: University of California Press, 1985.

STARK, Werner. *The Sociology of Religion: A Study of Christendom,* Vol. 4. New York: Fordham University Press, 1970.

SWANSON, Paul L. "*Shugendō* and the Yoshino-Kumano pilgrimage: An example of mountain pilgrimage." *Monumenta Nipponica* 36/1: 55–79, 1981.

SWYNGEDOUW, Jan. "Japanese religiosity in an age of internationalization." *Japanese Journal of Religious Studies* 5: 87–106, 1978.

TAKATORI Masao and HASHIMOTO Mineo. *Shūkyō izen* [Before religion]. Tokyo: NHK Books, 1969.

TAKAYAMA, K. Peter. "Enshrinement and persistency of Japanese religion." *Journal of Church and State* 32/3: 527–47, 1990.

TAKEDA Chōshū. *Minzoku bukkyō to sosen shinkō* [Folk Buddhism and ancestor veneration]. Tokyo: Tōdai Shuppankai, 1971.

TAKIZAWA Nobuhiko. "Religion and the state in Japan," *Journal of Church and State* 30: 89–108, 1988.

THELLE, Notto R. *Buddhism and Christianity in Japan: From Conflict to Dialogue, 1854–1899.* Honolulu: University of Hawaii Press, 1987.

TSUSHIMA Michihito, et al. "The vitalistic conception of salvation in Japanese New Religions: An aspect of modern religious consciousness." *Japanese Journal of Religious Studies* 6/1–2: 139–61, 1979.

TUBIELEWICZ, Jolanta. *Superstitions, Magic and Mantric Practices in the Heian Period.* Warszawa: Wydawnictwa Uniwersytetu Warszawskiego, 1980.

TYLOR, Edward Burnett. *Primitive Culture.* New York: Harper & Row (reprint), 1958.

UCHIDA Mitsura and Hans H. BAERWALD. "The House of Councillors election in Japan: The LDP hangs in there." *Asian Survey* 18 (March) 301–308, 1978.

UCHIMURA Kanzō. *Uchimura Kanzō zenshū* [The collected works of Uchimura Kanzō], vol. 1 (1886), vol. 18 (1911), vol. 22 (1916), vol. 25 (1920). Tokyo: Iwanami Shoten, 1981.

UI Hakuju. *Bukkyō jiten.* Tokyo: Daitō Shuppansha, 1980.

VAN BRAGT, Jan. "An uneven battle: Sōka Gakkai vs. Nichiren Shōshū." *Bulletin of the Nanzan Institute for Religion & Culture* 17: 15–32, 1993.

WEBER, Max. *The Sociology of Religion*. Trans. by Ephraim Fischoff. Boston: Beacon Press, 1964 (Orig. ed. 1922).

WEISSBROD, Lilly. "Religion as national identity in a secular society." *Review of Religious Research* 24: 188–205, 1983.

WILLIAMS, George M. *Amerika ni okeru shūkyō no yakuwari* [Role of religion in America]. Tokyo: Ushio Shuppansha, 1989.

WILSON, Byran R. "The New Religions: Some preliminary considerations." *Japanese Journal of Religious Studies* 6/1–2: 193–216, 1979.

WOODARD, William P. *The Allied Occupation of Japan 1945–1952 and Japanese Religions*. Leiden: E. J. Brill, 1972.

YAMADA, Yutaka. "Healing, conversion, and ancestral spirits: Religious experiences among the Japanese-American members of the Church of World Messianity in Los Angeles, California." In YANAGAWA Keiichi, ed., 1983, 197–239.

YAMAMOTO Soseki. *Kaisei no bōkensha—Sai Sai-kan* [Choi Jae-Whan: An adventurer in renewal]. Tenri: Tenrikyō Dōyūsha, 1982.

YAMAZAKI Masakazu. "Signs of a new individualism." *Japan Echo* 11: 8–18, 1984.

YANAGAWA Keiichi, ed. *Japanese Religions in California*. Tokyo: Department of Religious Studies, University of Tokyo, 1983.

YANAGAWA Keiichi & ABE Yoshiya. *Shūkyō riron to shūkyō-shi* [Theories and history of religion]. Tokyo: Nippon Hōsō Shuppankyōkai, 1985.

YANAGAWA Keiichi and MORIOKA Kiyomi, eds. *Hawai nikkei shūkyō no genkyō to tenkai* [The current situation and future prospects for religion among Hawaiian Japanese-Americans]. Tokyo: Tōkyō Daigaku Shūkyōgaku Kenkyūshitsu, 1979.

———. *Hawai nikkeijin shakai to nikkei shūkyō* [Japanese-American society and Japanese-American religion in Hawaii]. Tokyo: Tōkyō Daigaku Shūkyōgaku Kenkyūshitsu, 1981.

YANAGITA Kunio. *About Our Ancestors: The Japanese Family System*. Trans. by Fanny Hagin Mayer and Ishiwara Yasuyo. Tokyo: Monbushō, 1970.

———. *Yanagita Kunio zenshū* [Collected works of Yanagita Kunio]. Tokyo: Chikuma Shobō, 1973.

YASUKUNI JINJA SHAMUSHO, ed. *Yasukuni Jinja*. Tokyo: Yasukuni Jinja, 1975.

YINGER, Milton J. *The Scientific Study of Religion*. Toronto: Collier-Macmillan, 1970.

YOUNG, Richard F. "From *gokyō-dōgen* to *bankyō-dōkon*: A study in the self-universalization of Ōmoto." *Japanese Journal of Religious Studies* 15: 263–86, 1988.

———. "Jesus, the 'Christ', and Deguchi Onisaburō: A study of adversarial syncretism in a Japanese world-renewal religion." *Japanese Religions* 15/4: 26–49, 1989a.

———. "The little-lad deity and the dragon princess: Jesus in a new world-renewal movement." *Monumenta Nipponica* 44: 31–44, 1989b.